Charles Tennant

Utilitarianism explained and exemplified in moral and political

government

Charles Tennant

Utilitarianism explained and exemplified in moral and political government

ISBN/EAN: 9783742818027

Manufactured in Europe, USA, Canada, Australia, Japa

Cover: Foto ©Suzi / pixelio.de

Manufactured and distributed by brebook publishing software
(www.brebook.com)

Charles Tennant

Utilitarianism explained and exemplified in moral and political government

UTILITARIANISM

EXPLAINED AND EXEMPLIFIED

IN

MORAL AND POLITICAL GOVERNMENT.

"The Welfare of the People is the Highest Law."

LONDON:

LONGMAN, GREEN, LONGMAN, ROBERTS, & GREEN.

1864.

NOTE FROM THE AUTHOR.

In offering to the Public these pages in answer
to a small volume by Mr. John Stuart Mill, entitled " Utilitarianism," the Author thinks it necessary at the same time to offer his apology for
the introduction of many subjects which, at first
sight, may seem to have little or no relevancy to
the main subject.

It may, however, to thoughtful readers, be
unnecessary to point out the connection between
the abstract reasoning and its application to im
portant current events concerning human government.

How far the reasoning and its application are correct, is another question, which Public Opinion must determine.

The impartial judgment of the Public is now invited, between an Author of deservedly high repute, and an Author without a name.

January, 1864.

CONTENTS.

UTILITARIANISM,

EXPLAINED AND EXEMPLIFIED,

IN

MORAL AND POLITICAL GOVERNMENT.

———◆———

CHAPTER I.

GENERAL REMARKS.

THE object of this treatise is not so much to refute the false philosophy under this name, as to draw practical conclusions from a higher and true source.

It is true, as Mr. John Stuart Mill says, that " from the dawn of philosophy the question concerning the *summum bonum*, or what is the same thing, concerning the foundation of morality, has been accounted the main problem in speculative thought, has occupied the most gifted intellects, and divided them into sects and schools, carrying on a vigorous warfare against one another.

B

And after more than two thousand years the same discussions continue, philosophers are still ranged under the same contending banners, and neither thinkers nor mankind at large seem nearer to being unanimous on the subject, than when the youth Socrates listened to old Protagoras, and asserted (if Plato's dialogue be grounded on a real conversation) the theory of Utilitarianism against the popular morality of the so-called sophist."

Rather a strong ground of presumption this, that there is something wrong in the philosophy!

The Utilitarians may say what they please, but the truth remains the same, and they are only repeating the doctrine of the ancient Epicureans, a doctrine which never made much progress even among Pagans.

The wonder is not that it has made so little progress, but that it has found advocates among enlightened and thinking men in the 19th Century of the Christian Era!

Mr. John Stuart Mill, who may be regarded as the living chief of the small sect of modern Epicureans, is more careful in defining "What Utilitarianism Is," by saying, what it is not, than by saying, in intelligible terms, what it is.

But he is hardly fair to his opponents, when he refers to their "shallow mistake."

He says (p. 8)—"Those who know anything about the matter are aware that every writer from Epicurus to Bentham, who maintained the theory of utility, meant by it, not something to be contradistinguished from pleasure, but pleasure itself, together with exemption from pain; and instead of offering the useful to the agreeable or the ornamental, have always declared that the useful means these, among other things. Yet the common herd, including the herd of writers, not only in newspapers and periodicals, but in books of weight and pretension, are perpetually falling into this shallow mistake. Having caught up the word utilitarian, while knowing nothing whatever about it but its sound, they habitually express by it the rejection, or the neglect, of pleasure in some of its forms; of beauty, of ornament, or of amusement."

Their mistake, according to this, is shallow enough; but, whether shallow or not, their objection is something more than this.

The present object is to state their objection more clearly than Mr. Mill has here stated it, and, perhaps, he will see that the ground of objection to his favorite philosophy is then removed, and that he is still left in possession of all that he desires to establish.　　　D 2

With this view Mr. Mill's work on "Utilitarianism" will be closely followed as the text, on which this treatise will be the Commentary; and it will be concluded with practical remarks in application to Human Government.

CHAPTER II.

Mr. Mill, (p. 9) says: "The creed which accepts as the foundation of morals, Utility, or the Greatest Happiness Principle, holds that actions are right in proportion as they tend to promote happiness, wrong as they tend to produce the reverse of happiness. By happiness is intended pleasure, and the absence of pain; by unhappiness, pain, and the privation of pleasure."

Referring to some supplementary explanations, he adds:—"But these do not affect the theory of life on which this theory of morality is grounded—namely, that pleasure and freedom from pain, are the only things desirable as ends; and that all desirable things (which are as numerous in the utilitarian as in any other scheme) are desirable either for the pleasure inherent in themselves, or as means to the promotion of pleasure, and the prevention of pain."

Mr. Mill then goes on, very properly, to add :

"Now, such a theory of life excites in many minds, and among them in some of the most estimable in feeling and purpose, inveterate dislike."

He also, but not so properly, gives the reasons for their dislike. Those, as Mr. Mill truly says, are foolish reasons; and those are not the reasons which will be given here. This gets rid of a great deal of Mr. Mill's waste reasoning, which it is needless here to follow.

According to Mr. Mill, (p. 17) "the Greatest Happiness Principle, as explained, the ultimate end, with reference to and for the sake of which all other things are desirable (whether we are considering our own good or that of other people), is an existence exempt as far as possible from pain, and as rich as possible in enjoyments, both in point of quantity and quality; the test of quality, and the rule for measuring it against quantity, being the preference felt by those who in their opportunities of experience, to which must be added their habits of self-consciousness and self-observation, are best furnished with the means of comparison. This being, according to the utilitarian opinion, the end of human action, is necessarily also the standard of morality; which may accordingly be defined, the rules and precepts for human conduct, by the observance of which an existence such as has been described might be, to the greatest extent possible, secured to all mankind; and not to them only, but, so far as the nature of things admits, to the whole sentient creation."

This is a very comprehensive, though not a very clear explanation; but it is given in Mr. Mill's own words, and he is bound by them. He feels the difficulty of defining Happiness, and tries to avoid the difficulty by the use of negatives rather than of affirmatives; by showing what Happiness is not, rather than what it is; by showing that it "is an existence exempt as far as possible from pain, and as rich as possible in enjoyments,"—but without explaining what he means by pain or enjoyments. He assumes Happiness as a principle, though he admits Happiness to be the end and object of all principle. This, coming from a Master of Logic, deserves notice. He cannot mean that a principle and its consequences are one and the same thing. And yet this is what he has said! He must mean that Happiness is the consequence, or result, of the principle. But,—What principle? The Utilitarian principle. Be it so. But, let us see how this will bear examination.

He says, (p. 16) in reference to his previous reasoning:—" I have dwelt on this point, as being

a necessary part of a perfectly just conception of
Utility, or Happiness, considered as the directive
rule of human conduct."

Here he makes Utility and Happiness synonymous terms. But just before he made Happiness the principle, and also the consequence, or
result!

Assuming that he meant to say, Utility, the
principle, and Happiness, the consequence or result, how can Utility and Happiness be synonymous terms? If so, Utility and Happiness
are convertible terms, and a perfectly just conception of one is a directive rule of human conduct for both; or, a perfectly just conception of
Utility is a directive rule of conduct for Happiness, and a perfectly just conception of Happiness
is a directive rule of conduct for Happiness;
which seems very much like saying that, a perfectly just conception of what is right is a directive rule of conduct for what is right;—a proposition which no one is likely to dispute, though
the difficulty of obtaining that "perfectly just
conception," seems to be left precisely where it
was before this new "directive rule of human
conduct" was given.

But, for this new "directive rule," we must
have a "just conception" of what Utility is, or
what Mr. Mill means by it. The only explana-

tion which he has given is that, " Utility holds
that actions are right in proportion as they tend
to promote happiness, wrong as they tend to produce the reverse of happiness."

There is nothing new in this, and nobody ever
disputed it, but there is not much explanation in
this. It would have been something more to the
purpose if Mr. Mill had told us more clearly what
he means by Utility.

It would have been something new, and might
have helped his argument, if he had given us
some clear and definite rules by which we might
determine this question. But on this he has no
where ventured, and he has left us only where we
were before, and that is, under the guidance of
our reason.

We will endeavour to give the answer as we
understand it.

What is Utility?

Every created thing is a Utility.

But nothing is of any use, until used. How
far anything is useful depends on the use of it.
Improperly used it is hurtful, and useful only
when properly used. Therefore, the Greatest
Happiness results from the proper use of everything.

This is what Mr. Mill and the Utilitarians mean,
though it is not what they say; and it is what

every body means, whatever they may say, or
do. But this may be said in fewer words, the
meaning being simply that,—'What is right is
best!'

To say that, the Greatest Happiness is Utility,
is a mere jumble of words, which would read as
well backwards as forwards. Utility is the
Greatest Happiness. And this is just what the
Utilitarians do say. They say it backwards and
forwards, and it is as true one way as the
other.

To simplify this, let us reduce it.

The Vegetarians say, Health is the Greatest
Happiness:—Vegetables are most conducive to
health; therefore, Vegetables are the Greatest
Happiness Principle.

The Tee-totallers say, Temperance is the
Greatest Happiness:—Milk and Water are most
conducive to Temperance: therefore, Milk and
Water are the Greatest Happiness Principle.

These words may be said backwards or forwards with as much meaning.

There is no more Principle in Happiness or
Utility, than there is in a Potatoe, or in Milk and
Water, or any other utility.

Mr. Mill and the Utilitarians seem to have a
strange notion about utilities, and in this notion
seems to lurk a great deal of their error.

They seem to regard utilities as given by man ; as if mankind were the givers, instead of being the receivers.

Man never gave anything useful to man, in the correct sense of the word, as here used, and never can give anything useful to man in this world. He can only use and adapt, for himself and others, the gifts of God. · Man can give nothing useful, in the true sense of utility. He can give only his efforts or services, in his labour and skill, to make available for human use the gifts of God to man. To give a utility he must create. The various adaptations by man of God's gifts are great services to man, because great conveniences, but are nothing more. "The Earth and the fulness thereof" are gifts of great utility, but even these are made useful only by labour and skill, and are of no use to man without his efforts or services.

Water is a great utility, but not to the man dying of thirst, without any one to bring the water to him. This is no play upon words. This is a grand distinction which, when clearly seen and followed out, blows to the winds all the Epicurean and Utilitarian doctrines, which men in all ages have been trying to maintain, as some wise and beneficial discovery, but which means nothing more than, '*what is right is best.*'

This is Mr. Mill's Utilitarianism, and this view reconciles all difficulties, but tells us nothing new, and leaves us where we were before.

CHAPTER III.

UTILITARIANISM.—ITS SANCTIONS.

MR. MILL, in his Chapter III., treats "Of the Ultimate Sanction Of The Principle of Utility."

It is not necessary here to follow Mr. Mill through all his reasoning under this head. He says, (p. 39) :—"The principle of utility either has, or there is no reason why it might not have, all the sanctions which belong to any other system of morals."

Without admitting that there is any principle of utility, there can be no objection to admitting the truth of this position in its fullest sense, for the sake of examining it.

If every utility be a gift of God to Man, it requires no evidence to prove that the use of that gift, as it was intended to be used, must be sanctioned by the moral standard, and must be conducive to Happiness. But this is not the argument of the Utilitarians, nor is it their meaning.

It is arguing in a circle' to attempt to prove

that the gifts of God to man were intended to
be conducive to the happiness of man ; but it is
confounding the meaning of words, and, moreover, is contradicted by facts, to say that the
gifts of God to man constitute happiness, or are
even necessarily conducive to happiness.   They
never were intended to constitute happiness, but
were intended to be conducive to happiness, and
always would be so if used as intended.   But
we see that they are often, and perhaps as often,
conducive to misery as to happiness, and thence
we may infer that they are not used as intended.
They are more frequently used for convenience
and pleasure, and are conducive to both, but
that is not happiness, or necessarily conducive to
happiness, and is often quite the contrary.

Riches, as a means of obtaining human efforts,
or services, are conducive, as a necessary consequence, to convenience and pleasure.   That may
be said to be a necessary consequence of Utility.

But Happiness is no necessary consequence,
and this shows that Happiness is not dependent
on Utility, but is quite independent of it, though   .
it may be conducive to Happiness.   But riches
are a necessary means to convenience and pleasure, these being dependent on the means.
Riches, more or less, are one of the means for
obtaining possession of those services or efforts

which render Utilities useful, or available for use,
and, as such, riches are desirable for convenience and pleasure, and are, practically, essential,
to some extent, for the means of subsistence;
but riches are not necessary, or even desirable,
for Happiness, unless rightly used, and then
only can they be, and even then not necessarily,
conducive to Happiness. For convenience and
pleasure there is no such condition.

This shows that there is a very great distinction between convenience and pleasure, and happiness. This distinction is lost sight of by the
Utilitarians, and is fatal to their Philosophy.
This is a grand distinction which should never
be lost sight of, as may be shown in innumerable ways. The drunkard, it must be supposed finds pleasure in getting drunk. So of
the Opium Eater. And so of all who avail
themselves of the Utilities, or God's gifts, in any
manner contrary to their intended use. But all
these, if used as intended to be used, are very
precious gifts, and are conducive to Happiness,
as well as to convenience and pleasure.

In this view it will be seen that, all the gifts
are from God to man, and that Man never has
given, and never can give anything to God in
return, but thanksgiving; and never has given,
and never can give anything to man, but labor

and services, or efforts, to make available God's
gifts, for the convenient use and pleasure of man;
and that by so doing he is rendering the best
return in his power to God, by so far forward-
ing His design for the Happiness of all mankind, and that mankind are thereby making themselves instruments in God's hands for working
out, so far, their own happiness. But only so
far as Human efforts are in accordance with the
Divine Will, through God, and by His means
given to them by Him, and not given by themselves, for they have given nothing but their
efforts, to make available for their use His gifts
to them, and which are given equally to all. If
the efforts be not made through Him, or in accordance with His Will and design for Human
Happiness, they must fail in obtaining Happiness for themselves, though they may not fail in
the object of convenience and pleasure. And as
we may assume that the Divine Will can never
be frustrated by Man, we must suppose that the
design in the creation of Man will be ultimately
carried out to completion, according to the Will
of the Creator, though that completion, for man's
benefit, may be deferred, according to our notion of time, by human instrumentality.

Thus, it may be seen that the Greatest Happiness, or any Happiness at all, can never be

obtained by following out what the Utilitarians
call the "Greatest Happiness Principle," though
an increase may thereby be obtained of what the
world in general calls convenience and pleasure,
and these, if used only on the Utilitarian Principle, will surely lead away from, instead of bringing nearer to, what the world in general under-
stands by Happiness.

Therefore, the " Utilitarian Principle," as Utilitarians interpret it, is not sanctioned by God's
moral standard, but is opposed to it, and is more
in accordance with the Mahometan than with
the Christian doctrine.

Happiness means a sensation of happiness, and
though that must be pleasurable, yet it is something different from, and much more to be desired
than, what we call pleasure, and we all know that
Happiness may exist quite independently of pleasurable circumstances, even under great bodily
suffering, and even under mental suffering through
great worldly affliction.

This, once established, may be sufficient to
show that Utility has no necessary relation to
Happiness ; for, although Utility has a very direct
and necessary relation to convenience, and thereby
to pleasure, and may be even essential for both,
convenience and pleasure are not happiness, and
are not essential for happiness, though these may

c

be conducive to it ; therefore Utility has no necessary relation to Happiness.

Thus, it may be seen, the error of the Utilitarians, in their Greatest Happiness Principle, is
in confounding Happiness with Utility, or the
Spiritual with the Material.   And this is a very
great error, for its tendency is to keep out of view
that higher quality of the human being, called
the Spirit, or Soul, which is above and quite independent of all material objects.   No doubt,
the Utilitarian philosopher denies any such tendency in his doctrine or arguments, but then his
own words contradict him, and his only escape
from this dilemma is, that his words are misunderstood.

But the Utilitarian doctrine rests on the assertion,—an assertion entirely assumed,—that Utility has relation to Happiness,—and that assertion is here denied and disproved.   One must
be wrong, and the other right.   Both cannot be
right.   That Utility has a great deal to do with
convenience and pleasure, is admitted on both
sides ; and this admission may be made with
perfect safety, for this involves none of the solemn
consequences of the great error that Human
Happiness is dependent on material circumstances, or, what the sect call, ' Utility.'

To be forced to admit that there is more Human Happiness in fine carriages than in common carts ; or, in all the appliances of wealth, than in the destitution of poverty; is a sad conclusion to be driven to, seeing that fine carriages are confined to a comparative few, and that the great masses of mankind, all over the world, are struggling against the ills of poverty. If Human Happiness be in any way dependent on external circumstances, over which human beings individually have no control, it would be a difficult matter for us to reconcile that arrangement of human affairs with our ideas of the Divine Attributes of Justice and Mercy. But, if we separate Human Happiness from all external circumstances, we at once get rid of this difficulty. If we can only believe that there may be as much Human Happiness in a common cart as in a fine carriage, in the roughest fare as in the most delicate dainties, we can at least contemplate these Divine Attributes with more composure in this view, than we can through the medium of the Epicurean or Utilitarian Doctrine.

If this be the true view,—and who can doubt it?—then, what becomes of the Utilitarian doctrine? It neutralizes that doctrine, or reduces it to this simple truism,—*the right is the best.* It leaves Human Happiness untouched by outward or material circumstances. It proves that human happiness is something distinct from human convenience and pleasure, and that these have no necessary connection with it. It leaves all the reasoning of the Utilitarians applicable to convenience and pleasure, but inapplicable to Human Happiness; and it shows that Happiness lies beyond either pain or pleasure. It leaves the hope which is not of this world, and makes intelligible the meaning of St. Paul, when he said:—"If in this life only we have hope, we are of all men the most miserable." Here we are expressly told where to rest our hope,—where to look for the Greatest Happiness Principle,—and we are told that it is not in anything in this world.

Many will think that this is conclusive against the Utilitarians, because it proves their doctrine to be in direct opposition to the word of God, and, therefore, false: and because ingeniously contrived to deceive and mislead, therefore, dangerous. But many who profess to be are really not Christians, so that this reasoning will not hold them.

It is a glorious hope for all mankind, and far too precious to be trifled with, that Happiness lies beyond either pain or pleasure, and no play upon words should ever be allowed to dim the glorious radiance which this life throws over our sorrowful world. But it is far from the meaning of these remarks to impute any such intention to all those who, in these times, advocate the Utilitarian Doctrine. As a guide for human actions, to the things of this world, it is excellent; but Happiness is not to be reached by this Philosophy. A French writer expressed this idea, perhaps without intending it, in these words: "Ce qui est moins que moi m'éteint, et m'assomme; ce qui est à côté de moi m'ennuie et me fatigue. Il n'y a que ce qui est *au dessus* de moi qui me soutienne et m'arrache à moi-même."

CHAPTER IV.

UTILITARIANISM: HOW PROVED.

Mr. Mill in his Chapter IV. treats "Of What Sort Of Proof The Principle Of Utility is Susceptible."

He says, (p. 51): "The Utilitarian doctrine is, that happiness is desirable, and the only thing desirable, as an end; all other things being only desirable as a means to that end."

He then proceeds to the proof by a process of reasoning which is open to no objection, and comes to the conclusion, (p. 60) that "nothing is a good to human beings but in so far as it is either itself pleasurable, or a means of attaining pleasure or averting pain;" and then he adds: "If this doctrine be true, the principle of utility is proved."

Now, the Utilitarian doctrine, as here laid down, is not controverted, being incontrovertibly true. But the conclusion from this, "that the principle of utility is proved," is not true.

What is proved is this:—that all good is de-

sirable, and that Happiness is a good. Happiness
is the ultimate end.

But this is proved by universal assent, and
not by reasoning.

Mr. Mill very properly says, (p. 51.) : " Questions about ends are, in other words, questions
what things are desirable."

And again he says, (p. 51.) : " Questions of
ultimate ends do not admit of proof, in the ordinary acceptation of the term ;" these being " the
subject of a direct appeal to the faculties which
judge of fact—namely, our senses, and our internal consciousness."

This he well illustrates thus (p. 51.) :—" The
only proof capable of being given that an object
is visible, is that people actually see it. The only
proof that a sound is audible, is that people hear
it : and so of the other sources of our experience.
In like manner, I apprehend, the sole evidence
it is possible to produce that anything is' desirable, is that people do actually desire it."

Exactly so. Happiness is a good, and is an ultimate end, which does not admit of proof, in the
ordinary acceptation of the term. But all people
desire happiness, and that is the only proof capable of being given, that it is a good.

But this proves nothing for the Utilitarian
doctrine, if it be established that Happiness is

in no way dependent on, and has no necessary relation whatever to, Utility. As already
shown, Utility can have relation only to things
created, and as Man never has created, and
never can create, anything, and can avail himself of the utilities of nature only by the
efforts of himself or others, Happiness must be
something quite independent of Utilities, otherwise Utility must be synonymous with Happiness, or must be the source of Happiness, and
then the greater amount of Utilities, or services,
man can control, the greater must be the amount
of his Happiness.   In that case the greatest
amount of riches, which now commands the
greatest amount of services, ought also to command the greatest amount of Happiness.

This is what the Utilitarian doctrine means, if
it mean anything, but, of course, this meaning
will be repudiated, nor is it for a moment to be
supposed that such is the meaning of all those
who maintain this doctrine.   But, nevertheless,
this is what the doctrine leads to, and from this
there is no escape.

It is of the highest importance to distinguish
between the material and the spiritual good in
this life, and the Utilitarian doctrine not only
confounds this distinction, but actually declares
the material to be essential for the spiritual.

It may be safely admitted that the material may be, and is intended to be, conducive to the spiritual good, but it is of the utmost importance to be clearly seen that the material is not necessarily conducive to the spiritual good, and we know, as a fact, that it is often quite the reverse.

If it were not so, but if the material were necessary for the spiritual good, then, as before said, it would be impossible for us to reconcile that necessity with our notions of the Divine Attributes on any conceivable grounds of justice and mercy.

We know that all the Utilities of Nature are given gratuitously and equally to all mankind, and we know that these are necessary for human existence; but we also know that these are not equally available to all mankind, and never can be in the present state, or in any conceivable state, of human society. If the greater amount of the Utilities of Nature at the service of a man, secure to him a greater amount of Happiness than is enjoyed by the man who possesses these Utilities in a smaller amount, then these utilities are essential for Happiness, and the greater the command over the gratuitous services of Nature, the greater the Happiness. But, then, to be consistent with our notions of justice and mercy, the command over these services should be equal to all, which, we know, never can be, consistently with the present dispensation of this World's affairs.

It is, therefore, impugning the Divine Attributes of Wisdom and Justice and Mercy, to make Human Happiness dependent on those gratuitous services of Nature, which though given equally to all, are not equally shared by all, but are commanded in a much larger share by some than by others, and in a much larger share by the few than by the many. That this is so, no one pretends to deny, and that the disproportion is so great is one of the greatest reproaches against civilized society. But this ground of reproach will be treated of hereafter. The present inquiry is into the proof of the Utilitarian doctrine, and this proves it to be untrue, because inconsistent with the Divine Attributes, and contradicted by every Law of Nature.

It results from the preceding considerations, as Mr. Mill says, (p. 56) " that there is in reality nothing desired except happiness. Whatever is desired otherwise than as a means to some end beyond itself, and ultimately to happiness, is desired as itself a part of happiness, and is not desired for itself until it has become so."

Happiness is desired not as a means to some end beyond itself, but as the ultimate end.

Utility is desired as a means to some end beyond itself, but that end is convenience and
pleasure, and not Happiness. Utility may or
may not be conducive to Happiness, but it
never can be Happiness, and is more frequently
conducive to misery than happiness. Virtue is
Happiness, or brings the sense of Happiness;
but Utility is not Happiness, nor does it bring
the sense of Happiness. Utility, or the gratuitous gifts of Nature, does not bring even convenience and pleasure, without human efforts,
and it is the virtuous use of these gifts alone
which makes them conducive to Happiness.
Therefore, it is the virtuous use of these gifts,
and not the utility of the gifts, which constitutes, or conduces to, the happiness. Therefore,
there is no relation between Utility and Happiness. The relation is between Utility and
convenience and pleasure, and between Happiness and Virtue, or, Happiness and Virtue are
synonymous, rather than Utility and Happiness.

Those who desire virtue for its own sake, desire it not because the consciousness of it is a
pleasure, or because the consciousness of being
without it is a pain, or for both reasons united,
but because the consciousness is Happiness.

Mr. Mill and the Utilitarians say, they desire
virtue because the consciousness of it is a plea-

sure, or because the consciousness of being without it is a pain, or for both reasons united; but
this is contradicted by experience, as we all know
that pleasure or pain, or both united, may exist
without virtue, and, therefore, can have no relation to virtue, though a consciousness of virtuo is
a consciousness of pleasure, as Happiness is a
consciousness of pleasure, but quite independently
of pleasure or pain, in the ordinary sense of these
terms.

Mr. Mill and the Utilitarians also say that,
virtue, if it gave no pleasure, and the absence of
virtue, if it gave no pain, would not be desired.

This is an undeniable conclusion from the Utilitarian doctrine; but this is not the conclusion
to be drawn from the Christian doctrine. According to the Christian doctrine, virtue is to be
desired for itself, without reference to pleasure or
pain, and if virtue be happiness, this is compre-
hensible. And this alone is sufficient to show
that, happiness is something different from pleasure—something higher and more to be desired
than pleasure—something beyond the reach of
pain, and, therefore, quite independent of pleasure or pain, in the ordinary acceptation of these
terms.

This shows that Utility has immediate and necessary relation to convenience and pleasure, but

no necessary relation to virtue, or happiness. In
fact Utility exists only in relation to convenience
and pleasure. In the absence of human efforts
there is no Utility. All the gratuitous gifts of
Nature are made useful only by human efforts.
Nothing further is required to make these available for convenience and pleasure. But for Happiness, we know that, human efforts alone will
not avail. These may be conducive as means to
an end, but are not necessarily so, and, we know,
are frequently otherwise. Thus, we may know
that, Happiness is beyond the reach of Utility,
and the one has no relation to the other.

If this distinction be psychologically true,—if
human nature be so constituted as to desire
something more than Nature has given in Utilities for convenience and pleasure,—something
more that we call Happiness,—we can have no
other proof, and we require no other, that Happiness is distinct from convenience and pleasure,
and is independent of all Utilities, having no necessary relation thereto. But " we know that all
things work together for good to them that love
God, to them who are the called according to
His purpose." If so, not Utility but Happiness
should be the sole end of human action, and the
promotion of it the test by which to judge of all
human conduct; whence it necessarily follows

that Happiness, or Virtue, which are synonymous
in effect, and not Utility, must be the criterion of
morality, and as Utility is desirable as a means
to an end which may be conducive to Happiness,
and may thus become a part of Happiness, Utility is included, since a part is included in the
whole.

"And now," as Mr. Mill says, (p. 57) "to decide whether this be really so; whether mankind
do desire nothing for itself but that which is pleasure to them, or of which the absence is a pain;
we have evidently arrived at a question of fact
and experience, dependent, like all similar questions, upon evidence. It can only be determined
by practised self-consciousness and self-observation, assisted by observation of others."

To the judgment of self-consciousness this
question is now left, with confidence that, "the
principle of Utility is proved" to be unfounded,
as a criterion of morality.

CHAPTER V.

UTILITARIANISM: HOW CONNECTED WITH JUSTICE.

In this Chapter, Mr. Mill treats of "The Connexion Between Justice And Utility"; and
he commences with the following startling assertion, (p. 61):—" In all ages of speculation, one
of the strongest obstacles to the reception of the
doctrine that Utility or Happiness is the criterion
of right and wrong, has been drawn from the
idea of Justice. The powerful sentiment, and
apparently clear perception, which that word re-
cals with a rapidity and certainty resembling an
instinct, have seemed to the majority of thinkers
to point to an inherent quality in things; to show
that the Just must have an existence in Nature,
as something absolute, generically distinct from
every variety of the Expedient, and, in idea, opposed to it, though (as is commonly acknowledged) never, in the long run, disjoined from it
in fact."

It may be that the sense of Justice is a powerful sentiment, resembling an instinct, in every rational human being, as the instinct of self-preservation ; but how this should "have seemed to the majority of thinkers to point to an inherent quality in things," is not so clear, being not very intelligible.

Whatever may be meant by "the sense of Justice pointing to an inherent quality in things," this powerful sentiment which so resembles an instinct, shows "that the Just must have an existence in Nature as something absolute, generically distinct from every variety of the Expedient."

A passage in Plato's treatise De Legibus, p. 757, quoted in a note by Browne, p. 116, shows how far the views of the great Master and his distinguished pupil, Aristotle, coincided on this subject of particular justice. As far as regarded universal justice, the theory of Plato was as follows :—

"He considered the soul a republic (De Rep. IV.) composed of three faculties or orders. (1.) Reason, the governing principle. (2.) The irascible passions. (3.) The concupiscible passions. When each of these three faculties of the mind confined itself to its proper office, without attempting to encroach upon that of any other; when reason governed and the passions obeyed,

then the result was that complete virtue which
Plato denominated *Justice.*   Under the idea of
universal justice will be comprehended the "*justitia expletrix,*" and "*justitia attributrix,*" of
Grotius ; the former of which consists in abstaining from what is another's, and in doing voluntarily whatever we can with propriety be forced
to do; the latter, which consists in proper beneficence, and which comprehends all the social
virtues.   This latter kind has been by some
termed "distributive justice," but in a different
sense from that in which the expression is used
by Aristotle.   With respect to particular justice,
distributive justice takes cognizance of the acts of
men, considered in relation to the State, and
comprehends what we call criminal cases.   Corrective justice considers men in relation to each
other, and comprehends civil cases."

According to Aristotle,* a man is termed unjust for two reasons :—Firstly, as being a trans-
gressor of the law, whether that be the written
or the unwritten ; and, Secondly, as being unequal or unfair, as taking more of good and less
of evil, which comes to the same thing, than he
has a right to.   Hence injustice ; and, therefore,
justice is of two kinds : (1) a habit of obedience
to law ; (2) a habit of equality.

* Ethics, Book v. c. v.

D

Now, as law, in the most comprehensive acceptation of the term, implies the enactment of all the principles of virtue which are binding on mankind as members of a social community (which, be it remembered, Aristotle considers their proper normal condition), the only difference between universal justice (1) and universal virtue is, that the habit of obedience to the fixed principles of moral rectitude is, when considered absolutely, termed virtue, when considered relatively to others, justice.

The history of the human race never presents man to us except in relation to his fellow-man. Even in savage life, the rude elements of civil society are discoverable. If we could conceive the existence of an individual isolated from the rest of his species, he would be a man only in outward form, he would possess no sense of right and wrong, no moral sentiments, no ideas on the subject of natural justice. The principles of natural justice are doubtless immutable and eternal, and would be the same had the man never existed; but as far as man is concerned, the development of them must be sought for in him as we find him; that is, in his social condition and no other.

Aristotle, in his 5th Book, 10th Chapter of Ethics, treats of Equity, the principles of which furnish the means of correcting the imperfections of law. These imperfections are unavoidable, because, from the nature of things, the enactments of law must be universal, and require adaptation to particular cases.

As Aristotle observes, if we attend to the definition, it appears absurd that equity should be praiseworthy, when it is something different from justice, for either justice must be not good, or equity must be not just, that is, if it be different from justice; or, if they be both good, they must be both the same.

But, as Aristotle nicely discerns, these considerations are in one sense true and not inconsistent with each other; for, "the equitable" is just, being better than a certain kind of "just;" and it is not better than "the just," as though it were of a different genus. Just and equitable, therefore, are identical; and both being good, "the equitable" is the better. With wonderful power of discrimination, the Greek Philosopher describes the cause of ambiguity to be, that "the equitable" is just, but not that justice which is according to law, but the correction of the legally just. And, as he points out, the reason of this is, that law is in all cases universal, and on some subjects it is not possible to speak universally with correctness. In those cases where it is necessary to speak universally, but impossible to do so correctly, the law takes the most general case, though it is well aware of the incorrectness of it. And the law is not, therefore, less right; for the fault is not in the law, nor in the legislator, but in the nature of the thing; for the subject-matter of human actions is altogether of this description.

When, therefore, the law speaks universally, and something happens different from the generality of cases, then it is proper that where the legislator falls short, and has erred, from speaking generally, to correct the defect, as the legislator would himself direct if he were then present, or as he would have legislated if he had been aware of the case. Therefore, the equitable is just, and better than some kind of "just;" not, indeed, better than the "absolute just," but better than the error which arises from universal enactments.

And this is the nature of "the equitable," that it is a correction of law, wherever it is defective owing to its universality. This is the reason why all things are not according to law, because on some subjects it is impossible to make a law. So that there is need of a special decree: for the rule of what is indeterminate, is itself indeterminate also. It is clear, therefore, what "the equitable" is, and that it is just, and also to what "just" it is superior. And from this it is clear what is the character of the equitable man; for he who is apt to do these things and to do them from deliberate preference, who does not push the letter of the law to the furthest on the worst side, but is disposed to make allowances, even although he has the law in his favor, is equitable; and this habit is equity, being a kind of justice, and not a different habit from justice.[*]

This is the meaning of the well-known proverb:—"Summum jus summa injuria."

Our Court of Equity is formed and conducted on this principle, for this corrective purpose; and, in this respect our administration of the law approaches more nearly to equitable justice than that of any other country.

The Greeks recognized the principle that it was the duty of their State to support the sanctions of virtue by legislative enactments; consequently, the moral education of the people formed part of their legislative system. Hence the rule which Aristotle states; "Quæ lex non jubet vetat." The principles of our law, on the contrary, are derived from the Roman law, which confines itself in all cases to forbidding wrongs done to society. Hence the rule with us is

[*] Aristot. Eth. Book v. cap. x.

exactly the contrary; "Quæ lex non vetat per-
mittit."

Aristotle roughly defines justice as, the habit
from which men are apt to perform just actions
and entertain just wishes.

Injustice is the contrary habit.

The same capacity and science comprehends
within its sphere contraries, but a habit cannot
be of contraries.

And if we have the things connected with a
habit, we have the habit itself.

Therefore, if we have what the unlawful and
the unequal mean, we know that the just is the
lawful and the equal.

The object of the law is to direct and enforce
virtue; therefore, justice, which has to do with
law, is perfect virtue, considered not absolutely,
but relatively.

Justice implies equality.

The equal is a mean between more and less.

Therefore the just is a mean.

Justice differs from all the other virtues in
the following respect: Justice is a mean state,
not in the same manner as the other virtues, but
because it is of a mean, and injustice of the
extremes.*

"The other virtues are mean habits between

* Aristot. Eth., Book v. c. v.

two extremes; *e. g.*, courage is a mean between rashness and cowardice; justice, on the other hand, is not in the mean between two extremes, but its subject-matter is a mean between too much and too little." (Browne's Note.)

And justice is that habit, according to which the just man is said to be disposed to practise the just in accordance with deliberate preference, and to distribute justly, between himself and another, and between two other persons; not so as to take more of the good himself, and give less of it to the other, and inversely in the case of evil; but to take an equal share according to proportion; and in like manner between two other persons. But injustice, on the contrary, is all this with respect to the unjust; and this is the excess and defect of what is useful and hurtful, contrary to the proportionate. Wherefore injustice is both excess and defect, because it is productive of excess and defect; that is, in a man's own case excess of what is absolutely good, and defect of what is hurtful; but in the case of others, his conduct generally is the same: but the violation of proportion is on either side as it may happen. But in the case of an unjust act, the defect is the being injured, and the excess to injure.[*]

* Aristot. Eth., Book v. c. v.

It is not necessary here to follow this wonderful heathen Philosopher further in his incomparable views of Justice, and these are here introduced only for the purpose of pointing out the superior clearness and definiteness of these to Mr. Mill's views of the same subject.

No doubt, these views of Aristotle are quite consistent with Mr. Mill's, so far as his views are consistent with truth, because truth must always be consistent with itself; but the substantial difference between them is this:—that the views of the heathen Philosopher are clearly defined and founded on practical virtue ; whereas the views of the Christian Philosopher are necessarily undefined and not very intelligible, because not founded on virtue, but on the vague and general principle of utility, as he calls it, and which admits of no clear definition, or of which, at least, he has given none, and from which, therefore, can be drawn no practical result.

Another object in here referring to the Ancient Greek Philosopher for his definition of Justice is, to lead modern philosophers and politicians to consider how far our code of Christian laws is conformable with Justice according to this definition; and how far our laws are made consistently with "that feeling which" Mr. Mill properly says (p. 61) "is bestowed on us by

Nature, but which does not necessarily legitimate all its promptings." But he adds: "The
feeling of justice might be a peculiar instinct,
and might yet require, like our other instincts,
to be controlled and enlightened by a higher reason."

What does Mr. Mill mean by "a peculiar instinct," applied to the human "feeling of justice"? What are "our other instincts"? What
does he mean by, "might require to be controlled and enlightened by a higher reason"?
Are not all instincts "controlled and enlightened
by a higher reason"? And, if this be an instinct,
is it a question whether or not this is so "controlled and enlightened"? Does Mr. Mill mean
that, the feeling of justice, bestowed upon us by
Nature is an instinct? Or, does he mean that
it is a sense of virtue, imparted to us by the
Divine Spirit?

If an instinct only, it may "not necessarily
legitimate all its promptings." But, if a sense
of virtue imparted to us by the Divine Spirit,
how can it fail "to legitimate all its promptings"? If the Spirit of God be in us, "the spirit
itself beareth witness with our spirit, that we
are the children of God." (Rom. c. viii. 16.)
"Hereby know we that we dwell in Him, and
He in us, because He hath given us of His

Spirit." (1 John, iv. 13.) If it do "not necessarily legitimate all its promptings," it cannot
be of "His Spirit." If it be of "His Spirit,"
it cannot require to be controlled and enlightened by a higher reason, because there can be
no higher. If it be not of "His Spirit," it cannot be justice. If it be justice it is just. If it
be not just it is not justice. Does Mr. Mill
mean to say what Aristotle said some thousands of years before? If so, why not say, as
he said, that justice is one of the virtues, emanating from the one universal source of all virtue?
What does Mr. Mill mean by "instinct," applied
to the Holy Spirit of God in man, as representing one of the Divine Attributes? If he mean
"an innate moral principle," or an emanation
from "the energy or activity of the soul," according to Aristotle, why not say so? This Mr.
Mill has not attempted to explain, or to make
intelligible, and many will think that he is bound
to do both, or to retract what he has so inconsiderately or loosely expressed.

If our animal instincts may mislead us, there is
no necessity that our intellectual instincts should
be more infallible in their sphere.

That is, probably, all that Mr. Mill means, but
he has said much more, and left it in such obscurity that it is impossible to know what he

does mean.   This is the more astonishing from
one who is supposed to have studied the writings
of Aristotle.

But every one will agree with Mr. Mill that
it is of high importance to determine how far our
natural feeling of justice may be acknowledged
as an ultimate criterion of conduct.

It may be sufficient for the present purpose,
without following Mr. Mill through all his reasoning, to admit his conclusion ; (p. 64.) " that it is
just to respect, unjust to violate or withhold the
legal or moral rights of any one," unless those
rights have been justly forfeited.   It follows from
this, that it is just to bestow that which is deserved,
and unjust to bestow that which is not deserved.

It is also unjust to break faith with any one :
to violate an engagement, either express or implied, or to disappoint expectations intentionally
raised.

It is also inconsistent with justice to be partial.
Justice implies equality.

The Laws can interfere only in a very small
degree with the details of private life, and no one
wishes for this interference more than is necessary
for the protection of private rights, and public interests.

This is a true, and may be a sufficient, account
of the common sense of justice.   But this con-

tains nothing to distinguish between the legal
and the moral sense. All persons must feel that
there is a great distinction between legal and
moral wrong; that there are many legal wrongs
which are not moral wrongs, and many moral
wrongs which are not legal wrongs. We acknowledge that there are Duties which may be
exacted, as we exact a debt, though many of
these are not recognized by our Laws. But
these, as moral or social duties, are not the less
binding.

Then, there are exactions, enforced by our
Laws, which are not founded on any moral right,
but which reasons of prudence may induce people
to submit to.

Then, again, as Mr. Mill says, (p. 71.) "There
are other things which we wish that people should
do, which we like or admire them for doing, perhaps dislike or despise them for not doing, but
yet admit that they are not bound to do; it is
not a case of moral objection; we do not blame
them, that is, we do not think that they are proper objects of punishment."

Mr. Mill is right in saying that, these ideas of
deserving and not deserving punishment is a distinction which lies at the bottom of the notions
of right and wrong; and, as he remarks, the character is still to be sought which distinguishes
justice from other branches of morality.

He is also right in saying, (p. 73.) that, " Justice implies something which it is not only right to do, but which some individual person can claim from us as his moral right. No one has a moral right to our generosity or beneficence, because we are not morally bound to practise those virtues towards any given individual."

Mr. Mill, (p. 75.) thinks, " that the desire to punish a person who has done harm to some individual, is a spontaneous outgrowth from two sentiments, both in the highest degree natural, and which either are or resemble instincts ; the impulse of self-defence, and the feeling of sympathy."

Our Laws proceed more upon the principle of suppressing present wrongs by the intimidation of punishment, than of righting the wrong by compensation, which was the principle of the Laws of our Saxon ancestors. The old Saxon Laws compelled the wrong-doer to right the wrong by compensation. And this seems to be the better principle wherever it can be enforced. Justice is but imperfectly obtained by the punishment of the wrong-doer without compensation for the wrong done. But it seems to be the principle of the English Criminal Law to right the wrong done to society, rather than to the individual sufferer. The sufferings of individuals

are supposed to be compensated by the promotion
of the public good. But in most examples of
punishment there is some tincture of injustice.
This was said so long ago as by Tacitus:
"Habet aliquid ex iniquo omne magnum ex-
emplum, quod contra singulos utilitate publica
rependitur."

Mr. Mill says, (p. 77.): "The idea of justice
supposes two things; a rule of conduct, and a
sentiment which sanctions the rule." This is
admitted.

Then he goes on to say: "The first must be
supposed common to all mankind, and intended
for their good." This also is admitted.

But then he adds: "The other (the sentiment)
is a desire that punishment may be suffered by
those who infringe the rule." This is denied.
The desire is for righting the wrong, if that be
possible; and for preventing a repetition of the
wrong, as far as that may be possible. The
desire of punishment is vengeance, and that is not
the common feeling of mankind. It is often the
first impulsive, but very rarely the permanent,
feeling. This is shown if the criminal escape,
and be brought to justice after a long lapse of
time. Few would advocate putting to death a
criminal for any crime, after the lapse of fifty
years from the commission of his crime, even

though that crime should have been murder.
This may be sufficient to show that vengeance is
merely the impulse of passion, and that our sense
of justice does not require punishment as a gratification of vengeance, but only as a compensation
for the wrong committed, and to deter others
from the commission of the like wrong.   How
far the punishment of death has that effect, is a
very open question, and many believe that it has
an effect contrary to that which is intended.
But this is another and different inquiry, and is
here adverted to only to show that the *sentiment
of justice* is not, as it appears to Mr. Mill to be
(p. 78), " the animal desire to repel or retaliate a
hurt or damage to oneself, or to those with whom
one sympathizes."

But Mr. Mill correctly lays it down, (p. 78.),
" When we call anything a person's right, we
mean that he has a valid claim on society to protect him in the possession of it, either by the
force of law, or by that of education and opinion.
If he has what we consider a sufficient claim, on
whatever account, to have something guaranteed
to him by society, we say that he has a right to
it.   If we desire to prove that anything does not
belong to him by right, we think this done as
soon as it is admitted that society ought not to
take measures for securing it to him, but should

leave him to chance, or to his own exertions.
Thus, a person is said to have a right to what he
can earn in fair professional competition; because
society ought not to allow any other person to
hinder him from endeavouring to earn in that
manner as much as he can. But he has not a
right to three hundred a-year, though he may
happen to be earning it; because society is not
called on to provide that he shall earn that sum.
On the contrary, if he owns ten thousand pounds
three per cent. stock, he *has* a right to three hundred a-year; because society has come under an
obligation to provide him with an income of that
amount."

He thence properly infers that, to have a right
is to have something which society ought to defend me in the possession of, on the ground of
general utility.

There is no good objection to this account of
the notion of utility; but it would be quite as
correct to say that, a sense of justice is inherent
in the human mind, totally independent of utility,
and is a standard *per se*, which the mind can
recognize by simple introspection of itself, although that internal oracle is so ambiguous, and
so many things appear just or unjust, according
to the light in which they are regarded.

But if that be an uncertain standard, Utility

is an equally uncertain standard, which different persons interpret differently. All standards must be uncertain which are dependent on the fluctuations of opinion, and there is as much difference of opinion about what is just, as about what is useful to society; and, therefore, as Mr. Mill remarks, (p. 81)—" Not only have different nations and individuals different notions of justice, but in the mind of one and the same individual, justice is not some one rule, principle, or maxim, but many, which do not always coincide in their dictates, and in choosing between which, he is guided either by some extraneous standard, or by his own personal predilections."

Mr. Mill gives numerous illustrations of this very plain fact, which no one denies, and these illustrations might be multiplied innumerably. But then he concludes, (p. 87.): "From these confusions there is no other mode of extrication than the utilitarian."

Now, if the right be made to rest on the ground of general Utility, as Mr. Mill infers, how is the question less ambiguous, or less open to difference of opinion, on this ground, than the right itself, as a standard *per se?* This, Mr. Mill has not attempted to show. He says only, that he can carry the inquiry no further, nor can he, but that amounts to nothing more than is expressed in

E

the vague uncertainty of Expediency, which is a merely imaginary distinction.

If there be confusion in these various opinions, the additional question of the Utility or Expediency does not seem to remove any of that confusion; but may be rather said to increase it.

It, therefore, seems that "Utility, or the greatest Happiness Principle," is without any foundation, and as a moral guide is useless, that "Principle" being a mere form of words without any rational signification.

That Justice stands very high in the scale of social utility no one denies, but that Happiness depends upon, or has any necessary relation to, Justice, is not only denied, but is contradicted by experience all over the world.   If happiness is to be measured by justice, there is very little happiness in the world.

The general maxims of justice, and their application for social utility, or the universal benefit of mankind, will be more expressly and fully treated of hereafter.

We have now followed Mr. Mill through the several chapters of his book, with running commentaries showing wherein we differ with him.

It may be convenient, in another Chapter to notice more particularly some of his leading fallacies, the tendency of which seems highly objectionable.

As a specimen of logical reasoning, coming from Mr. Mill, his book will be read by some with great interest, but by others with no less surprise; not so much that his reasoning should proceed on such false premises, as that his conclusions should be so illogically drawn.

There is something more in this question than can be reached even by Logic; but, on Mr. Mill's own showing, it is submitted that he proves his own conclusions to be wrong.

It has been considered unnecessary in these remarks to prove the absurdity of the old sophistry, that all good actions, being for the pleasure of a good conscience, originate in a refined sensuality.

That absurdity has been exposed by Coleridge in a very few words, and which, quoting from memory, are to the following effect :—

" So you object, with old Hobbes, that I do good actions *for* the pleasure of a good conscience ! And so,—after all, I am a refined Sensualist !

" Heaven bless you, and mend your logic ! Don't you see that if conscience, which is in its nature a consequence, were thus anticipated and made an antecedent, a party instead of a judge, it would dishonour your draft upon it. it would not pay on demand ? Don't you see that in truth the very fact of acting with this motive properly

und logically destroys all claim upon conscience
to give you any pleasure at all?"

This is a complete answer to the Epicurean
Philosophy, as the basis of Human Happiness.
It is strange that Mr. Mill does not see the error
of his philosophy when brought under this light.

CHAPTER VI.

FALLACIES OF THE UTILITARIANS.

UNDER the title of 'Utilitarianism' we are told that "the beliefs which have come down are rules of morality for the multitude and for the philosopher, until he has succeeded in finding better."

Mr. Mill earnestly maintains that philosophers may easily do this even now, on many subjects; and while he makes this declaration, which we understand to mean, that men are going onward in the wisdom of morality, he is taking up, as a good ethical doctrine, that of Epicurus two thousand years old. So that his progression seems to be one in a circle, rather than in a straight line.

We will receive Mr. Mill's definition (p. 8) of *utility*, as *pleasure* itself, together with exemption from pain; by which word, *utility*, he appears to mean *perfect utility;* while he might better say that, the measure of utility is that of the increase of pleasure with diminution of pain: for, if whole exemption from pain be an essential in utility, then there is none at all with the smallest pain among thousands of elements of utility.

Some one has given definitions of pleasure, and happiness, and blessedness, as differing all three one from another, and feeling that it was worth one's thought to keep them asunder, we are not quite ready to treat them, with Mr. Mill, as one; as in his proposition (p. 16) he seems to put the word, *happiness*, for the word, *pleasure*, in his definition (p. 8).

He writes, That the sanction of the standard of utility (p. 41) is the conscientious feelings of mankind at the time, as we understand his meaning, when that sanction is given as that of the standard: for, he would lead us to believe that neither such a sanction, nor utility itself is as yet a *truth*, taking the word *truth* as an offspring of the root, *to put up firm;* since he says, (p. 34) as already quoted; "the beliefs which are come down are the rules of morality for the multitude, and for the philosopher, until he has succeeded in finding better; that philosophers might easily do this even now, on many subjects; that the received code of ethics is by no means of divine right, I admit, or rather, earnestly maintain."

We must wait for the better rules of morality, till the philosophers, among whom we reckon Mr. Mill, shall have found them: but we should

like much to have from them answers to the questions of cases of conscience which have long since
been solved by Christian Ethics, so that we may
see how far the light of Utility outshines that of
the Gospel.

We should like to know how the Epicureans
would answer questions, such as many about oaths,
and others on vows; such as cases of anger, and
self-defence; such as, How a man may possess
and use riches?   What rule of moderation is to
be observed in eating?   What kinds of recrea-
tions are lawful? (of utility): Whether a wife
may give alms without consent of her husband:
and many others?

If the Utilitarian's answers to these and such
questions should be, as we think they would be,
of the same meaning as those of the Christian
casuist; How much are we yet the better for
Utilitarianism?

In many places Mr. Mill, in the answer of the
objections to his doctrine, shows, not that such
objections do not lie against it, but that like objections may be cast against other doctrines of
good and evil, right and wrong, or utility; so
that it often seems as if he were proposing only
that an allowed objectionable scheme should
stand among other objectionable ones; unless
we should rather understand that he wishes men

to accept his objectionable doctrine untried, for
their own, such as Christianity, of which they
most likely, by this time, know at least the
worst.

Mr. Mill's *tu quoque* arguments, *ad hominem*,
may be found, pp. 29, 36, 39, 42, 43, 44, 77.

He says, (p. 12) " Of two pleasures, if there
be one to which all, or almost all, who have experience of both, give a decided preference, irre-
spective of any feeling of moral obligation to
prefer it, that is the more desirable pleasure."

And again: " Now it is an unquestionable
fact that those who are *equally* acquainted with,
and *equally* capable of appreciating and enjoying,
both," (how many are they?) " do give a most
marked preference to the manner of existence
which employs their higher faculties."

Again: " Few human creatures would consent
to be changed into any of the lower animals, for
a promise of the fullest allowance of a beast's
pleasures; no intelligent human being would
consent to be a fool; no instructed person would
be an ignoramus; no person of feeling and conscience would be selfish and base; even though
they should be persuaded that the fool, the
dunce, or the rascal, is better satisfied with his
lot than they are with theirs."

We conceive that the minor proposition of this

reasoning must be, that a man (*homo*) who is intelligent and of feeling and conscience, is *equally*
acquainted with the utility known by a lower
animal, and a fool, or a rascal.

When we hear that Mr. Mill shall have been a
beast and a fool as long as he has been a man
and intelligent, we will believe that he knows
the compensations which Divine mercy has given
for intelligence to the beast and the born fool.

" It is better to be a human being dissatisfied,
than a pig satisfied," (p. 14.)

We may believe it with Mr. Mill; but, Why
is it better?

A man dissatisfied is so for in want of utility,
since Dissatisfaction is a pain, *pœna*, a sense of
evil.

As a Christian, I see, what, as a Utilitarian,
I might not see, that it is better to be in pair
under the loving Providence of God, than in
pleasure out of it.

In much of this reasoning there seems to be a
fallacy, through the want of a major-proposition,
or from the taking of a bad one, which seems
to be, as we understand it,—that if a being, as
a man, find a pleasure or pain in a deed, or in
a plight, which is common to him, in name or
form, with some other being, as a pig or a fish,
he thereby knows the pleasure or pain of the

other being in the like deed or plight, although
that other being differ from him in instincts and
in organs, and in fittingness for such deeds or
plights.

We deny it.

If Mr. Mill be a logician, he can give us his
major-proposition and his syllogism; but we do
not see what it can be but something of this
form :—

If one being find pleasure or pain, good or
evil, in any deed or plight, every other being
finds as much pleasure or pain, good or evil, in
a deed or plight of the same name. But man
is a being who finds pleasure, or good, in a bed
on a frosty night; and, therefore, every other
being, as a fish, finds the same pleasure, or utility, in a bed on a frosty night.

If a man, as a diver, may have been under
water in the mammoth cave, will he thereby
know the utility enjoyed by the eyeless fishes in
the cavern, or of a bat in the dark hole?

It does not seem likely that even a man who
has experienced a pleasure or pain of a deed or
plight common, in name, to him and other men,
can always measure their pleasure or pain in the
like deed or plight.

A man may have loved, and his wife may have
loved, yet we cannot see that a man can ever

know fully the pleasure of a mother's love of her new-born child.

I may toss a mouse, and a cat may toss a mouse; but I am not sure that I know the pleasure with which the cat may do the act of the same name as mine.

A man and a pig may eat and lie on straw in the same sty; but we do not believe that the man therefore knows what a quantity of utility, *i. e.* pleasure itself, together with exemption from pain (p. 8) is enjoyed by the pig.

It may seem to us that the pleasure enjoyed by a bird on wing, is greater than that of the mole in the earth; but we may be mistaken, as we have never been a bird or a mole, though we believe that, the love of God, by the fitness of beings to their settings in creation, affords the elements of utility to all of them; so far, as to utility which does not seem to reach beyond earth-life, they have no more grounds for wishing to be man, than man has to wish to be a lower animal.   Why should the dog wish to be man when out-running man, and out-witting him in the tracking of game; or the eagle in out-seeing him; or the cat in out-climbing him; or the swan in out-swimming him; or the lion in the use of his greater strength?   Why?

"For his mind:" the Utilitarian may answer.

Aye:—but man's mind is only just up to his
need of mind for the utility of his life amid his
many wants, more wants (p. 13) than those of
beings with less mind. For, Mr. Mill says, (p. 13)
"A being of higher faculties requires more to
make him happy, is capable, probably, of more
acute suffering, and certainly accessible to it at
more points, than one of an inferior type ; but
in spite of these liabilities, he can never really
wish to sink into what he feels to be a lower
grade of existence."

What then? There is more of utility in his
life than in the so-called lower one?

If an Englishman may not wish to be a Frenchman ; if a Frenchman would not be an Englishman ; if a white man would not be black, and a
black man would not be of our sickly pale hue ;
if a man may not wish to be a woman, nor a
woman to be a man ;—Is it, therefore, certain that
the man or woman, the white or black man, the
Englishman or Frenchman enjoys more utility, as
such, than the other of his pair?

No. Unless we can affirm a major proposition, that every state or form for which a being
would not give up his own, is, therefore, one of
less utility than his own ; or, by consequence,
that a man is infallible in the judgment of all
states or forms as rated by himself, against his
own.

Mr. Mill says, (p. 15.) : "From this verdict of the only competent judges, I apprehend there can be no appeal."

What verdict? The verdict which he seems to think he has shown in his propositions, which are greatly weakened by facts, and by his own last statement; that a case which he does not believe *may be questioned!*

We believe with Mr. Mill, though on Christian grounds, which we need not here set against his own, that the pleasures of the mind are better, or of greater utility, than those of sense ; but we deny that he has shown this truth by his arguments.

Neither mankind in full, nor all the men who have known both the so-called higher and lower pleasures have been polled for their opinions of them ; and though we may have more written records, from men of higher yearnings, of their preference for higher pleasures, than from sensual men of their preference for lower ones, it may be that one class of men are more often pen-teachers than are the others, who may not proclaim their happiness to many others than their companions or neighbours.

We are told, (p. 15.) "Men lose their high aspirations because they have not time or opportunity for indulging them, and they addict them-

selves to inferior pleasures, not because they deliberately prefer them, but because they are either
the only ones to which they have access, or the
only ones which they are any longer capable of
enjoying."

We believe that many men who have known
the higher pleasures of the mind, and can still
indulge them, as higher bred opium-eaters, or
smokers, in India and China, and misliving men
of scholarship or taste in England, such men as
Porson or Morland, or others of wit and wickedness, of high taste in Art and low joys in life,
have often preferred sensual pleasures to the
higher ones of the mind; and if the Divorce
Court, and some other Courts, show us anything,
they show us that many men, who have time and
opportunity, at least, for indulging the most refined bents of mind, do addict themselves to inferior and unrighteous pleasures, though they be
not the only ones to which they have access. Mr.
Mill's last clause, however, so weakens down his
former propositions that it is almost as needless as
it is hard to answer him.

He says, (p. 15.): "It may be questioned
whether any one who has remained *equally* susceptible to both classes of pleasures, ever *know-
ingly* and *calmly* preferred the lower."

What can we learn from this? As we are only

told that, " it may be questioned," we may leave
it as an open question, but still we may own that,
if a man like two things *equally*, he may not prefer either of them. We can see it, but not by
any new light of the doctrine of utility. If a
man get tipsy with grog when his wife wants him
to drink coffee, utility now instructs us that, he
so does since he has not remained *equally* susceptible to both pleasures, that of inebriation, and
that of harmlessly quenched thirst ; or, If a man,
a husband and father, choose the pleasures of
adultery, instead of those of the blameless head-
ship over an untainted house, Utilitarianism
may cry—' Yes ;' but he does not *calmly* choose it.

The writer says (p. 51)—"The only proof
capable of being given that an object is visible
is, that people actually see it. The only proof
that a sound is audible is, that people hear it."

In these propositions we note that *visible* and
audible mean, that *can* or *may be*, not *should be*,
or *ought to be*, seen and heard. Mr. Mill, however, writes on by what he seems to deem analogy.

" In like manner, I apprehend, the sole evidence
it is possible to produce, that anything is *desirable* is, that people do actually *desire* it."

Does the word ' *desirable*,' then, here mean
of utility, and of utility to the desirers, or to
man in full?

The analogy of the case with *seeing* and *hearing*, 'visible and audible,' would show us that, it means only *desirable* to the desirers; and, even then that, *desirable* means only *that can* be desired, not that *should* be, or *ought* to be desired, and thus the whole proposition falls into a trite truth, for which we need not the teaching of an Epicurean.

If, however, it be meant by the writer's word '*desirable*,'—*that ought* to be desired, or of utility to man in full, or, even to the desirers, we think the proposition is faulty from a fallacy of speech, and is not true, nor strengthened by the analogy.

Seeing and hearing are bodily acts, not need-fully mighty for further action; whereas, desiring is a mind deed, which is itself a yearning for some other deed which, again we hold, may or may not be of utility. It is true that the only evidence that John *could be* knocked down by Thomas was that, he *was* knocked down by him; but to say that, the only evidence that he *ought to be* knocked down, or, that it was of *utility* that he should be knocked down by Thomas, was, that Thomas knocked him down, is either to make Thomas a judge of the worthiness of men to stand on their own legs, or to give no evidence at all.

Children may desire to play, rather than learn;

thieves to steal, rather than earn their own liveli-
hood; and most men to take pleasure, rather
than work hard. But we do not think it is thereby
shown, that only to play, to steal, and to take
pleasure, are of utility; while to learn, to earn,
and to work hard, are not of utility.

In page 61, Mr. Mill himself says:—"That a
feeling is bestowed on us by Nature, does not
legitimate all its promptings."

"As to the objection that utilitarianism is only an
immoral expediency," (p. 31) he says: "It would
often be expedient"—in a low and bad way—
"for the purpose of getting over some momentary
embarrassment, or attaining some object, useful to
ourselves or others, to tell a lie." This, he holds,
is forbidden by his doctrine, as harmful to social
well-being, and human happiness: but (p. 27)
he had said that, in every other case than the exceptional one of the man who has it in his power
to multiply happiness on an extended scale,
private utility, the interest of some few persons,
is all that a man has to attend to.

He says: (p. 69)—"There can, I think, be no
doubt that the *idée mère*, the primitive element,
in the formation of the notion of justice, was conformity to the law."

The Romans, we think, distinguished *lex*, law
laid down, from *jus*, right, or equity. We believe

F

that the word *right*, *rectum*, *recht*, is from a root,
meaning, to reach forth, as a reached, or stretched,
or straight line; and that *wrong* is from *wring*,
to twist, as a bent line. So that *jus* and *right*
reject the doctrine of yielding expediency, with
the faith that what is not just is not of utility
("quod non justum,"—not, utile). " Fiat justitia
ruat cœlum," said the Roman; though it may be
that Epicurus might have discovered less utility
in *cœlum ruitum*, than in *justitia non facta*.

In answer to the charge against Utilitarianism,
that it is a godless doctrine, Mr. Mill answers that,
if it be a true belief that God desires, above all
things, the happiness of His creatures,—utility is
not only not a godless doctrine, but more pro-
foundly *religious* than any other. Without stop-
ping to ask the meaning of the word 'religious,'
we would answer that, as far as we understand
the doctrine of Utilitarianism from Mr. Mill, it is
a godless doctrine, inasmuch as it is not grounded
on any sanction of God, by name, or word, as
the thought of God is not needful to its fulness;
and as it stands on man's experience, and not on
any received wisdom of God; and what is *without God*, is *godless*. It may work out farther, or
less far,—as far as it goes,—nothing against the
will of God; but, so a Captain, going into a
known haven without a pilot, may steer as the

pilot would have taken in his ship ; but, still, the ship with no pilot on board, is *pilotless*.

How far the charge against Utilitarianism, that it is godless, should be taken as an evil report of it, is another question, to which the Christian, and the Utilitarian, as such, may give different answers.   A doctrine, or, at least, a science, as geometry, may be godless without being false, but it cannot be godly without God.

Why should Utilitarians be ashamed to be seen on the ground which they choose ?

If they shape a doctrine on the sanction of man's experience, without a needful thought of God ; why will they not hear it called godless ?

If their doctrine be only for man's life in the flesh, without a needful thought of him as an immortal soul ; why should it not be called carnal ?

If it be only for the earth ; why should they wish it to be called heavenly ?

If it do not look to a judgment to come ; why should it be called longsighted ?

If it never look for light to a Holy Ghost ; why should we call it Spiritual ?

Let them make it what they would have it called, or own it as they make it.

CHAPTER VII.

HAPPINESS, THE ULTIMATE END.

God designs the happiness of all human beings.
Some human actions forward that purpose, or
their tendencies are favorable to it. Other human actions are adverse to that purpose, or their
tendencies are unfavorable to it. God has enjoined the former as promoting His purpose, and
has forbidden the latter as opposed to His purpose. He has given us the faculties by which we
may collect the tendencies of our actions. By
these faculties we know His tacit commands.

This is a brief summary of the *true* Utilitarian
theory.

The late Mr. Austin, in his learned and profound work on Jurisprudence, gives the following
brief summary of this theory:—"Inasmuch as
the goodness of God is boundless and impartial,
He designs the greatest happiness of all His
sentient creatures: He wills that the aggregate
of their enjoyments shall find no nearer limit
than that which is inevitably set to it by their

finite and imperfect nature. From the probable
effects of our actions on the greatest happiness of
all, or from the tendencies of human actions to
increase or diminish that aggregate, we may infer the laws which He has given, but has not expressed or revealed."

We accept this explanation. But the Utilitarian theory is carried beyond this by its advocates. They maintain that we may not only infer therefrom the laws which He has given, but
has not expressed or revealed, but that we may
derive from the observance of the laws so inferred,
that Happiness which is their ultimate end or object. And such seems to have been the meaning of Mr. Austin. But this is the great error
of the theory. Those laws are for the Government of human actions, and the tendencies of
those laws are for bringing human actions into
conformity with the Divine Will. This would,
certainly, be conducive to temporal welfare, but,
as certainly, this would not constitute human
happiness, which is independent of temporal
welfare, and, therefore, is not necessarily connected with it.

Human Happiness must consist in a conformity of the human with the Divine Will, as the
ultimate end, and for that end we should regard
those laws as given for our guidance and help;

but obedience to those laws does not necessarily
imply that conformity of Will which constitutes
Happiness, though this observance may imply
temporal welfare, and so far may be conducive to
Happiness as the ultimate end.

The observance of human laws, we know, se-
cures us from the penalties which the infringement of those laws imposes, but gives us no security beyond, and this observance, though it
may be, is not necessarily, conducive even to our
temporal welfare. And so we may infer of Divine laws, though their observance may secure us
in temporal welfare, and is most likely to do so,
yet something more than temporal welfare is required for the ultimate end in Happiness. For
this end must be required not only conformity
with Divine laws, but also conformity with the
Divine Will, or Spirit, as evinced in those laws.
Some of those laws are expressly revealed to us ;
others, not revealed, are to be inferred by sentiments, or feelings, common to all mankind, which ·
arise spontaneously, instantly, and inevitably.
These are the proofs that the actions which excite them are enjoined or forbidden by the Divine Will. The agreement or disagreement of
our actions with the laws or will of God, is instantly inferred from these sentiments, or feelings, without the possibility of mistake. We

may infer a great increase to our temporal welfare from keeping His Commandments, but we
may not infer Happiness from any increase of
temporal welfare, though we may fear a diminution of our sense of Happiness therefrom, without
a conformity to the Divine Will, or Spirit. Accordingly we are not committed to the guidance
of our slow and fallible *reason*, but we are endowed with *feelings* which warn us at every
step, and pursue us with their importunate reproaches when we wander from the path of our
duties. From those feelings which arise within
us when we think of certain actions, we infer that
those actions are enjoined, or forbidden, by the
Deity.

The yielding and accommodating phrase, *Common sense*, has been used to express this feeling.

Considered as affecting the soul, when the man
thinks especially of *his own* conduct, these sentiments, feelings, or emotions, are frequently styled
his *conscience.*

Thus, we have revealed to us by express laws,
and by these innate sentiments, feelings, or emotions, the necessary and sufficient guides and
helps for so directing our actions as to secure the
attainment of our ultimate end and object in the
greatest possible Happiness, quite independently
of any question of general Utility, nor does this

question seem to arise as in any way necessary
for this end and object.

But as regards our temporal welfare, those
laws, sentiments, feelings, or emotions, are much
more vague and indeterminate, and, therefore,
leave the question of general Utility a necessary
inquiry for that end or object, and that object
may be defined, in general terms, convenience
and pleasure. Utility, therefore, has a direct,
immediate, and necessary relation to convenience
and pleasure, because, without utility, convenience
and pleasure, as we understand them, could have
no existence; but, we know that Happiness can
and does exist without convenience or pleasure,
in the general acceptation of those terms, and we
know that Virtue, which constitutes Happiness,
does exist even when all the conveniences and
pleasures of this world are withdrawn. It is,
therefore, a vain and delusive attempt by any reasoning to make Utility a criterion or standard of
Happiness, and if it be once admitted to be a
rule or guide for human conduct with a view to
the ultimate end or object of Human Happiness,
utility is thereby admitted to be a criterion or
standard of human happiness, which is a manifest
absurdity and a dangerous error.

But though Utility cannot constitute Happiness, or furnish any criterion or standard of Hap-

piness, yet the practice of the Utilitarian theory
may often tend to the prevention or mitigation
of unhappiness; for, doubtless much of the existing misery is to be attributed to the present
wretched education and wretched social arrangements.

It is, no doubt, true, that next to selfishness,
the principal Cause which makes life unsatisfactory is want of mental cultivation.

As Mr. Mill says, (p. 20.) " There is no reason
in the nature of things why an amount of mental
culture sufficient to give an intelligent interest in
the objects of Nature, should not be the inheritance of every one born in a civilized country.
As little is there an inherent necessity that any
human being should be a selfish egotist, devoid
of every feeling or care but those which centre in
his own miserable individuality."

There is every reason to hope that better education and better social arrangements would go
far to improve the social condition; but to suppose that the highest results can ever be attained by human means alone, is to attach more
importance to the utility of the things of .this
world than they were intended to carry, and far
more than it is in the nature of things to effect.

Mr. Mill is quite right in saying, (p. 21) that
" most of the great positive evils of the world

are in themselves removable"; but when he goes
on to say, in the same sentence; "and will, if
human affairs continue to improve, be in the
end reduced within narrow limits"; he gives no
reason for this assertion, which has no sanction
from anything that he has said before, or says
after; and which has no sanction from divine
authority.

In what sense he means that human affairs
will continue to improve, he does not explain.
In some sense the world's affairs may continue
to improve, whilst the great positive evils may
be increased, and the limits of evil may be enlarged instead of narrowed. Poverty, as he says,
in any sense implying suffering, may be completely extinguished by the wisdom of society,
combined with the good sense and providence of
individuals. This, in a worldly sense, though little
likely, may be, and to this extent is, within the
providence of the doctrine of utility; but all this
may be, and still be very far from the advancement of human happiness; and if it should be
attended with a diminution of human misery,
which is by no means a necessary consequence,
the very diminution of that particular description of human. misery may lead only to an ag-
gravation of human wickedness, and a further
removal from human happiness.

These are conclusions in no way unfavorable to the utilitarian theory, but only confining its application within appropriate limits, consistently with the nature and fitness of things.

The tendency of human actions on the general welfare is a very important inquiry in the question of human happiness; but it is of especial importance in this inquiry to distinguish between the tendency of human actions from the nature of things, and the tendency of human actions from the energy of the soul, which is beyond the nature of things, as we understand it.

It is confounding things different in their properties and purposes to attribute the operations of things material to influences purely spiritual, between which there can be no necessary connection, though they must be intended to be in perfect conformity. And although the purely spiritual influences must affect the operations of material things, yet it cannot be supposed that those operations, however conducive to spiritual influences can possibly control or govern them.

Mr. Austin is right in saying that to collect the tendency of a human action, as influencing the general welfare, we must not consider the action as if it were *single* and *insulated*, but must look at the class of actions to which it belongs. The probable *specific* consequences of doing that single act, of forbearing from that single act, or of omitting that single act, are not the objects of the inquiry.

The question is, if acts of the *class* were *generally* done, or *generally* forborne or omitted, what would be the probable effect on the general welfare or good?

Considered by itself, a mischievous act may seem to be useful, or harmless. Considered by itself, a useful act may seem to be pernicious.

For example,—If a poor man steal a handful from the heap of his rich neighbor, the act, considered by itself, is harmless or positively good. One man's poverty is assuaged with the superfluous wealth of another.

But if thefts were general, or the useful right of property were open to frequent invasions, property would be without security, and there would be no inducement to save. Without habitual saving there would be no accumulation of capital. Without capital there would be no fund for wages, no division of labor, no machinery, none of those helps to labor which augment its productive power, and multiply the enjoyments of every individual in the community. Frequent invasions of property would bring the rich to poverty, and would aggravate the poverty of the poor.

Again :—If the payment of a tax imposed by
a good government be evaded, the *specific* effects
of the mischievous forbearance are undoubtedly
useful. The money unduly withheld is convenient to the person who withholds it; and, compared with the bulk of the revenue, is too small
to be missed. But the regular payment of the
taxes is necessary to the existence of the government.

In these cases, the act or omission is good,
considered as single or insulated; but, considered with the rest of the class, is evil. In
other cases, an act or omission is evil, considered
as single or insulated; but, considered with the
rest of its class, is good.

For example : punishment, as a solitary fact,
is an evil : the pain inflicted on the criminal
being added to the mischief of the crime. But,
considered as part of a system, a punishment is
useful. By a few punishments many crimes are
prevented. With the sufferings of the guilty
few, the security of the many is purchased.

It, therefore, is true generally that, to determine the true tendency of an act, forbearance,
or omission, we must resolve the following question :—What would be the probable effect on the
general welfare or good, if *similar* acts, forbear-
ances, or omissions were general or frequent?

Such is the reasoning of Mr. Austin for the principle of general Utility. He infers that the tendencies of actions are the index to the will of God, and that if so, it follows that most of His commands are general or universal. The useful acts which He enjoins, and the pernicious acts which He prohibits, He enjoins and prohibits, for the most part, not singly, but by classes: not by commands which are particular, or directed to insulated cases; but by laws or rules which are general, and commonly inflexible.

Consequently, where acts, considered as a class, are useful or pernicious, we must conclude that He enjoins or forbids them, and by a *rule* which probably is inflexible.

To this reasoning in support of the theory of Utility, there can be no objection, but the only practical result seems to be this: that our motives to obey the laws which God has given us are paramount to all other motives, the greatest possible happiness of all His sentient creatures, being the purpose and effect of those laws.

Utility is indisputably a good guide for our conduct where the Divine Will is not expressly revealed, and our convenience and pleasure and well-being may be said to be dependent thereon; but for our Happiness we have express revelation, and for the attainment of that Utility is no

guide, nor is any such guide required for that
end ; and with reference to that end, there is no
more meaning in the theory of Utility, than that,
utility is utility, and right is right.

For the greatest possible Happiness we have
not to shape our conduct according to the principle of general Utility, but according to the
Divine laws as revealed. We may then be certain that our conduct is according to the principle of general utility, without any exception ;
but to make Utility a rule or guide to Happiness,
is to invest God's gifts of the utilities of nature
with a power and importance which they do not
possess, and which it is impossible for us to believe they were ever intended to exercise.

Admitting these premises, the following conclusion, drawn by Mr. Austin, is inevitable :—
"The *whole* of our conduct should be guided by
the principle of utility, in so far as the conduct
to be pursued has not been determined by Revelation. For, to conform to the principle or maxim
with which a law coincides, is equivalent to obeying that law."

To this conclusion there can be no objection ;
but much more than this is the conclusion drawn
by Mr. Mill, and also by Mr. Austin, and other
advocates of the Utilitarian theory, and by so
much more the *whole* theory is made erroneous,
confusing, and deceptive.

The final cause or purpose of the Divine laws
is the general happiness or good. But to trace
the effect of our conduct on the general happiness or good is not the way to know those laws.
It is sufficient to know, that by consulting and
obeying the laws of God we promote our own
happiness and the happiness of our fellow creatures. But, we should thwart their benevolent
design, and fail in our object or end of general
happiness, if we took the principle of general
Utility as the *guide* of our conduct. Not that
the principle of Utility is a *dangerous* principle
of conduct, but that this principle is not necessary to, however consistent with and conducive
to, our ultimate end or object in general happiness.

To say that ' the principle of Utility were a
dangerous principle of conduct,' is to say that,
' it were contrary to utility to consult utility,' or
that, right is contrary to right. But, to say that,
the principle of utility is applicable *only* to God's
gifts to man, through what is called Nature, is
another form of saying that, ' Utility is our *only*
index to the *tacit* commands of God'; and this
is what Mr. Mill, Mr. Austin, and other Utilitarians do say; though the opponents do not say,
or do not mean to say, as is imputed to them,
that, ' the principle of utility is dangerous.'

We say that, for our ultimate end or object in Happiness, we have the revealed Word of God, and that it is dangerous to confound this glorious fact with any human theory resting on deductions from the principle of utility, or our use of God's gifts in Nature, though it is admitted that we may recognize in these His benevolent purpose, and may infer therefrom his tacit commands.

We judge by a sure instinct that every way of God must be a good way, and the way of our own interest. But many think it the same thing to say that, every way which seems to be the way of their own interests is therefore proved to be a way of God. They too easily become content both with this sign of what is right, and with their own notions of what is really for their own good. In this way they almost imperceptibly become a law unto themselves; and, having no longer the fear of God before their eyes, follow the devices and desires of their own hearts. They cease to trouble themselves with the question what is godly, and pious, and reverent; they content themselves with asking what is profitable and agreeable, what is for their pleasure and convenience. They look to the utility of things, and to that only, and so far they are Utilitarians. They cannot fail to perceive sin, but they regard sin more as folly than as sin.

G

To convince of sin, is indeed, "the mission of the Comforter," but in the doctrine of the Utilitarians this mission, if recognized, is kept out of view; it is not denied by them, but, being kept out of view, it is apt to be forgotten by them.

The external life of a "worldly man," who looks to his pleasure and convenience in the utility of the things of this world, may be forbidden by no divine law, may, in fact, be required by the divine law; but not for that reason is he living in it. His external life may be in perfect conformity with the doctrine of Utilitarianism, but his inner life may tell him that he is still very far from the attainment of happiness.

Virtuous impressions, and our capacity for receiving them, are excluded by Utilitarians in their doctrine of utility, or, at least, form no necessary part of their teaching. They pretend to show the way to the attainment of the Greatest Happiness, but they show only their own way, and that is not the way of Him who said:—" I am the way." In this the modern Utilitarians are very far behind many of the ancient heathen philosophers.

According to Aristotle, we are born with a natural capacity for receiving virtuous impressions, and for forming virtuous habits. We are endowed with a moral sense, a perception of

moral beauty and excellence, and with an acute-
ness on practical subjects, which, when cultivated, is improved into prudence or moral wisdom.   Therefore, according to Aristotle, virtue
is the law under which we are born, the law of
nature, that law which, if we would attain to
happiness, we are bound to fulfil.   Happiness in
its highest and purest sense, is our "being's end
and aim;" and this is an energy or activity of
the soul according to the law of virtue : an energy
of the purest of the capacities of the soul, of that
capacity which is proper and peculiar to man
alone ; namely, intellect, or reason.

But this natural disposition is, according to
Aristotle, a mere potentiality ; it is possessed, but
not active, not energizing.   It is necessary that
it should be directed by the will, and that the
will in its turn should be directed to a right end
by deliberate preference ; *i. e.* by moral principle.   From his belief in the existence of this
natural capacity, or inclination towards virtue,
and moreover from his believing that man was a
free and voluntary agent, Aristotle necessarily
holds the responsibility of man.   Man has power
over his individual actions to do or to abstain.
By repeated acts, habits are formed either of
virtue or vice ; and, therefore, for the whole character when formed, as well as for each act which

contributes to its formation, man is responsible.
Not that men have always power over their acts,
when their character is formed; but what he con-
tends for is, that they have power over them
whilst their moral character is in process of formation; and that, therefore, they must, in all
reason, be held responsible for the permanent
effects which their conduct in particular acts has
produced, and which they must at every step have
been gradually resulting.*

Aristotle defines Happiness as a good of the
soul, and the chief good, because it is self-suffi-
cient; and Pleasure as giving a perfection, a
finish, as it were, to an energy; being, as he says,
in order to illustrate its nature, what the bloom
is to youth. But if so, pleasure must be active,
energetic; not simply rest; but rest as regards
the body, and energy as regards the mind. It
is an activity of the soul—not a mere animal activity.

This distinction enables us to mark the difference between true and false pleasures. Those
which are consequent upon the mere activity of
our corporeal nature are low and unreal; those
which attend upon the energies of our intellectual
nature are true and perfect, and worthy of the
dignity of man.

* See, Browne's "Analytical Introduction to the Nicoma-
chean Ethics of Aristotle."

But as happiness is an energy or activity of the soul according to its highest excellence, this must be that which is the characteristic property of man, namely pure intellectual excellence, and this must constitute the chief good of man.

Although happiness must be sought for and arrived at by the formation of habits of practical virtue, still all other virtues must be pursued with a view to the final gratification of our intellectual nature; the end of the cultivation of all virtue being to fit us for the enjoyment of pure and unmixed happiness.

It is by the gradual perfection of our moral nature, and by this method only, that we are brought into that state in which the intellectual principle is able to act purely and uninterruptedly. The improvement of our moral and intellectual faculties will go on parallel to one another. Every evil habit conquered, every good habit formed, will remove an obstacle to the energy of the intellect, and assist in invigorating its nature. Begin with moral training, and we shall attain to higher capacities for intellectual happiness, whether derived from the contemplation of abstract truth, or of the perfections and attributes of the Deity. The Christian philosopher will easily understand the value of this method of teaching; for he knows that it is re-

vealed to us, that in divine things moral training
is the way to intellectual cultivation,—that the
heart is the way to the understanding :—" If any
man will do God's will, he shall know of the
doctrine whether it be of God." (St. John vii.
17.)*

Here is no reference to the Epicurean doctrine
of Utility, and the Heathen Philosopher has,
better than some Christian Philosophers have,
pointed out the way to the attainment of Happiness, being more in accordance with the principles of human nature, and, therefore, with the
laws of Him who is both the Author of revelation, and of the moral constitution of man.

Aristotle connects the subject of ethics with
that of politics, by considering that the idea of a
State implies a human society united together
upon just, moral, and reasonable principles. These
principles are developed and displayed in its institutions; its end and object is the greatest good
of the body corporate ; and, therefore, so far as
it can be attained consistently with this primary
end, the greatest good of each family and individual. Now, on the morality of the individual
members, the morality, and therefore the welfare
and happiness, of the body depends ; for, as in a
free State, the source of power is ultimately the

* Browne's "Analytical Introduction to the Ethics of Aristotle," p. 11.

People, on the moral tone of the People the character of the institutions framed by their Representatives must depend.

What is the answer which, in the spirit of our modern political science, a man should give to this question; Who shall be my Representative in Parliament?

Many say : " He must be a man who, whether he can speak or not, must vote. He must vote exactly as I should vote myself, whatever his own convictions may be. He must take care of my local interests, and the protections or liberties by which my particular trade or commerce will be most effectually served. In fact, he must do exactly what I tell him to do. I shall give no man my vote who will be a party to compelling me to do what I do not in the least wish to do ; by passing laws that I do not approve. I shall give my vote to no man who does not distinctly understand that in the very act of becoming my Representative he gives up his own experience, judgment, conscience, religion, God, and take mine instead ; who does not clearly see and unambiguously acknowledge that he goes to the House of Commons for no purpose in the world but to deliver my message ; for no reason in the world but because I am not allowed to go there and deliver it for myself."

Such is very likely to be the answer of the Utilitarian Politician.

The answer that would be given in the spirit of the Platonic philosophy—an answer, let us hope, not altogether "unfit for this world"—is surely in a nobler strain. "I will seek for my Representative one who will represent all in me that is righteous, and wise, and brave, and unselfish; who will utterly scorn to give effect to my mean and covetous desires; whom I can trust because he will not condescend to flatter me and sell his conscience and his country for my vote. I will seek one who will represent my excellencies, not by an exact copy reproducing all the imperfections and flaws of the original, but by actually being and doing all that I have been able only dimly to see and anxiously to desire. I will seek one who will act on principle, not from expediency; who will not be misled by the clamour of those who threaten, or the sophistries of those who deceive, or the bribes of those who buy. I do not want a puppet who will move as I pull the strings—I want a man."

We may think our Platonists' vote will be long in suspense; but, possibly, even hunger may not be worse than poison.*

* "The Republic of Plato." By the Rev. W. Kirkus, LL.B., p. 172.

The reference here made to Aristotle's Ethical System is for the purpose only of showing, even from the experience of the most ancient heathen Philosophers, how very imperfect and fallacious must be the theory of Utility as a guide to Happiness; and how it may be made practically applicable to the purposes of Government, for the benefit of the State, and the welfare of the People, and, so far, conducive to Human Happiness.

The conclusion of the whole matter is that, not by the utility of the things of this world, but by fearing God and keeping His commandments, we may live a nobler life even than Solomon's; a wiser and a happier life than his whose wisdom and riches were the wonder of the world.

"Fear God, and keep His commandments: for this is the whole duty of man. For God shall bring every work into judgment, with every secret thing, whether it be good, or whether it be evil." This is no answer to a speculative Utilitarian; but it is a complete answer to a weary spirit.

CHAPTER VIII.

UTILITY, APPLIED TO GOVERNMENTS.

UTILITARIANS, who take the principle of utility as our index to the Divine commands, in the absence of express revelation, must infer that obedience to established government is enjoined by the Deity. For, without obedience to "the powers which be," there were little security and little enjoyment.

This is an inconvenient conclusion, and raises the difficult question, whether resistance to government be useful or pernicious,—whether it be consistent or inconsistent with the Divine pleasure.

Mr. Austin must have felt the difficulty when he called this, " an *anomalous* question." He says : " We must try it by a direct resort to the ultimate or presiding *principle*, and not by the Divine *rule* which the principle clearly indicates. To consult the rule, were absurd. For, the rule being general and applicable to ordinary cases, it ordains obedience to government, and excludes

the question." This is only what Aristotle said
so long before. In this question, Mr. Austin
says, we must dismiss the rule, and calculate
specific consequences. But can the consequences
be otherwise than evil, if we disregard the Divine
rule and act against it?

This "*anomalous* case" seems to beset the
principle of utility with many difficulties, which
may " well perplex and divide the wise, and the
good, and the brave." But whatever may be the
way out of these difficulties, it is not easy to see
how the principle of utility opens the way out.

For the present purpose it will be sufficient to
avoid these difficulties by not assuming the
Divine command of obedience to " the powers
that be," to extend to those Governments which
exercise their powers in a manner manifestly injurious to the general welfare, and contrary to
the Divine will; for as the judicious Hooker said :
"obedience, with professed unwillingness to obey,
is not better than manifest disobedience."

St. Paul and St. Peter in several places command slaves to obey their masters. But St. Paul
and St. Peter also command the masters themselves to obey their despotic rulers. " Let every
soul be subject unto the higher powers. For
there is no power but of God; the powers that
be are ordained of God. Whosoever, therefore, ·

resisteth the power resisteth the ordinance of God ; and they that resist shall receive to themselves damnation."

This passage teaches passive obedience to despotism more strongly than any text teaches the lawfulness of slavery. But no passage in the old or new Testament teaches the lawfulness of despotism or slavery. The teachers who taught the first Christians to obey despotic rule, and slaves to obey their masters, did not teach them to consent to be stripped of their rights—did not excuse tyranny or slavery because forcible opposition to it was generally wrong. They did not mean it to be inferred that bad institutions ought to be perpetual, because the subversion of them by force almost always inflicts greater evils than it removes. They believed then, as we believe now, that despotism was a wrong, notwithstanding the general obligation to obey, and that whenever the wrong was so universally felt as to demand its removal, the time for removing it had fully come. But to infer any sanction of the wrong from the doctrine of obedience, is to fix the wrong upon Christianity, instead of being the evidence of our faith in the Divine Founder.[*]

Channing says: "Slavery, in the age of the

* Channing, quoted by Goldwin Smith:—" Does the Bible sanction American Slavery ?" page 99.

Apostle, had so penetrated Society, was so inti-
mately woven with it, and the materials of servile
war were so abundant, that a religion, preaching
freedom to the slave, would have shaken the social fabric to its foundation, and would have
armed against itself the whole power of the
State.   Paul did not then assail the institution.
He satisfied himself with spreading principles,
which, however slowly, could not but work its destruction."[*]

On this part of the question the late Sir
George Lewis has expressed his opinion in his
'Dialogue on the Best Form of Government,'
as follows: "The history of forcible attempts to
improve governments is not, however, cheering.
Looking back upon the course of revolutionary
movements, and upon the character of their
consequences, the practical conclusion which I
draw is, that it is the part of wisdom and prudence to acquiesce in any form of government
which is tolerably well administered, and affords
tolerable security to person and property.   I
would not, indeed, yield to apathetic despair, or
acquiesce in the persuasion that a merely tolerable government is incapable of improvement.   I
would form an individual model, suited to the
character, disposition, wants, and circumstances

---

* Channing, quoted by Goldwin Smith:—" Does the Bible
sanction American Slavery?" page 103.

of the country, and I would make all exertions,
whether by action or writing, within the limits of
the existing law, for ameliorating its existing condition, and bringing it nearer to the model selected
for imitation ; but I should consider the problem
of the best form of government as purely ideal,
and as unconnected with practice, and should abstain from taking a ticket in the lottery of revolution, unless there was a well-founded expectation that it would come out a prize."

The proposition, " to acquiesce in any form of
government which is tolerably well administered,"
is so widely comprehensive and so vaguely defined
that it seems hardly to furnish any guide to a
practical conclusion.   But even this rests the
question on general Expediency, or what is called,
the principle of Utility.

But, though the principle of utility would
afford no certain criterion, yet the community
would be fortunate if their actions were regulated
by it. The adherents of established Governments
generally think it the most expedient to uphold
existing institutions, and to regard all changes as
dangerous innovations, and therefore inexpedient.
When they yield, it is more frequently from their
fears of the danger of resistance, than from any
expected benefit from the change.   But for their
fears, there would probably be no change.

"Every one who has tried has been compelled
to admit, with bitterness and indignation, that
if he desires to bring the Government to abandon
a mistaken system, or to adopt sounder views, it
is not to members of the Government that he
must address himself. Time so employed is
usually thrown away. He must convince the
Public—not the Ministers; and when the public
is enlightened and persuaded and grows noisy,
then the officials follow tardily, reluctantly, and
grumblingly in its wake."* And, as Mr. Mill
well says; (Essay on "Liberty," p. 126.) "The
despotism of custom is everywhere the standing
hindrance to human advancement, being in un-
ceasing antagonism to that disposition to aim at
something better than customary, which is called,
according to circumstances, the spirit of liberty,
or that of progress or improvement."

The party affecting reform, being also governed
by their notions of *utility*, most frequently accept concessions short of their notions and wishes,
rather than persist in the pursuit at the risk of
greater evils.

In this way, to a certain degree, the standard
of *utility*, is, practically, made a criterion of improvement.   It is much to be desired that this

* "Truth *versus* Edification." The Westminster Review,
April, 1863.

should be acknowledged as a universal standard
in this world's affairs. We should then hear
less frequent appeals to those unmeaning abstrac-
tions and senseless fictions,—"the rights of man,"
or, "the sacred rights of sovereigns;" of "unalienable liberties," or eternal and immutable justice;" of an "original contract or covenant," or
"the principles of an inviolable constitution."
We might then hope to appreciate these at their
true value. "A sacred or unalienable right," as
Mr. Austin says, "is truly and indeed, *invaluable*, for, seeing that it means nothing, there is
nothing with which it can be measured."

But arguments drawn from utility, though open
to doubt and difference of opinion, are quite as
likely to be right as wrong, and quite as likely to
be right from this standard, as from any unmeaning abstraction, or senseless fiction. As if a
right were worth anything beyond the good it
may bring.

In the absence of an express revelation of the
Divine Will, we are warranted in inferring it
from His visible acts in creation ; and when we
see the tendency of human actions is to thwart
His visible acts in creation, we are not only justified in conclusion that those human actions are
contrary to the Divine Will, but we are tacitly
commanded to alter and shape them according to

His Will, as revealed in all creation for the welfare and happiness of mankind. We may discern in the design of creation, why these were
left as tacit rather than express commands to
man, endowed with the knowledge of good and
evil, and with freewill to choose between the two.
We may see in the gifts of God to man in the
utilities of nature, that these were given gratuitously and equally to all, and we may properly
infer therefrom, the tacit command of God that
all His creatures should gratuitously enjoy those
gifts. But in human laws, which regulate civilized society, we do not see this principle recognized. We know that these gifts were given
gratuitously and equally to all, but subject to the
condition of making these useful for human purposes by human labor. On this the utility de-
pended. On this condition alone were these gifts
conferred. They were conferred gratuitously and
equally on all, but subject to this condition; and
by compliance with this condition only could
these gifts be of any value. Hence we may infer that these gifts were intended to be enjoyed
equally by all, subject only to this condition.

   This seems to be a very simple and natural inference, but in no part of the civilized world are
human laws made in conformity with this view.

   We are not called upon to assume that, in the

present dispensation of this World, it was intended that these gifts should be enjoyed equally by all; but that they should be enjoyed equally by all who could avail themselves of these gifts on this condition. We may fairly assume that those persons who by their own efforts, or by the efforts of others, have obtained a greater command over these gifts, than has been obtained by other persons, were intended to enjoy these gifts in a greater measure of amount.

This view may be considered to be consistent with the Divine Will, the only condition of the gifts having been complied with. The gifts, though given equally to all, could never have been intended to be enjoyed in the same measure by all, unless the condition were complied with in an equal degree by all, which, as mankind and the affairs of this World are constituted, is manifestly impossible.

It has pleased the Giver of all to bestow the Utilities of Nature equally on all His creatures, subject to the one condition of making His gifts available for their use by their own efforts. From this we may infer His tacit command that no other than the single condition which He has imposed, should be interposed between possession and enjoyment. From this tacit command we may confidently infer the Divine Will

and intention.   But in no civilized Government
in the World is this tacit command acknowledged, or the Divine Will and intention recognized or confirmed.   On the contrary, in every
civilized Government this tacit command is disregarded, and this Divine Will and intention is
frustrated, by many other conditions and obstacles of human interposition.

Labor and efforts are prevented from enjoying that share in the gifts of Nature, according to the condition of those gifts, by the inter-
vention of human laws, in contravention of the
Divine law and Will.   All human beings come
into this world with equal rights, and all are in
a state of equal helplessness.   But all come into
the world with different natural powers and ca-
pabilities, both physical and mental.   There is
no equality in Nature, but all the works of
Nature are marked with inequality.   The only
equality which we can discern is in the Divine
Will, that all creation should be for the equal
good of all created beings.   In this way we can
see that all inequalities are only apparent, and
are intended for the equal good or happiness
of all.   From this we may see that, the more we
govern our actions by this principle, the more
we promote the good or happiness of all ; and
that the more we depart from this principle, the

H 2

more we thwart the Divine Will for this end or object.

If Governments were formed to carry out this principle, it can require no further evidence to show that it must promote the welfare and happiness of the People, than to show that this principle is enforced by the tacit command of the Deity, and that by no other means can the Divine Will and intention be carried out for the good and happiness of all created beings.

It need not be shown that, human laws and contrivances which contravene the Divine Will, as manifested in the Laws of Nature, can never attain the object of human good, but must end in confusion and misery.

If it can be shown how the inequality in the distribution of the temporal goods of this world, may be made equal to all in the end or object of temporal welfare, and so rendered conducive to the ultimate end or object of Human Happiness, nothing further can be required to show that this must be for the equal benefit of all.

In this view, the principle of Utility is presented to us as the leading principle of universal creation, and is manifestly intended for our guidance; and this, to be consistent with our own freewill, is left an open question, without any express command, but not without Divine help in those sentiments, feelings, and emotions, which are given to us for our sure guides. That long neglect and disregard of these silent monitors may have weakened their influence, and admitted the unreasoning sway of prejudice, is to be expected; but though weakened and dormant from disease, they are not, and never can be, extinguished, and will certainly, before the end, prevail. It may require many calls before they are fully awakened, but these calls have already commenced, and they must be heard—must be regarded.

In all this there is nothing new. The voices of the dead still speak to us in their immortal works. Mr. Austin has justly remarked that:—
"If our conduct were truly adjusted to the principle of general utility, our conduct would conform, for the most part, to *laws* or *rules*: laws or rules which are set by the Deity, and to which the tendencies of *classes* of actions are the guide or index."

But, he adds:—"If the Divine must be gathered from the tendencies of actions, how can they, who are bound to keep them, know them fully and correctly?"

The answer is that, they never can. God has given us laws which no man can know completely, and Man has so far obscured these that,

the great mass of mankind has scarcely the
slightest access to the knowledge of them.

In so far as human laws are what they *ought*
to be, or in so far as they are in accordance with
the Divine commands, these have been framed
on the principle of utility, or by observation and
induction from the tendency of human actions.
If all whom they bind keep or observe them, the
ends are sufficiently accomplished, though the
reasons on which they were founded be unper-
ceived. If human laws were exactly what they
ought to be, that is, formed on the principle of
utility, and so far in accordance with Divine
laws, these, we may assume, would be observed
or admitted as rules of conduct, and would be
taken by the most uninstructed, as well as by the
most instructed, on authority, testimony, or trust.
We may assume this in reliance on the sentiments, feelings, and emotions, natural to the
human mind. In short, if a system of law were
framed exactly on the principle of utility, all its
constituent rules might be known by all or most,
although the numerous *reasons*, upon which the
system would rest, could scarcely be compassed
by any.

If this be an inconvenience, it is not peculiar
to law and morality. It extends to all the sciences, and to all the arts. As Mr. Austin has

well remarked :—" Many mathematical truths
are taken upon trust by deep and searching ma-
thematicians : and of the thousands who apply
arithmetic to daily and hourly use, not one in a
hundred knows or surmises the reasons upon
which its rules are founded. Of the millions
who till the earth and ply the various handi-
crafts, few are acquainted with the grounds of
their homely but important arts, though these
arts are generally practised with passable expert-
ness and success." And, as he adds, the powers
of single individuals are feeble and poor, though
the powers of combining numbers are gigantic
and admirable. Little of any man's knowledge
is gotten by original research. It mostly consists of *results* gotten by the researches of others,
and taken by himself upon *testimony*.

But, apart from this principle, the opinions of
mankind are so various and hostile, and there is
so little concurrence or agreement, that here testimony is not to be trusted ; nor can the bulk
of mankind, who have little opportunity for research, compare the respective merits of these
conflicting opinions, and hit upon those which
accord with utility and truth. Anxiously busied
with earning the means of subsistence, they are
debarred from every opportunity of carefully examining the *evidence;* whilst every authority,

whereon they may rest their faith, wants that
mark of trustworthiness which justifies reliance
on authority.

As Mr. Austin has remarked, and with a force
and clearness which will be best expressed in
his own words :—" Many of the legal and moral
rules which obtain in the most civilized communities, rest upon brute custom, and not upon
manly reason. They have been taken from preceding generations without examination, and are
deeply tinctured with barbarity. They arose in
early ages, and in the infancy of the human mind,
partly from caprices of the fancy (which are
nearly omnipotent with barbarians), and partly
from the imperfect apprehension of general utility which is the consequence of narrow experience. And so great and numerous are the
obstacles to the diffusion of ethical truth, that
these monstrous or crude productions of childish
and imbecile intellect have been cherished and
perpetuated, through ages of advancing knowledge, to the comparatively enlightened period in
which it is our happiness to live."

In civilized society nearly all offences originate
in property; and to property may generally be
traced the instigation to the greatest crimes.

Nothing but the diffusion of knowledge through
the great mass of the people will go to the root

of this evil. But much may be done to correct
their moral sentiments, and to bring them more
under the restraints which are imposed by enlightened opinion, by framing the laws which
govern them in more strict accordance with the
principle of utility.

Every man's public is formed of his own class,
or of those with whom he habitually associates.
The rich man's public is formed of the rich.
The poor man's public is formed of the poor.
The crimes which affect merely the property of
the wealthier classes, are certainly regarded with
little abhorrence by the poor and ignorant portion
of the working people. They do not perceive
that such crimes are pernicious to *all* classes, but
rather regard them as *reprisals* made upon
usurpers and enemies. They regard the criminal
with sympathy rather than with indignation, and
rather incline to aid his escape, than to lend their
hearty aid towards bringing him to justice.

There is no natural sympathy, in the mass of
the people, with the laws which govern them.
They see, in the laws which most concern them,
more of the principle of injustice, than of utility.
They know nothing of their glorious constitution,
because they have no perceptible part or share in
it. They know only of that which immediately
concerns their creature comforts, and, by com-

parison with the wealthier classes, they find their
share miserably small. They attribute this to
injustice—to unequal and unjust laws,—and in
this they are quite right.

To the *ignorant* poor, the inequality which
inevitably follows is necessarily invidious. That
they who toil and produce should fare scantily,
whilst those who neither toil nor produce should
enjoy the fruits, seems, to the poor and the ignorant, a monstrous state of things, and quite inconsistent with the benevolent purposes of Providence;
nor are they altogether wrong in this conclusion.

They find themselves deprived of their fair share
in the gratuitous gifts of nature. They know that
these were given equally to all, and for the benefit
of all, subject to the only one condition of making
these available for human use by human labor or
efforts. They know that they have given all their
labor or efforts, which is all they have got to give,
but they find that they receive in return only a
bare subsistence. They know that this result is
the effect of human laws and regulations, in the
making of which they have no voice, and over
which they have no control. The working class
know very little more than this, and, probably, as
the Working Class, never will know much more.

But it is very important that they should see a
just foundation for the laws which so materially

affect their temporal welfare. That never can be seen until the laborer be left in possession of the full reward of *his own* labor. This, at least, he has a right to expect; but by no civilized government in the world is this right recognized; and, less perhaps, than by any other is it recognized by our own Government.

As long as the Wages of Labor are diminished by a single tax on any of the necessaries, comforts, or conveniences, of life, this great injustice against the working class is committed. To that extent, at least, the laborer is unfairly dealt by, and to that extent, at least, human laws violate the Divine Laws, as far as we can interpret them in Nature, and are directly opposed to the Divine Will. Until this natural *right* be conceded, as a foundation, it is in vain to attempt to build up anything on the principle of Utility, or to pretend to take this as a leading principle for human government. It is a mockery to talk of the principle of utility as a guide, when the first dictate of that principle is rejected.

Now, if that principle be acknowledged and carried out, every Customs and Excise duty must be swept away; and not only those duties, but also every other tax which is now levied; with the solitary exception of the Postage Stamp which, for obvious reasons, is excluded. How the re-

venue is to be raised is another question : a very
important one, no doubt, but still quite another
question, and one which will be hereafter considered. If it can be shown,—as it clearly can
be, and already has been,—that the whole revenue
might be raised without, in the slightest degree,
infringing on this natural *right* and principle of
utility, that ought to be received as conclusive
evidence in support of the proposition, for that is
the only evidence which the case admits of, to
prove that the proposition is in accordance with
the Divine Law and Will, and that is the proof
that the human law is opposed to the Divine Law
and Will.

If the proposition, as here laid down, cannot
be supported in every part, the whole of the reasoning falls to the ground. But if it be proved
true in every part, then the whole fabric of existing systems of political government falls to the
ground, the foundation being overthrown. The
principle of Utility is, indeed, "a mockery and a
snare" if it will not stand the test of this application. It is idle, or worse,—it is fraudulent,—
to pretend to look to the principle of utility as a
guide for human actions, if the primary rule of
right in that principle, as established by Nature,
be denied and rejected.

If there be any truth in that principle, that

truth must be proof of the Divine Will, and no other proof can be adduced. It must, therefore, be sufficient, and if so, it must be proof of the tacit command of God to all mankind.

If so, is the confusion and misery, which prevails throughout the world, any matter of wonder?

If the basis of human laws be injustice against the greatest portion of mankind, can any system founded thereon be expected to work for the welfare of any portion; or can it be said to be working on the principle of the Greatest Happiness for the greatest number?

Human laws will never extinguish those sentiments, feelings, and emotions, which are innate in the human mind, and which find their confirmation in the laws of Nature.

Any human obstacles interposed between the free use and enjoyment of the free gifts of Nature, beyond the condition of human labor,—the only condition of these gifts,—will always be regarded by the mass of mankind, as an unjust interference with their natural rights. It is impossible to prove that their view is wrong. They will never be brought to see that there is any moral wrong in the breach of any of our Customs and Excise laws, or in evading any other of our many laws which interfere directly with their natural rights and enjoyments, those rights and enjoyments

being in no way necessarily connected with the
rights and enjoyments of property as held for the
benefit of the community. It is impossible, by
any teaching or by any penalties, to bring the
mass of the people to see the moral wrong, if
there be any, in the breach or evasion of any of
these laws, if these laws be founded on injustice;
and the real question then is, whether such
breach or evasion, provided it infringe on no
other and just law, be not highly meritorious
and deserving of all encouragement; but, certainly, it is impossible to maintain the contrary,
and to justify the acts of Hampden, and those
other Patriots, to whose successful resistance of
unjust laws we owe so much of our present freedom, and so many of our present enjoyments.

It is impossible to maintain that, the principle
of utility is applicable to individuals singly, and
not to individuals in the aggregate, or to the
community. If this test be good for individual
action, it must be, at least, equally good for universal action.

No one individual can properly set up himself
as the sole arbiter of this test, and, if he do so,
he must take the responsibility upon himself, with
the consequences. But he ought not to be otherwise prevented from doing so. And if the great
majority of mankind find a response to this test

in their sentiments, feelings, and emotions, this
is the safest and the surest sign to prove that the
test is good, and that the application is consistent
with the Divine will and intention for human
benefit.

If human laws were tried by this test, how few
of them would be left standing! But if legislation were more carefully governed by this principle, how many causes of crime would be removed, and how much misery would be spared!
Prejudices which now enslave the popular mind
would then be expelled by the broad principles
of the science of political economy, and those
simple, though commanding truths, would then
be capable of the easiest application.

The nicer points presented by this science will,
probably, never be understood distinctly by the
multitude; but, in civilized communities, these
principles would soon be apprehended by the
the multitude, and, as Mr. Austin has said, they
"would soon acquire the talent of reasoning distinctly and justly, if one of the weightiest of the
duties, which God has laid upon governments,
were performed with fidelity and zeal." Human
laws when seen through the light of these principles, would not only be better understood, but
would be more carefully regarded and observed,
as cherished institutions for the general welfare,

and being in accordance with the Divine will, as
far as that can be known through His express
command in His revealed Word, and through His
tacit command in the laws of Nature, human
laws would then find a responsive sympathy in
the sentiments, feelings, and emotions, of the
human mind, which would operate with more
force, for the due observance of such laws, than
could be obtained by any penalties or other
punishments which could be inflicted.   The
breach or evasion of such laws would be followed
by the almost unanimous disapprobation of the
people, and the moral power thus obtained would
be invaluable, because there would be nothing in
this world to compare with it, of equal value, for
the benefit of the human race.

This is no Utopian idea, or any new theory;
but it is a very old theory, founded on Divine
truth, and confirmed by the experience of ages.

The Utopian, or fanciful, idea consists in looking to this as a means of Happiness, instead of
looking to this as a means of government for
temporal welfare, and thereby conducive to the
ultimate end or object of Human Happiness.

The attainment thereby of the Greatest Happiness was the Utopian idea in the philosophy of
the ancient Epicureans ; and the same is the idea
in the doctrine of the modern Utilitarians.

This is Utopian or fanciful, because Human Happiness is beyond the reach of Human Philosophy.

Human wickedness and folly will ever be insurmountable barriers to Human Happiness, and these will never be removed by any human laws or contrivances. The Divine Spirit alone can give what is essential for Human Happiness. All that Man can do is to make his measures conducive to that end, by preparing the Human Mind for the reception of that Holy Spirit; and we know, as an undeniable fact that, the tendency of human misery is to human wickedness. We may, therefore, reasonably hope that, by admitting all into an equal participation in the gifts of Nature, so gratuitously and abundantly bestowed for the benefit of all, the tendency and effect of such proceeding, in accordance with the Divine will and intention, would be, to diminish human misery, and, so far, would be conducive to Human Happiness. But misery, though it would be abated, would not be extinguished, for wickedness and folly will still prevail, and the poor will always be with us. The wrong-doers would then be accountable for their wickedness and folly, and on themselves would rest that heavy portion of their guilt, which now falls on their careless, ignorant, or selfish rulers.

I

If the principle of utility be founded upon observation and induction applied to the tendencies of actions, it is a matter of acquired knowledge, and not of immediate consciousness, but the consciousness is a confirmation of the truth, and this consciousness would be kept continually alive in every human mind, if this principle were strictly observed and kept in constant action.

The multitude might then clearly understand the elements or groundwork of ethical science, by actual experience of the more momentous of the derivative practical truths ; and to that extent they might be safely freed from the dominion of authority : being provided with safely directing principles, they might be relieved from the necessity of blindly persisting in hereditary opinions and practices, and prevented from turning and veering with every wind of doctrine.

Nor is this the only advantage which would follow the spread of those elements amongst the great body of the people.

If the elements of ethical science were widely *diffused*, the science would advance with proportionate rapidity.

This is the sound remark of Mr. Austin, and his conclusion is worthy of all attention :—" If the minds of the many were informed and invigorated, their coarse and sordid pleasures, and their stupid indifference about knowledge, would be supplanted by refined amusements, and by liberal curiosity.   A numerous body of recruits from the lower of the middle classes, and even from the higher classes of the working people, would thicken the slender ranks of the reading and reflecting public."

As long as the bulk of the people continue to be indifferent to that which determines the result of their own labor, so long will the classes which are elevated above them by rank or wealth be indifferent to their welfare.

So long as the laborer surrenders the smallest portion of the wages of his labor to any tax-gatherer, (except only the tax for the protection of his person) he surrenders that portion of his labor to the other classes without any equivalent.   Moreover, those classes derive no real, though an apparent, benefit from his sacrifice, because the wages of labor being always on a level with the means of subsistence, among the mass of the mere laboring class, any diminution brings the level below the means of subsistence, and to that extent, at least, the deficiency must be made good by a corresponding demand upon the property of the wealthier classes ; or the natural strength of the country must be diminished by emigration. But the actual effect is, to make a much

greater demand upon their property than by the
Poor-rate, for then are brought into action many
other rates, consequent on the increase of crime,
and for its suppression. Nor is that all, for the
derangement of the labor-market, necessarily de-
ranges all the markets which the labor-market
supplies. This last loss is the greatest of all,
and this is incalculable.

Tried by the test of utility, the universal practice, in all civilized governments, of taking by
far the largest portion of the revenue of the State
out of the wages of labor, by the fraudulent contrivance of Customs and Excise duties, cannot
stand for a moment. Nor can it be justified on
any principle of justice or expediency to diminish, in the smallest degree, the labor-fund for
any State or other purpose. This is as gross a
violation of a natural right, as to deprive an innocent man of his liberty, and in many cases it
does deprive him of his liberty, and, what is
worse, in many cases, it deprives him of his
sense of moral right, which is of more importance to him even than his liberty. It tends to unfit
him for his place in civilized society, and such is
the effect. More than half the crimes and offences against society are attributable to this
cause alone. It is an infamous mockery and
deception in the government of any State to pull

down the working-man and his family to destitution and despair, and then to attempt to set
him up again by the Poor-Rate, the Prison, or
the Reformatory. But this is what Governments
in all States are doing, and attempting to do.
They do the first effectually : the last most inef-
fectually. They go on, nevertheless, trying to do
that which is impossible. They can pull down,
but they never can set up again.

If they would let alone the laborer of every
kind—the common and the skilled laborer, the
Manufacturer, the Trader, and the Professional
Man, until he had realized the profits of his
labor and skill, of his trade, and of his profes-
sion, most of these evils would be avoided, and
the duties and responsibilities of Governments
would be greatly reduced.

It is well for Governments to encourage the
Education of the People. But that is no part
of the duty of Government, or, at most, it is
but a secondary duty. The first duty is, to let
them live—to let them live honestly by their
own exertions—to let them enjoy their rightful
share of the gifts of Nature by their own efforts.

It is no part of the duty of Government to
educate the People, though it is the duty of
every Government to encourage the education of
the People. But it is the first duty of Govern-

ment to protect the People in their rights and
their property. Keep off the Tax-gatherer from
those who are the producers of property, and the
People will educate themselves. They will do
that for their own sakes when they find it worth
their while. But that will never be until their
social condition is raised; nor will any Government system of Education make much progress
in the meantime.

There is much talk about the Education of
the People, and a large sum of public money is
annually expended thereon. A very large sum,
if judged by the perceptible good; but a very
small sum, if measured as a means to the end.

But no Government is justified in filching
from the wages of labor for any such purpose,
or in applying a farthing of the public money
in the Education of the People whilst they are
deprived of any part of their Wages of Labor.
Those who labor have a just claim to spend
the produce of their own labor as they please,
and government has no right to interfere with
their pleasure, or to diminish their means.

This is an essential rule in the doctrine of
Utility, and the truth of this rule is confirmed in
all Nature. The gifts of Nature are bestowed
freely and equally on all, subject to the one condition of applying human labor to make them

available for human purposes. No Government
has the right to interpose any other condition.
Any other condition imposed must be a further
obstacle to the enjoyment, and must, to that extent, diminish the utility. The imposition of
labor is a sufficiently onerous condition. To the
sweat of the brow, need not be added the pain
of the heart. If no water could be used for
drinking, without first undergoing an expensive
process of purification, the utility of that useful
gift would be greatly diminished for human purposes. To tax water, would be to act contrary
to the law of Nature. That would be too infamous ; but, on principle, not more infamous than
to tax salt, or malt. To tax the laborer in his own
labor is, in effect, the same. It is equally infamous, only the infamous injustice is a little
more concealed. The Customs and Excise duties
leave the poor working-man less means to buy
salt for himself and family; and Salt is as necessary for life as Water. Malt, Sugar, Tea,
Tobacco, and other taxed articles are scarcely
less necessary for human use, and are, therefore,
abundantly supplied by Nature, and but for the
obstacles interposed by human ingenuity, would
be abundantly supplied to all civilized human
beings, at from the five hundredth to the thou-
sandth part of the present prices. But Govern-

ment steps in and imposes a duty of many hundred per cent. upon the natural price, and the poor are cut off from these necessary articles, or their supply is most cruelly and most injuriously diminished.

It is a common but foolish saying, and was lately said by a Cabinet Minister.[the Duke of Argyle] at a great public meeting in Scotland, that none of the necessaries of life are now taxed ; and then comes the discussion on what are necessaries of life; as if tea, sugar, tobacco, beer, wine, spirits, and all articles for. clothing, and timber for houses and implements, were not necessaries.   As if any articles given by God to man, for his use, were not necessaries.   But, whether or not ; on what principle of utility, or expediency, or morality, does Man interpose obstacles to the use of those gifts which, we may presume, God thought necessary for Man's use?

And how can any of these be taxed without diminishing the means for obtaining the others ?

·By what right do Rulers assume the prerogative of over-ruling the Divine command, and withholding any of God's gifts to His creatures ?

How long the People will submit to be thus deprived of their natural right, is for them to determine.   Probably, the time will be limited to their correct understanding of these questions.

How far a Government is justified in encroaching upon or curtailing the natural right
or liberty of the subject, is a question on which
no universal rule can be laid down; as that
question must always be very much dependent
on the necessity or emergency of the case for the
common welfare.

It is manifest that on any great emergency,
threatening danger to the whole community,
such as the sudden outbreak of the plague, or
the appearance of an invading enemy on the
native shore, or the discovery of a wide-spread
conspiracy for over-turning established order, the
assumption of larger powers than usual over the
ordinary rights and liberties of the subject, may
not only be proper, but may be the positive duty
of the Government, until the danger be removed.

On the same ground a considerable part of
the natural right or liberty of the subject must
always be surrendered for the maintenance of the
social state.

It is true that the necessity of the case will
be differently estimated by different persons, and
therefore no certain rule can be laid down for all
cases.

But the principle of utility, for the general
welfare, may, in all cases, afford some guide for
determining the question of expediency, and in

all these cases it must be a question of expediency only, to be determined only according to the circumstances.

To infringe upon the natural right of the Parent over the Child, on the ground of public good, can never be one of those cases. Any infringement of that natural right on a public ground must always be attended by more evil than good, because any such infringement must tend to weaken the natural tie, which must be stronger than any artificial tie substituted by law.

The only ground on which any such interference can be justified, is more for the prevention of a private wrong than for the promotion of a public good.

The truth of this is confirmed by all our experience, on the principle of general utility.

To compel Education by law is an interference with a natural right which must ever fail in the desired object. Not that the Education of the People is not a desirable object on public grounds, but that the preservation of the natural right of the Parent over the Child is a still more desirable object on every ground, public and private.

But to prevent a private wrong by a parent to a child, is not only justifiable, but is the duty of every Government on public and private grounds.

For a parent to neglect the education of his

child, is no infringement of the child's rights, and, therefore, is no ground for the interposition of the State. There is no diminution of the child's liberty, and no violation of the child's rights; the child's own will is free; therefore, there is no ground for an infringement of the parent's liberty, or right over his child; and, inasmuch as the taking away of his property to educate his own and other people's children is not needful for the maintaining of his rights, the taking away of his property for such a purpose is wrong.

If it be said that the rights of the children are involved, that cannot justify State-interposition until it be shown that their rights have been violated.

However open to condemnation may be the non-performance of a parental duty, that is no violation of a right, and, therefore, cannot properly be taken cognizance of by the State.

But the ground of the argument in favour of State-interposition is, that the interests of the State require it.

The answer to that is, that the State has no constitutional right to take away a man's property, or to infringe his natural rights, unless a special case of necessity can be shown. That never can be shown, for a universal system of public education by the State.

Every argument which can be used to prove that

the State is bound to educate a man's child, will
equally apply to prove that the State is bound to
feed, clothe, and house, the child. If the mental
wants of the rising generation ought to be supplied by the State, there can be no reason why
their physical wants should not also be supplied
by the State, and then all parental responsibility
is annulled.

But for a parent to neglect to feed, or clothe, or
house, or otherwise to ill-treat, his child, is both a
private and a public wrong.

However desirable education may be on public
grounds, it is impossible to say that a poor man,
who has barely the means of subsisting his child, is
committing a private or a public wrong by not educating his child. But it is impossible to deny that
a man who is pursuing a course likely to destroy
or to shorten the life of his child, is committing
both a private and a public wrong.

This is a very important question, and is open to
much diversity of opinion.

On this subject of human government there is
no express Divine command. There is no express
command to *educate* a child. The command is to
" train up a child in the way he should go."

We must, therefore, take the principle of utility
as the index to the Divine will. A child trained
up by his parents in the Christian doctrine,
which includes all the social duties of his or her

station in life, though unable to read or write, is more likely to be a good and useful member of society than a child taken away from parents and taught to read and write.

It is no answer to say that the child, whose education is enforced by the State, may still be under the training of the parent.   No one can say what may be the consequences of this interference between the child and the parent ; but it may be said that the tendency of such interference is to weaken the moral affections of the child ; and it cannot be denied that it is an interference with one of the most solemn of all the natural ties.

But what says Mr. Mill, the Utilitarian Teacher, on this subject ?   So far from concurring in this view, he says :—

" It is in the case of children, that misapplied notions of liberty are a real obstacle to the fulfilment by the State of its duties.   One would almost think that a man's children were supposed to be literally, and not metaphorically, [Why not suppose so ?] a part of himself, so jealous is opinion of the smallest interference of law with his absolute and exclusive control over them ; more jealous than of almost any interference with his own freedom of action : so much less do the generality of mankind value liberty than power."[*]

* Mill, "On Liberty," p. 188.

May not this "jealousy of opinion" be expressive of a natural instinct in parents? May not this instinct of parental power be the strongest evidence of the inherent love of liberty?

Mr. Mill thus proceeds: "Consider, for example, the case of education. Is it not almost a self-evident axiom, that the State should require and compel the education, up to a certain standard, of every human being who is born its citizen?"

No. It is not; and for the reason which Mr. Mill has just before given.

He goes on to ask:—"Yet who is there that is not afraid to recognize and assert this truth?"

If it were a truth, nobody would be afraid to recognize and assert it. But it is not a truth, and of this Mr. Mill has himself given the best evidence when he says that "opinion,"—meaning public opinion,—denies it.

He then goes on to say: "Hardly any one indeed will deny that it is one of the most sacred duties of the parents, after summoning a human being into the world, to give to that being an education fitting him to perform his part well in life towards others and towards himself."

Probably, no one denies *that*; if by "education," Mr. Mill mean *moral training.*

But if, by education, moral training be not meant, where does Mr. Mill learn that "it is one

of the most sacred duties of the parents" to educate their children according to his notion of education?

Mr. Mill goes on to say: "But while this is
unanimously declared to be the father's duty,
scarcely anybody, in this country, will bear to hear
of obliging him to perform it. Instead of his
being required to make any exertion or sacrifice
for securing education to the child, it is left to
his choice to accept it or not when it is provided
gratis!"

From this it seems that Mr. Mill does mean by
"education," something more than *moral training.* If Mr. Mill mean by "education,"—reading, writing, and arithmetic, with the use of
the globes, why not say so? He says nothing about the kind of education which is "to
fit him to perform his part well in life." But
he says: "It still remains unrecognized, that
to bring a child into existence without a fair
prospect of being able, not only to provide food
for its body, but instruction and training for its
mind, is a moral crime, both against the unfortunate offspring and against society; and that if
the parent does not fulfil this obligation, the State
ought to see it fulfilled, at the charge, as far as
possible, of the parent."

Here Mr. Mill has changed his term from edu-

cation to "instruction and training." Assuming
this to mean *moral training*, the answer is, that
the State never can "fulfil this obligation," and
therefore it is no part of the duty of the State to
undertake it, or "to see it fulfilled." How far
it may be the duty of the State to undertake it,
or to see it fulfilled, when there is no parent, or
no parent fit to be entrusted with this duty, is
another question.

But, mark the strange inconsistency of Mr.
Mill's reasoning, and his illogical conclusion. He
says: "Were the duty of enforcing universal
education once admitted, there would be an end
to the difficulties about what the State should
teach, and how it should teach, which now convert the subject into a mere battle-field for sects
and parties, causing the time and labor which
should have been spent in educating, to be wasted
in quarrelling about education."

Why so? These difficulties would remain the
same; but would then probably be found to be
insurmountable, by open resistance to the law.

But how does Mr. Mill come to his conclusion?
"If the Government would make up its mind to
require for every child a good education, it might
save itself the trouble of *providing* one. It might
leave to parents to obtain the education where
and how they pleased, and content itself with

helping to pay the school fees of the poorer class of children, and defraying the entire school expenses of those who have no one else to pay for them."*

It is left to parents to obtain the education where and how they please, and Government does now pay the school fees of the poorer class of children, and does now " defray the entire school expenses of those who have no one else to pay for them."

But if the Government did make up its mind to *require* for every child a good education, how would that save the Government the trouble of *providing* one? How does Mr. Mill reconcile this last opinion with his former opinion, that "scarcely anybody, in this country, will bear to hear of obliging the father to perform this duty?"

Why does Mr. Mill assume that the law of Parliament would be more compulsory than the law of Nature?

If Mr. Mill will try this question by logic, let him state his proposition clearly, and draw his conclusion fairly.

* Mill, "On Liberty," p. 190.

K

CHAPTER IX.

UTILITY, APPLIED TO DOMESTIC POLICY.

IF the principle of *general* utility be the index
to God's commands, it must therefore be, next to
His express commands, the proximate guide of
all human conduct ; and we ought to adjust our
conduct to rules formed in conformity therewith.

This index must necessarily be imperfect, because often vague and uncertain. The laws established by the Deity are signified to us obscurely,
and many of these being known, so far as they
are supposed to be known, only by observation
and induction from the tendencies of human actions, are subject to inevitable and involuntary
misconstruction. Consequently, until the effects
of human actions shall have been observed and
ascertained with perfect completeness, and these
actions classed with the same completeness, the
rules formed on the principle of utility, must be
more or less defective, and liable to error. These
actions being infinitely various, and infinitely diversified, the work of collecting their effects com-

pletely, and classing them completely, must tran-
scend the limited faculties of finite beings.

But, for this result, we are conscious that there
is something more to guide us than the principle of utility can furnish. That which we understand by the Divine Spirit, breathed into man
with the breath of life, must ever be regarded as
our highest guide, to which the principle of
utility, as we can possibly understand it, must be
subordinate.

To expect to attain to a complete or correct
understanding of the laws established by the
Deity, by construing them by the principle of
utility, without the Divine Spirit, must be less
possible than to construe an Act of Parliament,
without entering into the spirit or meaning of the
Legislature. But it is impossible to argue from
the obscurity of an Act of Parliament, that it is
not an index to the meaning and intention of the
Legislature. And so, admitting the imperfection
of utility as the index to the Divine will, it is impossible to argue from its admitted imperfection,
‘that utility is *not* the index.’

To argue that the principle of utility is *not* the
index to the laws of the Deity, because the principle of utility is an *imperfect* index, is to argue that all His works are *in fact* exempt from
evil, *because* imperfection or evil is inconsistent

with His wisdom and goodness. This objection
proves too much, and, therefore, is untenable.
All the works of the Deity which are open to
human observation, we know, are rendered imperfect, to our senses, by evil, though the cause
of the evil be hidden from human understanding.
But we know that we have the power of distinguishing the good from the evil, and we may accept the principle of utility as a safe guide, in
making our selection, in the absence of any express command.

The very notion or idea of evil or imperfection
is involved in the notions of law and duty. For,
seeing that every law imposes a restraint, every
law is itself an evil; and, unless it correct a
greater evil, must be an unnecessary evil. The
question of utility ought, therefore, to be a primary consideration in all human legislation.

But, how do human laws stand this test?

In civilized society, all the relations of man to
man are necessarily connected together by the
principle of utility, for the common welfare of
all, or for the equal convenience and pleasure
of all.

Accepting this as the meaning of those who
advocate this principle for the Greatest Happiness of all, or of the greatest number, how far
are we justified in assuming, from practical re-

sults, that this principle has been followed in the laws and regulations of our Domestic Policy?

Admitting that the chief, if not sole, objects of human laws are convenience and pleasure, it follows that, security of person and property are of primary importance.

How far are these objects attained?

It still remains one of the undetermined questions, whether the actual enjoyments of life be greater in the civilized, than in the uncivilized state of society. It is unnecessary here to pursue that inquiry. That human wants are increased by civilization, is undeniable. That the civilized man would perish, where the savage subsists in enjoyment, is admitted. Therefore, civilization fails in one of its essential objects, if it do not provide for those increased wants.

England being the most highly civilized country in the world, it follows that the wants of the English People are greater than the wants of any other People.

Are those wants provided for in proportion to the increased necessity?

In no civilized country in the world is there so much human misery from a deficient supply of the conveniences, comforts, and pleasures of life, as in England.

There is greater actual destitution in Ireland
and Scotland. But there the standard being
lower, the deficiency is less in proportion. The
English laborer and his family would starve and
perish, where the Irish and Scotch laborer and
his family subsist and thrive. But then, the
Irish and Scotch laborers would starve and perish,
on the ordinary dietary of the French and German Peasantry, and on which they dance and
sing.

If, then, Civilization be a desirable object, and
if the higher the civilization the greater the wants,
the principle of utility points out the necessity for
providing for those increased wants. Otherwise,
civilization must be retarded, or misery increased.

The doctrine that the tendency of population
is to increase beyond the means of subsistence,
is true only if the means of subsistence do not
increase in proportion with the increase of population. But the means always would increase in
the required proportion, if human laws and regulations did not interpose obstacles. There can
be no greater disgrace to a Nation than when it
is otherwise. If it were necessarily otherwise,
the wisdom and justice of the Deity would be
impugned, according to human understanding.
It is impossible for us to suppose that the Divine

command, "to increase and multiply," means, to multiply misery.

The correction of this old Malthusian error is to be found in the doctrine of Utility. The true application of that doctrine, or applying the gifts of Nature as intended by the Giver, would remove or mitigate nearly all the misery of this world.

It is not that there is any deficiency of means, but that the means are unequally, and therefore unfairly, distributed. This defective distribution is to be attributed entirely to human laws, which are opposed to Divine laws, as far as we can discern them in Nature. This inequality is quite different from the inequality in nature. There is no equality in nature. The gifts are infinite, and as various as infinite. But they are given gratuitously and equally to all.

In the uncivilized state they are enjoyed equally by all, or all are free to enjoy them equally. But in the civilized state that equality disappears.

If that were a necessary consequence of civilization, a very serious question would arise as to the advantages of civilization, according to the ' Greatest Happiness principle,' as it is called.

But such is not the necessary consequence. On the contrary, civilization greatly extends the

utilities of nature, as we see, in the greater com·
binations of industry and skill in the civilized,
than in the savage, state.

But why should not the freedom of the civilized
state bear some nearer approach than it does, to
the freedom of the savage state?

Man, in the savage state, acquires a right of
property in the wild game which he has run
down, or otherwise caught.

Why should not a man, in the civilized state,
enjoy the same freedom, if he invade no other
man's ground?

The savage, when he has caught his game,
cooks it and eats it as he likes best, without any
interference.   He drinks what he likes best, and
compounds it to his taste, as he pleases.   He
clothes himself, and builds his habitation as he
pleases.   For all these and other purposes of his
life, he uses freely the gifts of Nature, as he
pleases, without any interference.

Who can confidently say that the sacrifice of
this freedom is compensated by the benefits of
civilization, to the great mass of mankind in
what are called the civilized countries of Eu·
rope?

Who can truly say that freedom and plenty in
the wild abundance of Nature, is not a preferable
state, to the condition of the poor in the cities,

towns, villages, and rural districts in all or any
of the civilized countries of Europe?

And why should civilization necessarily exclude the free use and enjoyment of the gratuitous and blessed gifts of Nature?

Why should the producers of the wealth of
nations be the slaves and outcasts of civilized
society?

How is this state of things reconcileable with
the principle of utility, or the 'Greatest Happiness of the greatest number'?

This is reversing the principle, and sacrificing
the Happiness of the greatest number for the
smallest number.

But why is any sacrifice necessary, *if* the good
of all be intended?.

If! There lies the question.

Who believes that the good of all is intended,
or cared for?

Would the poor working classes be left to
crowd together in their pestilential dwellings, if
they were cared for? Would they be made to
pay from their scanty and hard-earned wages
of labour, to spare the pockets of the rich and
idle? Would they be made to bear, as they are
made to bear, the greatest portion of the burden
placed upon the People, by the profligate expenditure of Governments in all the civilized nations

of Europe? Would they be so treated, if they were cared for?

They are not cared for.

In no civilized Country are the working classes cared for.

They are deceived and plundered by the rich.

The principle of Utility is applied not for them, but against them. Not to make them free and happy, but to enslave and ruin them, body and soul.

If the principle of utility were better understood, it would be more clearly seen that, anything which has a tendency to diminish the strength of the human sinews, must tend to diminish the labor-power, which is the strength and measure of prosperity to every Country; for, without this, the gifts of nature are not available for any useful purpose to man. In no way can the principle of utility be more efficiently applied than in making the most of human labor, by preventing waste, and preserving it from exhaustion, by removing all obstacles, and encouraging its fullest and freest exercise. For this purpose is all machinery, art, and science, brought to bear for the general good, and in this way only, as applicable to machinery, for the saving of human labor, is it productive of any good. But even this utility, of machinery, is obtained only by labor, and the labor, applied to the construction of machinery, is the necessary condition, or drawback, imposed by Nature on the benefit thereby conferred. Nor is this, in many cases, an inconsiderable drawback, the labor and capital, which represents labor accumulated, being, sometimes, nearly equal in amount to the labor saved. But, if the object of saving human labor be so great, as it is generally admitted to be, it is remarkable that human labor itself should be so little cared for, as it appears to be. It is astonishing that the laborer should be so little cared for, and that, in addition to the burden of labor necessarily imposed upon him by Nature, Government should impose upon him so great a share of the burden of the State. According to the principle of utility, he ought to be entirely free from any State burden, whilst he is wholly engaged in making available the gifts of Nature by his labor, on which every State must depend.

It must be at direct variance with the principle of utility to interpose obstacles between the laborer and his means of subsistence. And if, in addition to providing the means of subsistence for himself and his family, he be required to contribute largely, or at all, to the demands of the Government, for the purposes of the State, it needs no logic to prove that his means of subsistence for himself and family must be thereby diminished, and that his labor or services must be thereby diminished in the same or a greater proportion. Experience proves, what theory and common sense sufficiently shows, that the proportion is very often much greater; for the over-tasked and broken-down laborer, from insufficient wages, and, consequently, insufficient nourishment, very often comes to the Union, and with him come all his family. Unsuccessful efforts are apt to produce dejection, something like despair, and despair is apt to produce desperation, the consequences of which are generally very terrible.

What helpless folly, to preach to the broken-down laborer about his moral duties, when the highest duty to him is broken by the whole nation!

What weakness to talk to that man about the blessings of education, when his starving children around him in his wretched dwelling are crying for food, and he has none to give them!

What miserable comforters are they all who say,—this is the laborer's lot, and he ought to bear it with submission, because there is no remedy!

Do they really believe what they say?

They know, or ought to know, that this is not the laborer's intended lot, and that he ought not to bear it, because there is a remedy.

They know, or ought to know, that the remedy is in relieving the laborer from all the exactions of the State, and thereby leaving him free to enjoy the lot which was intended for him, and which, when free, his own exertions could procure for him.

They know, or ought to know, that the laborer is taxed by the State, that the Land-owner and the Capitalist may be saved, in their pockets; for, they believe in this, though in this they are mistaken.

There is a great deal of talk about the Capitalist forming the labor-fund. That is true. But that has nothing to do with this question.

This is the question of the laborer's right. His right is to be free from every exaction of the State. It is impossible, on any principle of utility, justice, expediency, policy, or morality, to dispute this right.

Exactions of the State, for State purposes, can be properly made only upon the realized property of the country.

It is absurd to talk of this reducing the capital, if it save that by which all capital is produced.

State exactions, when wastefully expended do
reduce capital, and do thereby diminish the labor-fund of the country. That is a real loss to
the country. But much greater is the loss when
those exactions are made upon the wages of labor, and the profits of trade, before those profits
are realized, and become capital.

It is most probable that, when the exactions
are made directly upon capital, and upon capital
only, the Capitalists will be more careful to limit
those exactions. They can control, but the working classes cannot. The great bulk of the working classes have no power, because they have no
voice in the making of the laws. They are oppressed and crushed by the laws. They are
ignorant, and have no other power than in brute
force. They have that power in their superior
numbers, and, fortunately, they are too ignorant
to know how to use it.

It were not wise to enlighten them, unless at
the same time to liberate them. To educate
them and to keep them in their present condition is an impossibility ; and, if it were possible,
force would then prevail, where reason and argument have failed.

The civilized Governments of Europe are trying to maintain a system which the progress of
human advancement in knowledge must break

up. It is only a question of time, and whether the break up shall come through revolution by force, or by reason.

The principle of Utility points to the remedy for most of the existing evils of civilization which are under the possible contol of human Governments.

It is not sufficient to provide for mere subsistence. Civilization creates new necessities, which must be provided for, to make civilization conducive to temporal welfare.

The tendency of civilization is to diminish equality of enjoyment in the gifts of Nature, and if the tendency be not also to increase the supply of the necessaries of life to all, and to add to these many additional comforts and conveniences, unknown in the less civilized state, the highest civilization is a very questionable gain over the lowest, as regards temporal welfare, if by that be meant—Happiness.

But if the progress of civilization be accompanied by wisdom and justice, or a strict observance of the principle of utility, then the tendency is not only greatly to increase the supply of all the necessaries, comforts, and conveniences of life, but also to equalize the enjoyment of them.

The enjoyment of these does not depend so

much on their equal division, as on the equal
distribution of the means for the comforts and
conveniences of life, in proportion to the wants
of the progressive state of civilization.

The wants in the tenth century were very
different from the wants in the nineteenth century.

Beyond a certain extent, the equal distribution
is not to be attained under any human system,
nor is it to be desired. That certain extent is
best defined by human exertions. But human
exertions must be left free, or there is no rule for
guidance, and where there is no rule, there must
be confusion.

The rule is given to us in the condition of the
gifts of Nature,—the single condition of human
labour, or efforts, to make those gifts available
for human use and enjoyment.

That is a rule which must apply to every
state of society, in all times. But if another
condition be imposed in the civilized state, that
rule is altered and destroyed. Its simplicity is
gone, and with it are gone all its good effects.
Disorder is let in, with all its ill effects. Pauperism, discontent, and misery, with all the consequences ensue, and against these the wit of
man has proved powerless.

The rule of Nature has been disregarded : the

principle of utility has been neglected : no substitute ever has been, or ever will be, found. We must revert to the original rule, which is better observed in the least civilized, than in the most civilized state of society, though, in the least civilized, this rule is outraged in many ways, by ignorance of the higher principle of the Christian doctrine. But, in the most civilized state of society, the principle of utility is scarcely recognized, in practice, as an essential part of the Christian doctrine. The working or producing classes are nowhere treated according to that doctrine. They are treated more like Slaves than free men. They know freedom only by name. They are more free to die, than free to live. They are denied the freedom of the natural state, and are not admitted to an equal share in the freedom of the civilized state. They are restrained in the enjoyment of nearly all their natural liberty, and they are inadequately remunerated by their share in civilized liberty. They are prevented from enjoying their fair share in the gratuitous gifts of nature, because they are prevented from enjoying the full fruits of their own labor, or efforts. They are the Slaves of the Land-owners and Capitalists, who have been made Land-owners and Capitalists by the labor of the Slaves. The Land-owners and the Capitalists

make the Laws, and they make them, as they
suppose, in their own favor. In this they are
mistaken. They only make confusion, to the
injury of themselves, and to the ruinous degradation and misery of all the working classes.
They try to correct that confusion by many ingenious contrivances, all of which utterly fail in
the object, and always must fail. They are trying, in fact, to defeat the original design of the
Deity, by overruling His beneficent law, and
substituting their own selfish law. They may as
well try to stop the flowing and ebbing of the
tide !

If they would turn to the natural law of
liberty, and leave the working classes free to
employ their capital, which is their own labor,
as they pleased, free from all restrictions, and
undiminished in its produce by any deductions,
free to buy in the cheapest market, and to sell
in the dearest, they would manage their own
affairs better for themselves, than others could
manage for them. The working classes, then,
would require no further protection than the
laws afford equally to all, and for which protection they would then be willing to pay, and
could then afford to pay, their equal share.

They would then be less concerned in, because
less affected by, State affairs ; and, if all Govern-

ments were conducted on the same principle, it would little concern them under what Government they lived. It little concerns them now, because under all Governments they are equally miserable; it would less concern them then, because under all Governments they would be equally comfortable.

If the object of human Government be, to promote the general welfare for the Happiness of the greatest number, it cannot be conducive to that object to make the greatest number, who bear the burden of labor for the general welfare, also bear the greatest portion of the burden of expenses for the maintenance of the State. Manifestly, on the principle of justice as well as policy, nearly the whole of those expenses ought to be borne by the Landlords and Capitalists, who have realised their property out of the labor and skill of the laborers employed. When the Capitalist has paid the wages of labor, he is at quits with his laborers. He has no right to make them pay for the protection of his property, which he has acquired through their means. On every principle of justice, it must be sufficient if they pay for the protection of their own persons. The mass of the People have no property to be protected, and those who have any should pay for it in equal proportion. For this purpose all that is required is, to define the description of property which should contribute, and that is sufficiently defined by the description of *realised* property, which excludes the wages of labor, and exempts the profits of trade until realised.

If all State charges were thrown upon realised property, the mass of the People who have no realised property, paying equally, *per capita*, as nearly as may be practicable, the machinery of the Government would be greatly simplified, and the cost would be incalculably reduced ; but the gain from this incalculable loss saved, great as it would be, would be small in comparison with the gain from the increase in all the sources of profit which this increased freedom would open, and the removal of so many complicated and conflicting laws, now required for the Collection of the State revenue, would not only render the administration of justice more simple and sure, but would actually remove a very large portion of offences which those laws create.   Abolish all existing Revenue and Game Laws, and the calendar of crimes and offences is at once greatly reduced.

But keep off the Tax-gatherer from the laborers of every description, and confine his duties to the owners of realised property, and the laborers of every description are then independent, and comparatively rich. Pauperism will then be disgraceful to the able-bodied pauper, instead of being, as it now is, disgraceful to the State.

There will still be pauperism, because there will still be evil; but many of the present evils will disappear, and with them much of the pauperism. The pauperism which will remain will be only the results of improvidence and affliction. The present results are frightfully but incalculably aggravated by human laws, which are thwarting the designs of a beneficent Providence, as clearly shown to us in the laws of nature, but which we disregard as guides for our self-government.

The enjoyment of wealth is the just reward of honourable and successful exertions, but the drawbacks to this enjoyment are very great, in the midst of a half-starved population, struggling for the means of subsistence. And that is the state of a very large mass of the population in every civilized country of Europe, and in none more so than in our own country, which commonly ranks highest in the scale of civilization.

This is a strong fact, unfavorable to civilization, if this be a necessary result. But who believes this to be a necessary result? It is the result of the folly and injustice of Governments.

It has been a great and very general mistake in our country to regard with jealousy the freedom of trade, and its exemption from the burdens of the State.

Hence has arisen the common mistake about our excessive population, which, if ever excessive, has been so only through the impolicy of our laws which have reduced and limited our powers of production, and, consequently, our means of subsistence.

It was well said a long time ago, by William Paterson, (the originator of the Bank of England) when recommending his 'Darien Expedition' (then a wild enough and disastrous scheme, though worthy of a better result), that—"Trade will increase trade, and money will beget money, and the trading world shall need no more to want work for their hands, but will want hands for their work. . . . . People and their industry are the true riches of a Prince or Nation ; and in respect to them all other things are but imaginary. This was well understood by the people of Rome, who, contrary to the maxims of Sparta and Spain, by general naturalization, liberty of conscience, and immunity of Government, far more effectually and advantageously conquered and kept the world, than ever they did or possibly could have done by the sword."

The truth is that we, in this country, have been sadly over-governed, and we should have been much better off than we are if we had been left more free to follow our own devices, as long as these were riskful only to ourselves.

Something like this has been said by Archbishop Whately in his Commentaries on Lord Bacon's Essays, and as the Commentary is equal to the text, no excuse can be needed for here giving the Commentator's own words :—

" Over-governing may be reckoned a kind of puerility ; for you will generally find young persons prone to it, and also those legislators who lived in the *younger*, *i. e.* the earlier ages of the world. They naturally wish to enforce by law everything that they consider to be good, and forcibly to prevent men from doing anything that is unadvisable. And the amount of mischief is incalculable that has been caused by this meddlesome kind of legislation. For not only have such legislators been, as often as not, mistaken, as to what really is beneficial, or hurtful, but also when they have been right in their judgment on that point, they have often done more harm than good, by attempting to enforce by law what had better be left to each man's own discretion.

" As an example of the first kind of error,

may be taken the many efforts made by the
legislators of various countries to restrict foreign
commerce, on the supposition that it would be
advantageous to supply all our wants ourselves,
and that we must be losers by purchasing anything from abroad. If a weaver were to spend
half his time in attempting to make shoes and
furniture for himself, or a shoemaker to neglect
his trade while endeavouring to raise corn for his
own consumption, they would be guilty of no
greater folly than has often been, and, in many
instances, still is, forced on many nations by their
governments, which have endeavoured to withdraw from agriculture to manufactures a people
possessing abundance of fertile land, or who
have forced them to the home cultivation of such
articles as their soil and climate are not suited ·
to, and thus compelled them to supply themselves with an inferior commodity at a greater
cost.

"On the other hand, there is no doubt that
early hours are healthful, and that men ought
not to squander their money on luxurious feasts,
and costly dress, unsuited to their means ; but
when governments thereupon undertook to pre-
scribe the hours at which men should go to rest,
requiring them to put out their lights at the
sound of the Curfew-bell, and enacted sumptuary

laws as to the garments they were to wear, and
the dishes of meat they were to have at their
tables, this meddling kind of legislation was
always found excessively galling, and, moreover,
quite ineffectual; since men's dislike to such
laws always produced contrivances for evading
the spirit of them.

"Bacon, however, was far from always seeing
his way rightly in these questions; which is certainly not to be wondered at, considering that
we, who live three centuries later, have only just
emerged from thick darkness into twilight, and
are far from having yet completely thrown off
those erroneous notions of our forefathers. The
regulating prices by law still existed, in the
memory of most of us, with respect to bread;
and the error of legislating against engrossing
of commodities has only very lately been ex-
ploded."

CHAPTER X.

UTILITY.—TAXATION.

Mr. Mill says : " How many and how irre-
concilable are the standards of justice to which
reference is made in discussing the repartition of
taxation." He then enumerates some of the
many differences of opinion, and adds : " Since
the protection of law and government is afforded
to, and is equally required by all, there is no injustice in making all buy it at the same price.
... The principle of justice which this doctrine
invokes is as true and binding as that which can
be appealed to against it."
· This would be true if the protection of law
and government were afforded to and equally
required by all. But this is not true. It is
neither equally afforded to, nor equally required
by all. The protection afforded to labor, is not
equal to the protection afforded to the capital
accumulated by labor; neither does the laborer
require any protection for his own labor. He
requires only the protection of his person, and

the principle of justice requires him to pay only for that protection equally with all other persons. He, therefore, ought to pay his equal share, with others, of the expenses of the State for the protection of his person;—but nothing more. He has no personal interest in any other expenditure of the State, and he pays his full share, if he pay the same for the protection of his person, as the wealthy Landlord or Capitalist pays for his.

This is consistent with the principle of Utility, as well as of justice. For, if the laborer's sole capital, which is his physical strength, be so reduced by taxation that his physical strength fail, or be not replenished by a sufficient return for the expenditure, the source of all capital is diminished, and the loss thereby to the Nation must be greater than if he were not taxed at all.

The physical strength of man was the gratuitous gift of the Creator, and was, we must assume, intended for man's free use and enjoyment, without any condition, beyond the necessity of using it, in order to preserve it.

In the same way, all the gifts of Nature were gratuitous, and these, we may assume, were intended for man's free use and enjoyment, without any condition beyond the necessity of making them available for human use and enjoyment, by a certain expenditure of human strength.

This condition, we know, was imposed, and we must assume that, subject to this condition only, it was the Divine and beneficent intention that these gifts should be enjoyed by all mankind. If so, we must assume it to be contrary to the Divine will and intention that any other condition should be imposed by man, and we must assume that man cannot frustrate the Divine will, nor attempt to frustrate it with impunity.

If these positions be admitted, and they can hardly be denied, they seem to point to Nature for a rule, or, as an index to the Divine will, which admits of no exception, for human government.

It can only be inferred that gifts freely and abundantly given to all equally, were intended for the equal use of all who would take them on the single condition imposed, of employing human labor.

On that single condition, the right to take and use God's gifts was vested in man by Divine command.

The fullest and freest exercise of that right by those who complied with the condition, could not be prejudiced because some preferred to avoid the condition, by rendering other services in return.

The interchange of services between man and man in the social compact, could in no way justify the imposition of any restriction on the right conferred by Divine command, as against those who were no parties to the compact. Whatever advantage might be acquired on either side by the interchange of services in the social compact, that could in no way affect the natural right, which must remain for ever inalterable. None can obtain an exclusive right of property in that which is given gratuitously and equally to all for ever. No social compact could diminish the benefit of that right. A man may sell his own labor, but he cannot sell the labor of another man against his will; or, if he do, he cannot find a sanction for this under any Divine command, expressed or implied. The fact of the existence of Slavery does not justify Slavery.

Neither does the fact of the existence of a social compact to infringe upon a right, conferred by Divine command, justify the infringement.

A Divine right cannot be purchased, because nothing can be given in return for it.

The right to take and use the gifts of Nature is a Divine right, and is inalienable.

Human efforts or services may be bought or sold, or exchanged for other services; but human arrangements can in no way set aside or interfere with Divine commands.

The right to take and use the gifts of Nature is, therefore, a universal and inalienable right conferred by the Deity on all Mankind, and to impose any obstacle or impediment to the full and free use and enjoyment of that right, must be a violation of the Divine command, with a view to frustrate the Divine will and intention for the benefit of all mankind, and this must be opposed to the principle of utility.

The conclusion, therefore, is, that to impose a tax, directly or indirectly, on any gift of nature, or on the labor employed in making any gift of nature available for any human purpose, must be a violation of the Divine Command, and must be opposed to the principle of utility.

Consequently, all the duties of Customs and Excise, and all the Assessed Taxes, come directly within this category, and are wholly unjustifiable on any principle of morality or policy.

All other Taxes, as now levied, are wholly unjustifiable on any principle of justice or policy.

The Income Tax is unjust, because it is unavoidably unequal, and is opposed to every principle of sound policy.   Moreover, it infringes on the natural and moral right, and creates inextricable confusion, and incalculable loss, besides being an encouragement to perjury, and other offences, and innumerable frauds.

Inasmuch as it takes away from the profits of trade, before those profits are realised, it is, indirectly, a tax on labor, or wages.

Inasmuch as it is levied on growing crops, it is a tax on food, or necessaries.

Inasmuch as it is levied on live and dead stock, machinery, tools, ships, carriages, carts, and other implements, it is a tax on all trade and industry.

Inasmuch as it is levied on manufactures, trades, professions, and other employments, it is a tax on industry and skill, on learning, the arts and sciences.

Inasmuch as it is an equal rate tax on all Incomes, however precarious and uncertain, it is, in its operation, unequal and unjust.

It is in the nature of a tax on the person who possesses the income, rather than on the property which the person possesses.

It is, therefore, impossible to make the tax equal in its operation, and inequality is injustice.

It necessarily involves a complicated and costly system of collection, and the cost, thus increased, is a pure and unnecessary loss to the nation.

It practically tends to encourage fraud and perjury, and, therefore, to demoralization and discontent.

The Income Tax, therefore, is opposed to the

principle of utility, and, as far as that is an index to the Divine command, is opposed to the Divine will and intention.

The same objections, to a great extent, are applicable to all the Assessed Taxes, and Stamps, except Postage Stamps. Tried by the principle of utility, all these taxes are proved bad, because unjust to the parties paying them, and injurious to the best interests of the Nation.

The taxes levied on the property of the dead, in the form of Probate, Legacy and Succession duties, are a gross violation of the principle of utility, and of every principle of justice, morality, and sound policy.

It is a gigantic system of legalized fraud ; for the whole of the property so taxed has already paid the tax to which it was liable when in the possession of the living owner.

It is making the act of God, on the dead owner, the occasion for the most oppressive tax on the living owner.

It is the robbery of the rich, under pretence of benefit to the poor, but it operates in every way to the greater injury of the poor than of the rich, and on this false pretence the unjust taxes on the poor, in Customs and Excise duties on the necessaries comforts conveniences and decencies of life, are pretended to be justified on the principle of compensation; but the principle of general utility being outraged by all these taxes, there can be no compensation by setting one class of common injuries against another class of common injuries.

If all these taxes be injurious to the community, as they are shown to be, there can be no compensation, nor any remedy, but by abolition.

It is impossible to measure the amount of the injury, by the amount raised by any particular tax, because that furnishes no criterion for estimating the whole loss, the indirect loss of a gain being, in many cases, much greater than the actual direct loss. And so, it is impossible to measure the indirect gain to the poorer classes, by a direct loss to the richer classes, through the imposition of an unjust and impolitic tax; for, in every community, an injustice to one class must be an injustice to every class composing the community. By the beneficent wisdom of Divine arrangements for the protection of natural rights, for the equal benefit of all, no part of these arrangements can be disregarded without injury, directly or indirectly, to all. Any tax levied directly and injuriously on the rich, because they are rich, will be no less injurious to the poor, than if levied directly on them. The taxes now levied on the poor react against the rich with a

M

force as great, if not greater, than if the whole were levied on the rich.

The time will come when it will be universally seen and admitted that, all *indirect* taxes levied on the poor fall ultimately on the Land-owners; and that all *direct* taxes on property levied on those who have no property, fall ultimately on those who have property. It is strange that anything so self-evident as this is, should be disputed, but this is much more generally disputed than admitted.

This is no newly discovered principle. It was seen and acknowledged so long ago as by Adam Smith, and, before him, by Turgot, and before either of them by other Economists, English, Scotch, and French. And yet, our system of Taxation is framed on a denial of this principle!

It is said by some advocates of our present mixed system that, if Indirect Taxation be unequal and oppressive, so may be Direct Taxation. Of course, it may be so, but the difference is this, that Indirect Taxation must be unequal and oppressive; whereas, Direct Taxation is not necessarily so.

There is no possible way of avoiding inequality and injustice, if the tax be in the nature of a personal tax,—as all *indirect* taxes must be,— instead of being a direct tax upon property fairly taxable, unless the tax be in a fixed sum, *per capita*, and fixed at the minimum amount, proportioned to the means of the poorest.

In the case of a tax for the protection of the person, that is properly a personal tax, and this principle is strictly applicable, the person of the poorest being, to himself, of equal value with the person of the richest, to himself.

The same principle is equally applicable to property, properly taxable, and is preserved by a tax of equal rate on the value of the property taxed. In no other way can this principle be preserved. This is in strict accordance with general utility, being founded on justice, which must always be sound policy and expediency.

It is manifestly unjust and inexpedient to levy a tax on a graduated scale rising in proportion to the value of the property taxed. This is unjust because it is a penalty on successful industry, and inexpedient because unjust.

But there is no injustice in an equal tax on a certain defined description of property. If the tax be equal, it is no injustice if it be not equally convenient to all to pay it. Neither is there any injustice if they escape the tax whose property does not come within the defined description. If it be proved to be inexpedient to tax any other description of property, to tax their property

M 2

would be unjust and injurious not only to them,
but also to the whole community.

Therefore, if it be shown to be injurious to
tax property before it is realised as capital, and
if that description of property be clearly defined,
it must be as unjust as injurious to tax any other
description of property. Any benefit to the
party escaping the tax can have nothing to do
with this question.

The benefit, if any, to the party escaping, must
be shared by him with the whole community.

This has been fully shown in " The People's
Blue Book," as also the description of property
properly taxable under the definition of *realised*
property, and that property of every other description ought to be exempt from taxation.
Also that all existing taxes ought to be, and may
safely be, abolished, and the proposed tax on
realised property substituted, with a separate and
fixed tax, *per capita*, as a personal tax, for the
protection of the person, to be fixed, for the convenience of collection, on all House-holders, and
to be regulated by a scale, according to the value
of the House, rising from £1 on the smallest
cottage, to £10 on the largest mansion.

To this scheme of Taxation the only objection
which has ever been made in terms sufficiently
definite to admit of an answer, was that of Lord

Derby, who candidly rested his objection on the ground that, on extraordinary occasions of great emergency, requiring larger levies than usual on the people, this direct resort to the Capitalists and Land-owners would not be so easily tolerated. That is extremely probable, but that is not an objection to the principle, and it is quite as reasonable to assume that, if the emergency be such as really to require the extraordinary demand supposed, it will be readily answered by the owners of realised property in this Country. They have never been found backward on any emergency requiring the appeal to be made directly to their class.

In this point of view, the objection on this ground is converted into a strong ground of argument in favor, for it may be fairly assumed that those who pay, being of the better educated and more influential classes, will look more closely into the necessity for the demand, and also into the application of the money, than when they are, as now, Contributors only in a small proportion in comparison with the very large share now paid by the great mass of the people who have no voice in the question, and who are too ignorant to exercise much judgment in such a question.

This is the only objection which, to the knowledge of the Writer, has ever been made in a

form admitting and deserving of an answer, and
this, coming from such an authority, ought to
be encouraging to Financial Reformers.

If this scheme of Taxation, or any other scheme
formed with an equal regard to the same principle, were fairly carried out in practice, it would
be found that the principle of general utility is
only another form of expression for justice and
sound policy, for nothing contrary to justice can
be used consistently with general utility, and
whatever is so used must always be conducive
to human welfare and happiness ; for, there is
nothing more evident to us in this life than
that, for the purposes of the great human community, nations and men alike have been so made
as to be dependent on each other.

It is not possible to show that Happiness, in
its true sense, will be the result of any human
arrangements ; but it is quite possible to show
that human arrangements may be conducive to
Happiness.   It is easy to show that existing
arrangements are conducive to much misery, to
much poverty, and to many crimes and offences
against society, as inevitable consequences of
poverty and misery in the social state.

That poverty and misery will always exist, and
that crimes and offences will always follow, in
every state of human society, is to be expected,

until the perfection of all things. But it is also to
be feared that these evils will go on increasing at
a greatly accelerated rate, and in new and greatly
diversified, perhaps aggravated, forms, with the
increase of population and knowledge, if not
accompanied with an increase of useful knowledge, and a more equal distribution of the necessaries, comforts, and conveniences of life.

One of the worst classes of crimes, the increase
of which is to be expected, is Infanticide. For
some years past this crime has been frightfully
on the increase, and is still more frightfully increasing. Moreover it is much to be feared
that public horror at this crime is fast diminishing,
and giving way to a morbid sympathy for the criminal.

But the public are acquainted with only a very
small proportion of the actual cases,—perhaps,
not more than 1 in 20. In these cases detection
and prevention are alike difficult.

From the Returns to Parliament, it appears
that during 18 months, ending June, 1862, Verdicts of " Wilful Murder,"—" Found Dead,"—
in ditches, ponds, etc., were returned—in London, .
297 Children, and in England and Wales, 624,
total 921 Children, under two years of age, all of
whom were most probably murdered ; and that
the total number of Children under two years of

age, who had met with untimely deaths within
that period was 5,547.

It is well known that Coroners' Juries are anxious
to avoid giving a Verdict of "wilful murder,"
even though against "some person or persons
unknown," and that they prefer such Verdicts as
"found dead."

This is some of the bitter fruit of man's own
planting, but is without a remedy under the existing system.

It is the reaction of evil, not against the evil-
doers alone, but against all the community. When
privation enters the cottage, degradation enters
with it. An impoverished population is always
a brutalized population.

The burden of taxation upon the laboring
population impoverishes and brutalizes them.
This is a necessary consequence of population
increasing beyond the means of subsistence. It is
proved to be so in China, and will be proved to be
so in England, if the existing system be continued.

There is no reason to suppose that the ties of
natural affection are less strong in China than in
England. They are known to be remarkably
strong, but they are not strong enough to resist
the pressure upon the means of subsistence.

In this way, we may see that, what is to us
evil, is really working out obedience to Divine

Command. We hope, by God's help, to remove the evil, through the preaching of His Word. But that is hopeless; for, that would be using His Word to break down His command. His command was ; 'to increase and multiply, and enjoy the fruits of the Earth, by the sweat of the brow !' Civilized Mankind have disobeyed that command, by introducing laws of their own which interfere with its due observance. They would invoke Divine aid to assist them in that interference. But they will be left to perish in their own confusion. Human wickedness will keep pace with human misery, and 'progress in civilization,' will be found to mean, progress in "confusion worse confounded." Thus will mankind be forced to consider the principle of general utility as an index to Divine Command.

There is, doubtless, in all human affairs, a natural law which rights itself by reaction against any wrong committed against itself. Every infringement of a natural right is ultimately redressed with unerring certainty by numberless and unforeseen evils which are let in to right the wrong. These are called evils, and really are so, but they work for good, by providing the remedy which by no other means could be brought about.

"An Irish famine repealed the Corn Laws. Irish outrage gave to the empire the benefit of a regularly organized Police. The desperate state of Irish property led to the passing of an Encumbered Estate Act. Ireland has introduced the system of mixed education.

"In Ireland the relations between landlord and tenant have been first made the subject of discussion, with some prospect of an equitable solution. In Ireland was promulgated the potent aphorism,—

"'Property has its duties as well as its rights.'"*

But for this mysterious and unerring power, rights of property could never have existed, or would have been long ago destroyed, and the weak would have been everywhere the slaves to the strong.

We see this natural law in operation in all the works of nature. The injury is repaired, or the defect is rectified, but still it is only a repair, or a substitution of something less perfect than the original design.

The beauty of the first creation is not restored, but the original design is not entirely frustrated. Nature supplies the substitute, and though that be not perfect, yet it is suitable for the occasion.

This idea, which has often been expressed in many ways, has, perhaps, never been better

* "Irish History and Irish Character." By Goldwin Smith, p. 197.

expressed than by the Rev. W. Barnes in his
"'Thoughts on Beauty and Art." He says:—
"Some have taken beauty to be a true quality
of things themselves, while others have held
that it is only a loving apprehension by the
mind, of the fitness of things for fulfilling its
own happiness. I would offer as my opinion
of the Beautiful, that which is less truly a definition than a theory, and say that the beautiful in nature is the unmarred result of God's
first creative or forming will ; and that the beautiful in art is the result of an unmistaken working of man in accordance with the beautiful in
nature.

"I do not understand, while I speak of God's
first will, that He has two sundry ones. God's
will is work ; but there are cases in which His
will takes form in what may be called after-
work, when a prior work of His forming will
has begun to be marred.

"A pea is planted, and there spring from it
a rootling and a plantling, the work of God's
first forming will. The plantling is cut off;
and, instead of it, there may outgrow two
others, the after-work of God's forming will,
which would not have acted in such work if
His former work has not been marred. Again,
the beauty of a species is the full revelation of

God's forming will—as, in an ash-tree, is shown
in the forming of one stem, with limbs, boughs,
and twigs, of still lessening sizes, and of such
forms and angles of growth as to the eyes of
a draughtsman are marks of its species. Then,
however, if an ash-tree is polled, there grow
out of its head more young runnels than would
have sprouted if the work of God's first will
had not been marred by the man-wielded poll- ·
ing-blade. So also, if a man's arm, the work
of God's first forming will, be broken, its bones
may be again joined by a callus, through that
Divine will which would never have taken form
in such work but on the marring of its first
work, the unbroken bone. If a man's hands be
worn by a tool, or his heel be rubbed by an
ill-fitting shoe, the evil may be warded off the
hands by a horny skin, and from the heel by a
water-filled bladder. God's first formative will,
then, is the fulness of every form of good, and
the after-work of His formative will is a filling
up of the losses of good from His primary work
by good of the same or other forms."[*]

We see this manifestation of the Divine will
in an infinite variety of forms, and, if we may
so express it, these are the substituted forms of
the permissive, rather than the original, will.

[*] " Thoughts on Beauty and Art." By The Revd. W.
Barnes. Macmillan's Magazine. June, 1861.

The struggle of the weak against the strong commenced, probably, very soon after the creation of man ; and out of this arose the institution of slavery, which has ever since existed. But there is no reason to infer from its long existence, that it was God's first forming will, or that it is, or ever can be sanctioned by long usage. The old struggle is still going on, all over the world, as in the time of the Israelites against Egyptian oppression. " Say unto Pharaoh, —Let my people go, that they may serve me." But Pharaoh harkened not, and refused to let the people go. He preferred to keep them in bondage. But the stubborn free will which resisted the Divine command, yielded at last to the overwhelming evils which followed. Not only was the King overwhelmed, but the whole Egyptian nation. The guilty and the innocent suffered alike.

Those evils, as we call them, worked out the Divine will for the everlasting good of all mankind; but the original evil in the human nature still remains.

That command—" Let my people go, that they may serve me,"—was given for ever, though the voice that pronounced it be no longer heard.

That command was only the old common Law of Nature, declared in all her works : That Man should be free to use and to enjoy all Nature's gifts.

How is that command observed in human laws?

The greatest portion of mankind, all over the world, is still held in Slavery by the smaller portion.

The Landlords, and the Capitalists are now, as then, the taskmasters of the people, and their officers say: " Ye shall no more give the people straw to make brick, as heretofore; let them go and gather straw for themselves."

If habitations fit for human beings are not to be found for men, prisons must be found for them.

It will be cheaper to find decent houses for them.

If they be not found in food and raiment, they will help themselves.

If they be let go free without the means of subsistence, they will provide means and all other necessaries for themselves.

If they be let go free, according to the terms of the original Deed of Gift, they will require no other help than their own labor.

But the burden of providing by labor the means of subsistence is all that the laborer can bear.

This was the sole condition of the original Deed of Gift to all. Man has no right to impose any other condition. He may impose any additional burden upon himself, but not upon any other man, without his consent.

The laborer has a natural and a just right to all the fruits of his own labor, and to deprive him of any portion of these fruits against his own free will, is a violation of the Law of Nature, and a wrong and injury to the whole community.

For this wrong and injury there is no human remedy, but in obedience to the Divine Law. If that obedience be refused, the time must come when it will be enforced in every Nation, as it was enforced against the Egyptian nation, through great national calamities. It is coming to that time in England and in France, and in other countries ; but, in the most civilized, it will come the soonest.

The Egyptians were the wisest people in their time, though they were poor economists. But neither their wisdom, nor their ignorance, saved them from the calamities consequent upon their disobedience.

If our ignorance be as great, our wisdom is far greater, and the consequences of our disobedience will probably be greater, in still greater and more lasting calamities.

The warning voice has been raised, and if good and true men will join in the cry for 'Justice to Labor,' the People may yet be Let go free, in time.

The Landlords and Capitalists will then be
the best friends of the working-people, instead
of being their taskmasters.

But the Landlords and Capitalists must take
upon themselves the chief part of the burden of
the State. They may then look to enjoy in
peace their honorable possessions; and all Nations,
desiring it, may look for the blessings of peace,
with prosperity before unknown.

All experience proves the inefficiency of human means to counteract the effects of a natural
law. No system of rewards and punishments
will ever extinguish the natural instincts, though
these may be so directed as to be productive of
good instead of evil. In most cases, and, perhaps, in all, the evil is the effect of circumstances, and not the cause. To suppose an evil
instinct in human nature, is a notion quite
inconsistent with the notion of Divine wisdom
and mercy. It is more consistent to suppose
that, all the natural instincts are good rather
than evil, and that the evil results from following
those instincts are the effects of circumstances
under human control. But, be this as it may, it
is impossible to suppose that human instincts for
evil have been given without a sufficient controlling power for good. Nor is it necessary to
suppose otherwise, for we have the Divine Word

for assuming this as a fact, and we have had evidence of its truth in the Divine Illustration.

This evidence is generally known and received in Christian Countries ; though in no country are the effects what might have been expected. But we are not to infer from this, that the controlling power for good is insufficient. The evidence proves that the power is all-sufficient. We may, without heterodoxy,—without doubting the all-sufficiency of that Divine power,—infer that through circumstances, under human control, all are not brought equally under the benign influence of that power, and that, the instincts, given for good, are thus made productive of evil. We may also, without offence, infer that those who mostly control the circumstances, will be held mostly accountable for the perverted consequences, when all accounts come to be settled. In this world we know that the evil-doers only are held accountable ; but many believe that their sufferings in this world will be taken to extenuate, if not held to expiate, their sins, when accounts come to be settled by the unerring and more merciful Judge, and that the Rulers in this world will have the hardest account to settle in the next.

Perhaps, very few really believe that, the helpless and neglected children, who are born and

N

brought up in scenes of infamy and misery,—
misery far greater than is suffered by the children
of the rudest savages,—will be held accountable,
as men and women, for their evil ways, by the
unerring Judge, as they are held by human judges.

Human nature revolts at the thought of holding these poor wretched creatures responsible for
their acts, and is only forced to make them responsible by another and still stronger instinct,
the sense of self-preservation. But for this, they
would be let go. Fear alone prevents the well-
to-do from taking that course. They know not
what to do with the outcasts. They know not
how to get rid of them. Formerly, they hanged
them all, and, perhaps, they would do so now, if
they dared. They did it as long as they dared.
But the more they hanged, the more they found
to hang. That seemed to be the shortest way,
and therefore the best way of getting rid of what
seemed to be of no use, and really was of no use,
as things were. But that was a great mistake,
and the shortest way was found to be the worst.
A common mistake, but a mistake which is still
continued, after all the long and dreary experience. At the bottom of this lamentable state of
things is the selfishness of the greedy, grasping
rulers. They rob the poor ignorant and deluded
working classes of their wages, and think thereby

to save their own pockets. They rob them' first‡
and turn them adrift afterwards, to seek their
means of living where and as they can. Those
who cannot find the lawful means,—which are
very difficult to find,—take the unlawful. Many
come back idle and reckless, some as hardened
criminals, and all are *then* provided for, at the
charge of the State; but what to do with them
nobody knows. As numbers increase,—and they
go on increasing,—the difficulty of knowing what
to do with them increases. The men and women.
fill the Prisons, and their children fill the Reformatories; and the weaker class of paupers, with
their children, the worn-out, helpless, and infirm,
sit enchanted in the Unions.

The wise rulers are at their wits-end. They
can no longer hang, nor get rid of their useless
rubbish by pitching it into one of the Colonies.
They were driven to the ingenious contrivance
of 'Tickets of Leave ;' but they forgot to provide
the holders with the means of subsistence, and as
nobody was disposed to provide the means, these
were, in effect, 'Tickets of Leave to rob or starve.'
In such an alternative, to rob became a necessity, and return to Prison and its enjoyments a
necessary consequence. In the meantime, the
throats and the pockets of the respectable com-.
munity, were found to be in peril, and even

N 2

Members of Parliament were not safe.   This was too much to be borne, something must be done.

The old, obsolete, and effete law for 'Whipping' these offenders is restored.   As if 'Whipping' would save starving, and its consequences !   But it is better than hanging, or transporting, and prison discipline with prison dietary were too good for those who had less comfortable quarters at home, and worse fare.

To make a home, with something like home comforts, has never been tried on this class.

Some think that such an experiment would be more successful in keeping this class at home, and at honest occupations, instead of sending them out into the streets and bye-ways, to throttle and rob honest folks.

Some think that infanticide is only the result of mother's love struggling with the agonizing sense of shame and misery.

Does any one really believe that human nature would be so perverted if men and women knew the comforts of a decent home, with means of subsistence honestly earned, and some few of the many enjoyments of civilized life ?

Who can say that the wretched mother does not destroy the new-born life to save it from the like of her own miserable existence ?

Who can say that this perverted nature is not

the instinct of maternal love, driven into another
form by the force of circumstances? And who is
responsible for those circumstances? Surely that
is an inquiry most proper to be made.

Many think that these consequences are to be
traced to the wrongs of Governments. And, if it
be so? Who should be held responsible? Surely,
not the poor ignorant sufferers!

But who are the gainers in a system which
leads to such consequences as these? And is
there any gain? In a merely political or worldly
point of view, can it be truly said that, in the
social state of a civilized community, there is any
gain to one class in the loss of another class? But
if the loss be to the class which *produces*, how
much greater must be the loss to the whole community, than if confined to the class which only
consumes?

What a practical reconciliation would be effected
between the wealthier and the poorer classes, if
only taxes were universally removed from the necessaries and luxuries of life, and these were left
open to the equal and fair competition of all as
the rewards of their own labor and skill!

As that excellent man and Political Economist,
Dr. Chalmers, said :—" What a death-blow would
be thus inflicted on the vocation of demagogues!
What a sweetening influence it would have on

British Society, after the false medium was dissipated, through which the high and the low now look on each other as natural enemies!"

It was the opinion of the same good and right-minded man that, "if the whole of our public revenue were raised by means of a territorial impost, it would ultimately add nothing to the burden which now lies on the proprietors of the land ; for they, when fighting against such a commutation, are fighting in defence of an imaginary interest."

This is the enlarged view which should be taken by statesmen in directing the legislation of a country, and if this principle were firmly relied upon and fully carried out, the results would soon dispel all fears for the consequences, and then all classes would soon find out that their true interests were identically the same, and inseparable.

If the landed Aristocracy, and the Capitalists, instead of their blind resistance to all change,—or, as they called it, *innovation*,—and their tenacious adherence to what they imagined, but mistook, to be their own indispensable interest, had paid all taxes, and had left all labor, and trades, and professions, unfettered, so far as human actions can be calculated upon by human motives, it may be confidently said that, no political sacrifice would have been required of them, and they

would have remained in the undisturbed possession of, and in the more full enjoyment of, their
rightful possessions as Landlords and Capitalists.

But, the democracy of England, fired by a sense
of injury, made head against them, and wrested
from them by force, what ought to have been
freely and willingly conceded in the spirit of an
enlightened policy.

May the Landed Aristocracy and the Capitalists
take warning from the past, for the protection
of their lawful rights for the future! There
yet lies before them a noble field of improvement in rightly shifting the burden of taxes,
from the working classes to themselves, in eman-
cipating manufactures, trade and commerce, agriculture, arts, sciences, and learning; and in providing amply and liberally for the Christian and
literary Education of the People.

It is not by Charitable Donations that wrongs
to the laboring classes are to be righted. By
depriving labor or trade of any part of its fair
wages or profits, charitable donations become a
necessity; but that necessity proves the evil, and
the evil is great, because it diminishes the necessity of labor to the recipients of the charity, and
thereby tends to neglect and non-observance of
the condition of all the gratuitous gifts of Nature,
and thus to thwart the Divine will and intention
for human welfare.

To suppose that charitable gifts can ever be substituted for the gratuitous gifts of Nature, is to suppose that the condition of Nature's gifts can be dispensed with.

This is a great mistake, and this is just the mistake under which all civilized society, under every human Government, is suffering. This system carried out to an extreme extent would bring mankind to the state of the Australian savages. But if such would be the result of the system carried out to its extreme extent, such must be its tendency, if carried out only partially. Charitable donations, therefore, which tend to destroy, or weaken the coercive power of the condition of Nature's gifts, must tend to diminish the benefit intended to be conferred on all by those gifts, and must also tend to reduce mankind to the savage state.

This is an inevitable conclusion, and all experience confirms it. There can be no doubt that, the large fortunes, accumulated by labor and saving, which the owners have left for the benefit of the poor, have, to those who receive the intended benefit, relieved them, to that extent, from the necessity of labor, and to that extent a permanent injury has been inflicted on the country. To that extent, the condition of the gift of Nature has been broken, and the loss

and injury have fallen, more or less, on all immediately concerned.

That is a certain consequence, as certain as
that night follows day. But, though as clear as
the sun at noon-day, attention to this glaring
consequence has only been lately called by the
Royal Commission appointed to inquire into the
State of Public Charities and Education throughout the kingdom.

The thinking part of the community are just
now beginning to see that these intended benefits
to a certain class, are no benefits at all to the
community as a whole, but positive injuries, and
very questionable benefits to the class intended
to be relieved.

But these mistakes would, probably, never have
been committed, if the people had been more
wisely governed, according to sound principles
and natural laws, as pointed out by the utility of
things. The occasion for these mistaken interferences with the natural law would never have
arisen, if the law of equal justice to all had been
more honestly observed.

These officious and mistaken interferences have
aggravated the occasion for them, and this has
been their most injurious effect; nor has this
been the only injurious effect, for it has greatly
increased them, and thereby rendered the injury

more permanent, by hiding from general observation the only real remedy.

But far be the inference that, the endowment of Hospitals, or other charitable institutions, for the relief of human afflictions, or for the diffusion of moral and religious instruction, comes under these observations.

These are England's most noble monuments, and have, more than all her armaments, sustained her national glory, and pre-eminence among nations.

But these will not continue to sustain the glory and power of England under the rapid increase of population, with all the misery and crime consequent upon the present system. The downfall of British power is as certain as the increase of population, misery, and crime, if the present system be continued, of defrauding the working classes by forced contributions, directly or indirectly, from their wages of labor, for any purpose of the State, beyond their equal and just proportion for the protection of their persons.

The great danger to be expected in the future is from the neglected children of imprudent, impoverished, and wicked parents. With a rapidly-increasing population under the present system, where so much is done for their impoverishment, and so little for their moral improvement, no forced

or voluntary charitable contributions, for their
temporary relief, will ever compensate the injurious consequences of this wrong, or counteract
the evils from this neglect, because, in the wisdom
and mercy of Providence, these are the inevitable
consequences and evils from the violation of divine
law, and must always be opposed to the principle
of utility, which is here the unerring index to divine command.

To repair these evil consequences in the adult
generation is a hopeless undertaking for human
Governments or Institutions. The extinction of
the evil is impossible : to diminish it by preventing
its extension in the rising generation is alone
practicable.

All that can ever be usefully done for the adult
poor is, to leave them in possession of the wages
of their labor, and to give them the rights of
free citizens. By this means the seeds of independence may be sowed, and the extension of
pauperism and its worst evils may be in a great
measure arrested. But though we have no ground
to hope for the extinction of human wickedness
and improvidence through any human means
alone, yet we have the surest ground to hope
that by human means the spread of the mischief
may be arrested in the rising generation.

There is nothing more deplorable, nothing

more pitiable, than the condition of destitute and
neglected little children, under all the most civilized Governments of the world. Whatever may
be said of the idle and worthless poor,—little
children, at any rate, cannot help being born.
It is not their fault that they are a burden to
society. It must surely be the duty of every
Government to regard the destitute orphans, and
the deserted children of unknown parents, as cast
by a higher Power upon the State, and it must
be even wise economy to provide that such children shall be thoroughly well-trained and disciplined to do the State good service.

How this may be best done is another question, but that it ought to be done by and at the
expense of the State there can be no question.

At any rate, it is a useless and wicked cruelty,
and, moreover, it is an unwise and a far more
expensive policy, to cast these children in the
midst of all kinds of knavery, and to leave them
surrounded by people and practices that can
hardly fail to demoralize them, and to unfit them
for social duties and the service of the State.

What neglect can be more cruel than our
Union and Work-house system for poor children?

The children of slaves are more cared for—
have more liberty—more joy of life. Can any

children be left in more utter destitution, bodily
and mentally, than the poor children in our
Unions and Work-houses? They are literally
penned up as cattle. Let any one who doubts
this only visit the work-houses in the London
Parishes. There will be seen the infant paupers
crawling on the floor, without a doll or a toy of
any description for the amusement of their poor
little minds; nor is the vitiated atmosphere which
they breathe better suited for their poor little
bodies. Then, look into the Bills of mortality to
learn how very short is the average duration of
their wretched little lives. Or, look at those
who have survived the perils of infancy in the
work-house, and have grown up boys and girls.
To look at them is enough to read the history
of their short lives, and of their probable future,
if they should, by chance, attain to manhood
and womanhood! But what can be expected
from manhood and womanhood so brought up?

How brought up? Go and see. See the
crowds of unhealthy, vacant-looking boys and
girls shut up apart in pens, or in narrow court-
yards, in a vitiated air, without book or toy for
their instruction or amusement, though many of
them can read and write, for that they have
been taught in their prison-school, and many of
the girls can sew, though these are too many to

find that employment for them all, and, perhaps, fortunately, even that employment is being rapidly diminished by the introduction of the sewing machines.

Why have these children never known the blessing of fresh air? Why are they taught for good, if left among nothing but bad?

Who, accustomed to life in London, has not wondered to see the children creeping forth from the foul mystery of their interiors, stumbling down from their garrets, or scrambling up out of their cellars, to swarm into the daylight and find all they know of personal purification in the nearest mud-puddle, and learn all they know from the guilt and wretchedness which surround them?

There is nothing which so much strikes the attention and shocks the humanity of foreigners in the streets of London, as the neglect of the children of our poor population.

A distinguished American Writer, in his observations on our "Old Home," says:—"It might almost make a man doubt the existence of his own soul, to observe how Nature has flung these little wretches into the street and left them there, so evidently regarding them as nothing worth, and how all mankind acquiesce in the great mother's estimate of her offspring.

For, if they are to have no immortality, what
superior claim can I assert for mine? And how
difficult to believe that anything so precious as a
germ of immortal growth can have been buried
under this dirt-heap, plunged into this cesspool
of misery and vice! As often as I beheld the
scene, it affected me with surprise and loath-
some interest, much resembling, though in a far
intenser degree, the feeling with which, when a
boy, I used to turn over a plank or an old log
that had long lain on the damp ground, and
found a vivacious multitude of unclean and
devilish-looking insects scampering to and fro
beneath it. Without an infinite faith, there
seemed as much prospect of a blessed futurity
for those hideous bugs and many-footed worms
as for these brethren of our humanity and co-
heirs of all our heavenly inheritance. Ah, what
a mystery! Slowly, slowly, as after groping at
the bottom of a deep, noisome, stagnant pool,
my hope struggles upward to the surface, bearing the half-drowned body of a child along with
it, and heaving it aloft for its life, and my own
life, and all our lives. Unless these slime-clogged
nostrils can be made capable of inhaling celes-
tial air, I know not how the purest and most intellectual of us can reasonably expect ever to taste
a breath of it. The whole question of eternity

is staked there.   If a single one of those helpless little ones be lost, the world is lost!"

This painful subject has recently engaged the
attention of the Commissioners appointed in the
early part of 1862 to inquire into the number
and condition of children under thirteen years of
age, employed in trades and manufactures not
already regulated by law.   In the course of their
inquiry much evidence was tendered to them
respecting the inefficiency and violation of the
"Chimney Sweepers Act," and the cruelty consequently inflicted upon a large number of unfortunate and helpless boys.   From the evidence
gathered in England, Ireland, and Scotland, it
appears that several thousand children, varying
in age from five, and even four to fourteen years,
and including many girls, are still condemned to
this life of slavery and frightful suffering.

The evil is greater throughout the country and
in the second-class country towns than it is in
London and the chief cities, but everywhere it is
being revived, and it is connived at by all classes,
from the highest to the lowest, even by Mayors
and County Magistrates, whose duty it is to inflict
the penalties prescribed by the law for the protection of these helpless little children.

The lord in his castle, the squire in his mansion-
house, the respectable father of a family in his pet

villa, the shop-keeper in his shop and warehouse, —lords, squires, mayors, magistrates, and shop-keepers, must have their chimneys swept, and all or most having great objection to the mechanical machine,—(though experience has proved that nothing can be more efficient,)—they take care to let this be known, and make no inquiries, but then shame, of course, prevents or makes them very unwilling to convict sweeps for using the human machine.

Consequently the poor little children of five or six years old continue to be forced up the chimneys almost as much as ever, and the Act of Parliament for their protection is almost a dead letter.

The Commissioners have just now laid the result of their inquiries, with all the evidence, before Parliament.

Let those who wish to know how the children of the depraved and destitute poor in this country are treated read this Report and Evidence—let them read,—if they can,—only the evidence of the sufferings of these poor children.

In all the accounts of all the horrors of slavery in the Southern States of America, there will not be found anything to exceed, if even to equal, the horrors detailed in this well authenticated evidence !

English mothers sell their little children of five and six, and even four years of age to this! Their own little boys and girls of four and five and six years of age they sell, for five and six shillings, and sometimes ten shillings a piece, to this! What this is, cannot be given here. It is too horrible. Those who have the nerves for reading it, will find it all in the evidence of George Stevens, now a master-sweep, and who went through all this fifty years ago as a climbing-boy.

But who is responsible—who is answerable to the country for this? Surely, there ought to be some department of our Government answerable to the country for this most foul outrage upon humanity!

What has our Home Secretary got to say for himself? What are the Representatives of the People about to leave these little children helpless in the merciless hands of those worse than high-way robbers and midnight murderers?

Who, but the Home Secretary, is the master of these Mayors and Magistrates, and why are they allowed to continue in an office of dignity which they have thus disgraced?

What confidence can be placed in the administrative powers of a Government which cannot find the remedy for such an evil as this? Why, even this same George Stevens, this master-sweep, tells of the remedy in his evidence, and no one who reads it can doubt that it is an effectual remedy!

Why are these children thus cast away by the State to which they properly belong?

Sooner or later the time must come when the Gentlemen of England will have to face this question.

If these poor children be cast by a higher Power upon the State,—and, surely, they ought to be so regarded, seeing that they have no parents, or proper guardians, or none that can or will provide for them, and are quite unable to provide for themselves,—how can the State be justified in so neglecting them?

But what and if the State have brought them to this condition!

How can the State expect good services from them, when the State has so cruelly neglected and wronged them!

Why should they not be taken and brought up as the children of the State, and be treated as unoffending precious human souls,—at least, so long as our present system continues to pauperize their natural protectors?

There are some who will say, the morals of the people would be depraved!

And others who will say, the cost would be too great!

But do they really believe this to be a question of morals or of cost?

They know or ought to know that, in this neglected and helpless portion of our population we are sowing broad-cast over the whole land the seeds from which must spring a plentiful crop of the most noxious weeds, the cost of rooting up which must be, of all costs, the greatest and the least productive of any profitable return.

Who can say what that cost is?

We know that the cost of providing maintenance for our paupers in idleness is about seven millions, sterling, a year. But who can say what are the costs of providing remedies for all those evil consequences which we find inevitably following pauperism? Who can say that these costs do not very far exceed the cost of maintaining our paupers? Who can say that the sum total of all these costs would be exceeded by the cost of a system which removed or greatly diminished these evils? But what if it were so? Who will venture to say that such a purchase would not be worth the cost at any price? Who raises these objections? Not the poor, but the rich. And if the parents of these children could be known, there would, perhaps, be found as many among the rich as among the poor.

The true answer is, that the rich parents care as little about morals as they care about these poor children, so that they never hear of them, and have nothing to pay for them. As to the poor, they are too poor to help them, or too indifferent to care for them.

The causes of poverty removed or diminished, the poverty would disappear or diminish in proportion, and with it would disappear a great deal of the roguery, which is much worse than the poverty, and, to the State, much more costly too.

Why should the State interfere with the Education of those children whose parents or natural guardians are able to provide it for them?

The State Family will be large enough, at least for a long time to come, and on these only can the State ever, in this country, apply compulsory Education with any good effect.

Government Establishments, all over the country, for the decent maintenance and education of destitute orphans, and children of the destitute poor, and convicted criminals, Ticket-of-leave men, prostitutes, and reprobates of every description, would close all the Reformatories in the kingdom at once, and would soon relieve all the Prisons,—moreover, would put a stop to that frightful and increasing evil of these times,—Infanticide.

This should be the only State Education, and
for this new department of the State a separate
Minister of the Government should be made
specially responsible. All such children should
be received into these State Establishments on
equal terms, without any distinction of class or
sect, and all should be taught in the same doctrine
of the Protestant Established Church, whether
such teaching be regarded with favor or dis-
pleasure, whether as a blessing conferred, or a
punishment awarded.

There is no Divine injunction for the Education of the poor, nor does it seem possible that
Education, to the great mass of the working
population, should ever be carried farther by the
State than the merely mechanical acquirement of
reading and writing.

But there is an express Divine injunction for
that teaching which leads to industrious, sober,
and thrifty habits, and these are the habits in
which our working population are mostly deficient.
It is these habits which are of the spirit of
pauperism. Saint Paul has described this spirit,
and given his opinion upon it.

"Neither did we eat any man's bread for
naught ; but wrought with labor and travail night
and day, that we might not be chargeable to any
of you, to make ourselves an example unto you to

follow us. For even when we were with you, this we commanded—that if any would not work, neither should he eat. For we hear that there are some which walk among you disorderly, working not at all, but are busy bodies. Now those that are such we command and exhort by our Lord Jesus Christ, that with quietness they work, and eat their own bread."

The injunctions of Christianity are wholly in opposition to the spirit of pauperism ; and those institutions of the Law which seem to encourage it, as well as those individuals who thoughtlessly encourage it, are in direct contravention of the wise and true spirit of Christian Charity.

· If the Laws were made more in conformity with that wise and true spirit, it would be clearly perceived that our Poor Laws tend much more to a premium on Pauperism than to a preventive, and, in fact, create much more pauperism than they relieve. It would then be perceived that we might with safety and advantage repeal our Poor Laws, and that we should thereby remove the greatest inducement to all those evil habits which lead to pauperism, by making more apparent the wisdom and prudence of industrious, sober, and thrifty habits.

No one who has any experience in the practical working of our Poor Laws can doubt that the

certain provision in old age which these Laws
secure, will, to the idle and improvident, outwork
any teaching for thrift and saving in earlier life or
better times ; nor will any prosperity, to the great
mass of the working people, ever counteract the
injurious tendency of the compulsory provision by
law. Not only do our Poor Laws work to discourage industrious, sober, and thrifty habits,
but they actually operate to bring down the
industrious, sober, and thrifty, to the level of
those who are content with the paupers' lot.

There can be no humanity in the Poor Laws ;
for, if wages be not sufficient, they are only paying what is due in a degrading and cruel manner ;
and, if wages be sufficient, they are a provision
held out beforehand to improvidence and all its
desolating evils. Even total relief from taxation
would not permanently better the condition of
the working classes without an increase of prudence. Not only are they, for the most part,
without thrift, but for providing resources for
casualties or old age they have no idea. How
could any reduction of taxation permanently
benefit those who become more thriftless, idle,
and profligate as the means of living become more
easy? How would they be better off for being
able to gain in four days as much as they
gained in six, if they only work in proportion,

or waste their money as fast as they get it ?
It is lamentable, but true, that to the pauper-
ized laborers of most of the agricultural districts,
any facilities for maintaining themselves beyond
drudging for the bare necessities of life, only
make them work the less, and multiply the faster.
This improvidence is mainly attributable to our
Poor Laws system, and yet it is this state of things
which makes it so generally believed that this
system cannot be dispensed with.   Those who
hold this opinion have formed it on the present
low standard.   They do not perceive that this low
standard is the result of unequal, unjust, and impolitic laws, and, therefore, they cannot trust the
only true remedy in raising the standard by wise
and just laws, which would render our Poor Laws,
now a necessary evil,—then wholly unnecessary.
If our Poor Laws promote the evil habits, there
is no reason, in the nature of things, why opposite
laws should not promote opposite habits.

One of the manifest evil effects of the laborers
having no resources to fall back upon, but that
provision of the Law which they never lose sight
of, is, in the claimants being so much increased
as to require an increase of the funds in aid.
This necessarily increases the distress, and this
distress goes on until it has in some degree reduced the population and allowed time for con-

suming the over-production. In a few years the same destructive course comes round again.

When government is carried on upon the principle that, "whatever is morally wrong, cannot be politically right," the standard of morals, individually, will soon be raised too high to admit of anything like a class of paupers, and there will be no destitution, for the relief of which private charity will not be far more than sufficient.

The result of all this is, that if there were no poor-rates, and the laborers were left in possession of their full wages, without any deductions by indirect taxes, they would then be both more industrious and more prudent, knowing that they had nothing else to depend upon. They would then be able to provide for old age, and to bring up decently their children, allowing for the ordinary casualties, and if, in some cases of extraordinary casualties, the resources fell short, though there might be some degree of privation, yet the voluntary assistance of those around would always prevent destitution. Under these circumstances, the few cases of poverty—not pauperism—so far from being considered burdensome, would be not only cheerfully but eagerly relieved. These are the legitimate objects of charity, and as they excite the kindly affections, and repay them with

gratitude, they tend to increase the general stock
of virtue and happiness. Every one who gives is
then the dispenser of his own charity, and he
feels the satisfaction which the rate-payer never
knows. But the tendency and effect of our
Poor Laws is to retard any material improvement, by debasing the one class, and making the
other believe that such debasement is inevitable;
besides keeping up a race of paupers even under
the most favorable circumstances. This is, in fact,
making Pauperism hereditary, and a perpetual
tax upon Land and Houses.

With respect to persons incapable of labor,
whether from infancy, or age, or from inability,
physical or mental, their natural rights cannot
be greater in a civilized than in an uncivilized
state, though in the former their chances of provision, independently of any compulsory maintenance, are much better than in the latter. But
the truth is, their claims are of a higher nature
than any that laws can enforce, and in a well-
ordered society are sure to be attended to without compulsion. In a state of nature, where
property is not appropriated, there can be no
compulsory provision for them, and their chances
of voluntary provision are much less than in a
state of civilization. But in a civilized state, as
to those who are capable of labor, and who, it is

said, are entitled to have employment found for
them, if they cannot get it for themselves, or to
subsistence, because all property is appropriated,
the answer is, that there could be no such class,
unless created or permitted by defective government.

The conclusion, therefore, is that, Poor Laws
are not founded on any natural right, but that
they involve merely a question of expediency;
and that no system of management will be ultimately productive of benefit, unless it have for
its object the total abolition of the principle,
the principle being, to supply the deficiencies of
wages or the waste of improvidence. If wages be
high enough to support the whole class of laborers, Poor Laws only encourage improvidence.
If wages be not high enough, Poor Laws operate
to prevent their becoming so.   Temporary want
of employment is no argument for the adoption
of a permanent principle, and permanent want of
employment implies an over-population, which
can only be the result of improvidence, for which
the Poor Laws are not the cure.

There is nothing new in this view of the effect
of our Poor Laws, for all these evils are most ably
pointed out by a Writer, less known than he deserved to be, in a little weekly publication, long
out of print and forgotten, called " The Origi-

nal," which, though at the modest price of
three-pence a number, appears to have received
but little support, and to have been continued
but for eight months ending with December,
1835.

It is strange that arguments so well advanced
thirty years ago, should have made so little
impression on the public mind. But the truth
is, that, our Poor Laws, bad as they are, could
not be wisely or safely dispensed with, under
our existing system of Revenue Laws, and reckless expenditure.

The condition of the laboring classes has
really never been considered. There has been
a universal avoidance of this subject. With
some there is a pretended dread that they may
be made too well off and become independent
of work, or so refined as to be above it, or
that their habits may be so raised as to require
much higher wages. Those who pretend to see
these dangers keep out of view the well known
truth that, competition and the demand for labor
must always keep up the supply, and keep down
the rate, so as to allow fair profit to the em-
ployer, which is all that he can fairly require.

Some others—but these are very few in number, and nothing in intelligence—pretend to see
danger in a general demand among the laboring

classes for a more equal division of the land of
the country. Our great popular Journal has
imputed to Mr. Bright that the tendency of his
remarks, in his recent speech at Rochdale, was to
excite the laboring classes to make this demand.
Some people, with glass eyes, "seem to see the
things which are not," and not to see the things
which are ; or to turn their blind eye to the real
danger. With regard to Mr. Bright, he never
spoke or thought such nonsense ; nor did the
people of any class in this country ever imagine
anything so much opposed to their own interests.
But the tenacity with which the great Landowners in general hold their own, and the per-
sistence with which they refuse to part with even
the smallest plot of ground to a laboring man is
a very proper subject for remark, and also for
censure. The true explanation is, not that the
Landowners have before them the fear of an
Agrarian Law, but the fear that their laborers
may acquire an independent position, and to this
fear they sacrifice not only the interests of the
laborers, but also their own.

In evidence of this the Writer has his own
experience.

Many years ago he was struck by the signs
of this want near his own property, in a thickly
populated manufacturing district, where the

land for many miles around was owned chiefly
by a few large Proprietors. No laboring man
could get a plot of ground to build his cottage
upon, or even for a garden, on any terms within
his reach, longer than from year to year, and no
man could prudently build his cottage on such a
term as that. To obviate this inconvenience he set
apart about thirty acres of ground, of a dry light
soil, on a breezy eminence overlooking the sea.
He made convenient roads, to it and through it,
most suitable to the plots into which it was divided, each plot large enough for two good cottages and two good gardens. The whole was
then laid down in a large Plan, on which each
plot was numbered. This Plan, with the terms
for letting, was hung up for public inspection in
a convenient situation near the ground. The
terms were as follows: For each plot one Guinea
a year; on the one condition that the houses
should be built within the lines described, and
not more than two houses together. The term
was for the lives of all persons then living in the
world, and a thousand years after the death of
the survivor. The price of the Lease and Coun-
terpart, to be paid by the Lessee, was 10s.
These plots were open to the first applicant. In
a short time all the plots were taken, and more
ground being from time to time required, several

successive additions were made in the same
manner, and on the same terms. Such was the
origin of the little Town of ' Skewen,'—so called
from the Welsh name of the locality—inhabited
chiefly by the industrious workmen in the neighboring Iron and Copper Smelting Works.

To the Landlord the clear profit is about £3
per acre per annum ; the value to let being about
10s. per acre per annum. He has never had any
difficulty in getting his Guinea a year. The
ground-rent is well secured by the building.
Many of the Lessees are the owners of several
adjoining plots, and they build their single house
or two cottages on each plot as they like, but
within the lines laid down in the Plan for unifor-
mity and the convenience of their neighbors.
The tenure being Freehold for Lives, each plot,
with its building, gives a Vote for a Member to
Parliament. These, being independent Free-
holders, vote as they think fit. The Lease is in
a printed form, on a small piece of parchment,
about the size of an ordinary sheet of note paper,
ready at all times to be completed by writing in
the name of the Lessee, and all that he covenants
is, to pay his rent. He, therefore, escapes the
Attorney.

Now, all this has worked very well for more
than twenty years.

Perhaps, Mr. Bright, when he referred to our Working Classes and Land Proprietors meant something like this, and not much more. But nobody really misunderstood his meaning, though times-serving politicians may think it suits their purpose to misrepresent it.

But, after all, whatever may be said or meant, the fact remains the same,—that the chance for the working man to obtain possession of the smallest bit of Freehold Land in this country is so inappreciably small as to be, practically, quite beyond his calculation.

This is a fact which nobody can deny, and it is suggestive, not of a more equal division of the land, but of throwing more of the burden of taxation upon the land, and off the labor, and if this can be done to the benefit of both, it is well deserving of dispassionate consideration.

In entering upon this question it is important to distinguish between Poverty and Pauperism.

Poverty has an independent spirit, and is silent and retiring—it strives to cure itself, and often stimulates to exertion.

Pauperism is a base and servile spirit, clamorous and exacting—it contaminates others and always paralyzes.

By confounding poverty and pauperism, poverty is dishonored, and pauperism countenanced.

P

Poverty supplied with means vanishes, but by the
same means pauperism is the more confirmed.

Our Revenue Laws and our Poor Laws have
dishonored poverty and established pauperism—
have done more to bring down the independent
spirit of our working people to the base and
servile level of disgraceful dependence than education can ever do to restore. It is now common
to hear them say,—" What is the use of saving?—
the parish must keep us." Unless it can be
made apparent that they who save will be able
to provide much better for themselves than the
parish will provide for them, it is almost hopeless
to think of creating a provident population.

Such being the existing state of things, no one
would be bold enough, or rash enough, to propose
the abolition of our Poor Laws whilst this state of
things continues.

But if the whole of our present system of
Revenue Laws were at once swept away, and the
wise and just system were substituted of raising
our Revenue directly from *realised* property,
many, who now cannot see, would then plainly
enough see, that our Poor Laws are not only unnecessary, but are actually making the very evils
from which we are seeking to escape. Many think
that all we want for this is Education, but what
we really want for the People is that they should

enjoy the full wages of their labor, and moral
training to bring them into thrifty and domestic
habits. They must first see themselves in the
secure possession and enjoyment of their full earnings, without any deductions, and they will then
learn to provide for themselves; but they will
never learn this if the strong necessity for industry and thrift, imposed by the nature of things,
be weakened by the interposing power of a compulsory provision by the Law.

Good training alone is good education, and it
is not enough to teach only those things which
are good or bad, as they are used. A woman
does not necessarily make a better helpmate to a
laboring man because she can read and write;
but it is otherwise if she have been taught arts
of life suitable to her condition. Both are desirable, but the latter are indispensable to domestic
comfort, and these are lamentably neglected.
Among the working classes waste and discomfort
are but too often the chief characteristics of their
mismanagement, the bitter consequences of which
are but too often strife, sickness, debt, misery,
recklessness and crime. Their purchases are often
bad in quality, small in quantity, and high in
price; their meals wasteful and unwholesome;
their clothes neglected, and everything about them
destitute of order and arrangement.

The want of good moral training is one of the causes which conspire to keep up this state of things; but the main cause, because it often creates and always aggravates the others, is in the policy of the Government to sacrifice the people to considerations of revenue, without any regard to consequences; and what has been the policy of the Government is in reality the policy of every party, because party can exist only by popular debasement brought about and fostered by fallacy and falsehood. The working classes being of no party and having no voice in the affairs of the State, are, in fact, without any Representatives of their interests, and are, consequently, without any influence in the State, otherwise than by their numbers, and the power which attaches to large numbers. But that power is to create fear and nothing more. That, in fact, is all the power which the People—the unrepresented, or great mass of the people—do exercise. Consequently, all that they ever gain is through the fear of that power. From what party have they ever gained anything worth having but through the influence of that power? And how could it be otherwise for those who have no party, and when all the parties are playing their own game, which never is the game of the People, but always is the game of the party, which never is for the welfare of the community—the common good of all?

It is not against individuals that these bitter words are directed, for there are in this country many earnest and honest friends of the People. It is against the political parties in the State who are struggling for the possession of power and its appendages. Whichever party succeeds is a matter of the utmost indifference to the People, for there is no party which, if in possession of the power, would think of exercising it by any wide reform for the permanent benefit of the People.

Who can hope to see the burden of the taxes placed upon the right shoulders, until the People have been fairly polled on this question; and how can that be until their votes be taken through Representatives of their own choosing; or even then, until they and their families be protected by the Ballot from the risk of ruin?

It is in vain to hope for any material improvement in the condition of the working classes of this country, until their interests be properly represented in the Council of the State; unless, indeed, some practicable measure, founded on sound principle, for the improvement of their condition, be openly placed before the country; such a measure as may unite the real friends of the people with the Landowners and Capitalists, and thus form a party powerful to control the Government and rule the State. Then the ' Fran-

chise ' and the ' Ballot' will so little concern
the People—the working people—that demagogues will be disarmed. These inscriptions
on their banners will then pass unnoticed, and,
being unnoticed, will soon be disused and forgotten. In the meantime, the friends of the
People can only continue to demand for them the
concession of those unquestionable rights which,
when obtained, will enable them to effect these
changes for themselves by constitutional means.

Who will say that this is hopeless, after the
experience in our own time of the first great
measure of Reform in Parliament, and after the
repeal of our Corn Laws? Either of these
sweeping measures of improvement, when first
proposed, was quite as hopeless of success against
the great Political Parties which then ruled the
State, as the sweeping measure of improvement
now proposed. When this is seen to be founded
on the great truth in the doctrine of Utility,
that it is for the equal benefit of all, there will
not be wanting in this country good men and
true to advocate it, and then a short time only
will be wanting to carry it by the force of reason.

What a mass of mismanagement and abuse—
what jealousies and enmities—what costs and
Government-patronage in useless, and worse than
useless, offices will then be swept away with

all our Revenue and Poor Laws! The clearance
away of all this old rubbish is essential for laying
down the new foundation, or we shall go on
groping about in this old rubbish, seeking for
what we shall never find, until it overwhelm us.

Such State Establishments as here proposed
would be no infringement of that wise policy
which has hitherto distinguished our country
from all other countries, in leaving our public
charities to be supported by the voluntary contributions of the benevolent rich.

The State Establishments here proposed would
not be charitable institutions any more than our
Unions and work-houses are charitable institutions ; but the destitute children being thus provided for, and the Poor Laws abolished, the aged
and infirm would find their resources in their
own savings, or in the aid afforded them by their
own children or children's children.

It is a mistaken view of the whole of this
question, to say that these expenses ought to be
borne wholly by the benevolent rich. There is
no more reason why they should bear the whole
of these expenses, than why they should bear
all the taxes of the State, for, more than any
other should the expenses of providing for the
destitute children of the Poor come out of the
pockets of the People. They are in every way

more deeply interested in the money so applied, than in any expenditure now made by
the State, and when taken directly from their
pockets for these purposes, they will, probably,
look more closely to the application of this money
than of any other.　But still more important will
be the lesson then taught to the People,—that
every tax-payer has a personal interest in these
now neglected and helpless children.

As the Children of the State, the State alone
would be responsible for their future as Men and
Women, and from these sources would be supplied the wants of the State at home and abroad,
in the various departments of the humble duties
of our social state.

To some parents these regulations would operate as a punishment, and, if so, might operate
beneficially; but, to far the greater number, these
regulations would be regarded with the utmost
indifference.

To the Children of the State themselves, these
regulations would be for their unqualified good,
and, instead of being turned loose, as outcasts on
society, they would be, or might be, marked
through life with this happy distinction—" THE
CHILDREN OF THE STATE,"—which would be, at
once, their best recommendation, and for deserving it the best security.　This would make them

to be sought for, instead of being, as now, rejected or suspected as Parish Apprentices,—and
would lead many of them to good fame and for-
tune, who might otherwise have been led to the
gallows.

To carry out this plan, or to proceed on some
such principle as this, would be a practical and
truly valuable application of the doctrine of
Utility; but nothing can be more idle than to
be drawing deductions from what is called the
principle of utility, and seeking Divine direction
for human government, if such plain and self-
evident rules of conduct as these be left neglected,
and the fruitful sources of all that is great and
good be left to be contaminated by the continual
in-pouring of all that is most vile. As well may
we expect the pure rills, which flow down the
mountain's side into the stagnant and unwholesome swamp, to come out a fertilizing stream, as
to look for healthy services from these poor neglected and destitute children of sin and sorrow.

Of all the evils that afflict the civilized States
of Europe, there is no one so full of menace as
this is against good order and the true welfare
of the People, nor could any greater misfortune
befal mankind than that these evils should cease
to be felt, without being removed.

We may all of us wisely believe that, every-

thing which befals us in this life to cause us any
great sorrow, although we see not the uses, has,
nevertheless, its definite object for good, which,
here or hereafter, will certainly be made visible.
For, if nothing in this world be accident, surely, all
that which affects us,—the only part of creation
upon earth to which immortality is announced,—
must have a distinct and definite purpose for our
ultimate and everlasting good.   In this way,
and in this way only, can we hope to reconcile
ourselves to the evils and sorrows of this life, and
if we would avert them or provide the remedy,
we should carefully seek through them their definite purpose, until we find the blessings, to
which, assuredly, they are leading us.

CHAPTER XI.

UTILITY.—COLONIES AND DEPENDENCIES.

SOME who have still faith in English statesmen
are beginning to ask, " whether the helm be
really in their hands and the compass really before
their eyes, or whether the ship be drifting before
the wind and tide to an unknown shore."

The recently revealed danger of the present
connection between Canada and England, has led
some to consider how far it is desirable that such
connection should continue.

The consideration of this question has led to
the same inquiry as regards other Colonies and
Dependencies.

If the same reasons, on principle, govern all
these questions, the only difference, as to any one
Colony or Dependency in particular, is of degree,
or emergency.

Colonies and Dependencies must be held on
the ground that they confer some benefit or
advantage, directly or indirectly, on the country
which holds them. It cannot be supposed that

the country holds Colonies and Dependencies for
the sole purpose of conferring benefits on them.
It cannot be supposed that the country which
holds them would continue to hold them at its
own loss, without some actual or prospective
gain.

The actual or prospective gain, therefore, are
the only points for inquiry in this question.

The actual loss or gain are simply questions of
fact, to be answered by figures.   The indirect or
prospective gain is a question not so much of fact,
as of opinion, on the ground of possible or probable benefit.

If it can be shown by figures that, our Colonies
and Dependencies are losing concerns, and that,
any benefits which we derive from them we could
equally enjoy without the loss involved by holding
them, the more difficult question of indirect or
prospective gain, which is possible, and more or
less probable, but never has been realized, is very
much simplified.

In this view, the force of the argument that,
foreign nations would take what we abandon,
would depend entirely on the correctness of our
conclusion on the before mentioned question.   If
the abandoned Colony or Dependency had been
abandoned because the benefit had never been
equal to the loss of holding it, and because, on

sound reasoning, no other result was probable, any argument from the acts of foreign nations must be deprived of all force, or, at least, could furnish no ground for altering our determination to abandon.

Assuming this very self-evident proposition to be admitted, the question, as proposed, will be considered without reference to the acts of foreign nations which, it is manifest, in this view, could in no way affect British interests.

If a Debtor and Creditor Account, of Profit and Loss, were fairly stated with Canada, how would the balance stand?

To state this Account with anything like accuracy is impossible, and if possible would not be worth the pains. It is sufficient to say that the balance of Loss is in millions.

If the Account could be carried back to include the expenses of our war with France, the Government Accounts of which are nowhere to be found, and, probably, are not in existence, it is manifest that the balance of Loss would be in many more millions.

To make out an account of our expenses for fortifications and works alone in Canada would be a formidable undertaking, and, after all, would only show an enormous expenditure without any return for it.

The cost of the Rideau Canal alone would form no inconsiderable item, and those large sums were voted by the British Parliament, and paid by British Tax-payers, on the ground that this was ·a work of necessary defence to Canada.

Then, again, who can say at what cost to the Mother-Country the rebellion in Canada was suppressed? Or, what sums are properly chargeable to that branch of the account?

This is one of the inevitable consequences of Colonial complications. A correct account of costs can never be made out; and the account which is made out can never be proved incorrect, because it can never be checked.

It is, practically, an open door to extravagant expenditure and misapplication of Public Money to an unlimited amount.

This should be regarded by British Tax-payers as an intolerable evil, unless it can be shown that they have, directly or indirectly, something like an equivalent.

But, unfortunately, this is not generally so regarded. With many, the larger the expenditure the stronger is the argument for holding on to the time of return; and often for spending more.

There might be something in the argument if that time could be seen within any reasonable period. But nobody, who knows anything about it, really believes that such a time ever will arrive, and nobody pretends that it has arrived. Everybody believes that the time will much sooner arrive when adult Canada will separate from the Mother-Country, and many think, the sooner that time arrives the better.

With such a prospect before us, there is not much use in making up an account of past expenditure of British Capital in Canada.

The only useful question is, the expediency of continuing the expenditure on the hope of any probable return.

This is a serious question for the Mother-Country, now maintaining 18,000 soldiers in Canada, for the defence of an open frontier of about 2000 miles, and which must be greatly increased in the case of a war with the United States. The costs and risks of war are greatly aggravated when the men and all the munition of war are to be transported 3000 miles; and, besides the land force, a powerful fleet must be kept on the station. Nor is this all, for, in this case, flotillas must be built and maintained on the frontier lakes, in the face of a powerful and energetic enemy at home on the Southern shore. What, then, becomes of England's boasted advantage in having no frontiers to defend? The advantage ought to be something great and substantial, and more clearly shown than by unmeaning words, for undertaking the responsibility and risk of defending 2000 miles of frontier in Canada.

. As Mr. Goldwin Smith asks : " Is it possible that with this on our hands we should be able to show a bold front in European questions, and do our duty as protectors of liberty, and right towards the community of nations in which nature has placed us, and to which we belong?"

That England has long been drifting into another American war, and that Canada is a primary cause, can hardly be doubted. That the Federal Government has long been plotting to annex Canada to the American States, is not doubtful. The *dénouement* has, perhaps, been deferred only by that want of union in the States which has terminated in political disunion and separation, and civil war. With the termination of the civil war the plotting for the same object may be expected to be resumed with more active operations. However and whenever that termination may be brought about, unless by the mediation of the European Powers, guaranteed by treaty, the position of Canada, and of Great Britain, as the Mother-Country and protector, must be perilous.

If the United States be divided into two independent Unions, North and South, now the most probable termination, the annexation of Canada to the diminished territory of the Northern Union will then appear to be a more imperative necessity.

If the Union of the North and South be restored, now the most improbable termination, the aggravated enmity of both parties against Great Britain will unite them for the seizure of Canada, on every ground which before impelled them, without any pretence, to effect this acquisition.

Thus, in any event, Great Britain seems to be drifting into another American war, and the timidity of British Policy, in withholding from all attempts to effect an amicable arrangement between the present contending parties by mediation, is rendering more probable that ultimate end.

That Great Britain could stand by a quiet spectator of the seizure of Canada, whilst Canada is under British protection, is a case which cannot be supposed, until Great Britain has lost her position among nations.

In the event of the seizure of this "precious gem of the British Crown" as it is called, war must be assumed as inevitable. But what would be the chances of that war, for the benefit of Great Britain, against the united efforts of the bold and

Q

energetic people of the United States, or of the
Northern States on their own frontier? Who can
say that the power of Great Britain, transported
three thousand miles to the scene of action, would
be more successful for retaining British Possessions in Canada, than it was, eighty years ago, in
retaining British Possessions in North America?
Who can say that failure in 1863, would not bo
even more disastrous to the British Empire, than
was the failure in 1783, when that disgraceful
war of eight years' duration terminated in British
humiliation, and the addition of One Hundred
and Five millions sterling, and upwards, to Great
Britain's National Debt, and a perpetual annual
charge of Four millions three hundred thousand,
sterling, and upwards, on Income?

Taking that as the cost of the American war,
though it was not nearly the whole cost, as that
war involved us in a war with France, who can
now say that it would not have been better for
Great Britain if she had never possessed any
American Colonies?   And who can now say that
the loss was not a great gain to us?   Who can
say that, if the whole of the North American
States had continued to be Dependencies of Great
Britain, the prosperity of those States, or our
trade with them would have been anything like
what it has been?

If experience in the past be any guide for human conduct in the present, here is much wisdom to be learnt, for our profit. We have paid dearly for our experience in wars, and we may well profit by it.

Whatever the *prestige* of England may be worth to her, even that may be paid for too dearly.

But why should that be brought into question for Canada?

Why should not the independence of Canada be declared, before England's *prestige*,—whatever that means,—is brought into question?

What opportunity could be more favorable than the present, for letting Canada hang on her own hook,—instead of hanging a dead-weight on England?

If the independence of Canada, on the basis of Free Trade, were now made part of the terms of mediation with the dis-united States of North America, and if the same basis were accepted by the States, either conjointly, as one Union, or, separately, as two or more Unions, and if the free navigation and use of all the Rivers, Harbors, and Seabord, were mutually guaranteed by treaty between the three or more independent Unions, a more real and substantial union would be formed between Canada and the American States than could be possibly formed by a hostile an-

nexation ; and much more real and substantial
would then be the Union between the North and
the South, than it has ever been since the day
when the Declaration of American Independence
was signed.

The only question of importance then remaining to be settled, or which could then be settled,
would be the line of separation between the
North and the South, if such separation should be
inevitable, as it must be assumed to be.

This question was settled by mutual concessions between the North and the South by the
admission of Missouri as a Slave State, in 1820,
well known as the " Missouri Compromise," under
the provisions of which Slavery was to be excluded from all the territory embraced in the
Louisiana purchase, north of 36° 30" latitude.

The Missouri Compromise was something
more than an ordinary legislative act. It was a
compact between two great opposing interests,
in virtue of which one of those interests obtained at the time valuable consideration on the
condition of abstaining from certain pretensions
in the future. It was, moreover, eminently a
slaveholder's measure. As Mr. Sumner, in one
of his speeches said : " It was brought forward
by a slaveholder—vindicated by slaveholders in
debate, finally sanctioned by slaveholding votes—

also upheld at the time by the essential appro-
bation of a slaveholding President, James Monroe,
and his Cabinet, of whom a majority were slaveholders, including Mr. Calhoun himself." The
measure was thus binding on the Slave Party by
every consideration of honor and good faith.

The line of demarcation, therefore, between
the Free and the Slave States, was deliberately
drawn and fixed by mutual agreement between
the North and the South, in the year 1820, and
the same line, continued across the Continent,
from the Atlantic to the Pacific, may now well
be taken as the line of separation between the
two independent Unions of the North and South,
and the increase of territory thereby given to the
North, would be amply compensated to the
South, by the vast increase of territory to the
South, from the continuation of the line of separation across the Continent, to the Pacific.

On this basis of sound policy, in which lies
real strength and the true foundation of prosperity, the Boundary Question becomes of no more
real importance to the States, than the question
of the boundary of a County.

It is important that the boundary should be
fixed, and clearly defined, within certain limits,
but of much less importance where. No doubt,
each State will struggle for extended territory,

and each Union for extended sovereignty ; but,
with the conditions prefixed, and guaranteed by
treaty, of Free Trade, and Free Navigation of all
Rivers, Lakes, Harbors and Sea-bord, any such
struggle will be for little more than the shadow,
the substance being already secured. When it
comes to a division of territories into two parts,
and each part is of nearly equal dimensions with
Europe, it seems like idle chaffering to be dis-
puting about a few hundred miles more or less
to the North or to the South. The real difficulty
in this part of the question is removed by the
two precedent conditions—Free Trade and Free
Navigation.

By drawing the Boundary Line between the
North and the South, as fixed by the Missouri
Compromise, for the extreme limit of Slavery to
the North, at 36° 30″ north latitude, the whole
of Virginia and Kentucky, and part of Missouri
to the north, would be in the Northern Union,
and the Metropolitan City of Washington would
then be more central. This would be no dis-
paragement to the South, but, on the contrary,
by extending the Boundary Line across the Continent, as proposed, a vast increase of territory
would be given to the Southern Union.

But if the mediation of England and France
were accepted on this principle, the details would

be easily settled by the Commissioners to be appointed by all the Parties, or by the Umpire to be selected by them. in case of difference.

It might well be part of the terms, for a more permanent union of mutual interests, that the Commissioners and Umpire should be empowered and instructed to fix on a more equitable boundary line, than that fixed by the Ashburton Treaty.

In this view, to purchase the willing concurrence of Canada, it would be no sacrifice to the North, if the present "crooked line" between the Northern States and Canada, on the Eastern side, were made straight, and so to unite Canada with New Brunswick, by drawing the boundary line on the parallel line of 45° latitude north, to 75° longitude west. The effect of this would be to annex to Canada the northern portion of the State of Maine, and the north-eastern corner of New Hampshire, thereby making a boundary line more convenient to Canada, without the smallest detriment to the interests of the Northern Union, but, on the contrary, to their manifest benefit, by bringing Canada in closer proximity with Boston and New York for all commercial purposes.

The Oregon Boundary Question, which, for the sake of peace, Great Britain consented to settle by the sacrifice of her manifest rights, even to the abandonment of the British possessions on the Columbia River, might at the same time, be put right, and settled for ever.

Thus would be formed and established on a firm basis, three separate and independent Unions, on the northern part of the Continent of America, all bound together by one common interest, and with no outstanding question or grievance, and no open ground for jealousy to lead to disunion. The old grievance, settled, but not wiped out by the Ashburton treaty, and the still pending grievance of the Oregon Question, would then be finally settled, and be remembered no more. The independence of Canada might then be safely conceded by Great Britain, and Canada might be safely left to settle her own form of government, and to manage her own affairs.

To make Canada an independent State, and capable of maintaining its own independence, would be no less for the interests of the Northern States of America, than of Great Britain. For this purpose, a convenient and well-defined boundary line between Canada and the Northern States would be of the greatest importance, and would go farther to unite these two nations in one common bond of mutual interests, than could possibly be attained, even by the annexation of the whole of Canada to the Northern States. But

this supposes the bond drawn up in the terms
proposed, for securing Free Trade in articles of
every description, and free access to all the Rivers,
Lakes, Harbors and Seabord.   In this mutual
interchange of natural advantages, all would be
obtained which could be acquired by annexation ;
and, the mutual rights being clearly defined and
acknowledged, this peaceful interchange would
form a Union too strong to be severed by ambition or jealousies, for which there would be no
longer any conceivable object.

So far as Great Britain is concerned, the gain
would be unqualified good, and all other nations
would participate in that good.   To Great
Britain, Canada has never been anything but a
dependent and a costly incumbrance.   But as an
independent State, carrying out the principle of
Free Trade with all the world, Canada would
become to Great Britain a most important and
valued Ally, and the North American States,
forming three independent Unions, bound together
by the close bond of mutual interests, would
together form the most powerful political union
in the world, and, as such, would at once rank
among its foremost Powers.

And what is to prevent the accomplishment
of these great objects, under the wise and temperate mediation of England and France?   With

the Mississippi a free outlet for the products of the
Western States in the South, and the St. Lawrence
a free outlet in the North, it is not easy to see the
ground of objection on the part of the Western
States. The St. Lawrence is now the outlet of the
greater part of that region, and the increasing
population in Wisconsin, Minnesota, Michigan,
and around the borders of the Lakes, renders
this more prominent every year. Yet the possession of that river by a Foreign Power has
neither checked the progress of those States, nor
disturbed their peace. We see in Europe the
separate Powers in the peaceable enjoyment of
the Rhine, with its outlet in Holland, and of the
Danube with its mouth in the possession of
Turkey. To assume that the Americans are
unable to live in harmony under the same conditions as the people of Europe, would be a reflection upon the national character without sufficient ground, and to refuse to make the attempt
on any such ground would be ridiculous.

The severance of the artificial union between
the North and the South, which has long ceased
to be a union of interests, will leave both free to
form a natural union on the firm basis of mutual
interests, when the independence of each is settled
and acknowledged.

For a time the commerce of the South may be

diminished, but in a few years, with free trade, with all the rivers, lakes, harbors, and seabord open to free navigation, the commerce of the South will have attained to a prosperity which under the old Union could never have been experienced, and all the natural advantages of the soil and climate of the South will be sources of wealth to the North, which will bind the North and the South together in a union more lasting than human power and contrivance alone could have effected.

Into this Union and share of profits Canada would be admitted, and each Union would stand in its own independent sovereignty, guaranteed in its integrity by England and France, with the acquiescence of all the other European Powers.

The North American States and Canada would then represent a power which must command the respect of all nations, and this combined power would be an example, as regards Free Trade, which must, sooner or later, be followed by all the civilized nations of the world.

The total magnitude of the territory of the Northern Union would be nearly three millions of square miles, and nearly three thousand miles across ; or more than four times as large as that of four of the five great European Powers ; more than twelve times as large as France, and more than eighteen times as large as eight kingdoms of Europe joined together

This should seem to be enough to satisfy any reasonable desire for space and power. Nor would the total magnitude of the Southern territory be much, if at all, less; and, certainly, not inferior in soil or climate with the Valley of the Mississippi, alone capable of supplying all the granaries of the world with corn.

This is a summary of the view taken by the writer of these pages in his Work, recently published, on "The American Question, And How To Settle It." He has there entered fully into the origin and progress of this Question, and he has shown the origin to be in Slavery. It is unnecessary here to enter into that part of the inquiry, or to show how he proposes to deal with the question of slavery, with a view to the immediate mitigation of its evils, and its ultimate extinction in 37 years, or, in the year 1900.

This view is here introduced only as a practical application of the Principle of Utility, for guidance through the unforeseen future, in the government of human affairs. This is the best guide we can have for answering the question of *cui bono*, and directing human actions to their right end; for this is the only index we can have to the Divine will, in the absence of all express command.

The burden of defending Canada has already been severely felt, but the past will be small in comparison with the burden to be expected in the future, if Great Britain is to continue to be the protector and defender of Canada.

To tax the British People for the benefit of Canada is as manifest injustice as it would be to tax the Canadians for the benefit of Great Britain.

But if it be shown that no benefit would be conferred on either country by the tax, then, not only the principle of utility, but common sense as well as justice is outraged. The Government which proposes a tax should, at least, show that there will be some chance of a benefit in return. That is impossible to be shown in the case of Canada.

As regards Great Britain, before it can be shown that the defence of Canada is of any importance, it must be shown that the possession of Canada is of any importance.

It must next be shown that Canada requires to be defended by Great Britain, and that any defence which she could afford, could be, on any rational ground, expected to be effectual against the apprehended invasion.

The first question is answered by the fact that, Canada, when a dependent possession of Great Britain, never was anything but a profitless loss ;

and that, since Canada became an independent
possession, she has been not only a loss, but has
exercised her independence in a manner so as to
prevent her from being otherwise than a loss to
Great Britain, by preventing any possible gain.

The dependence of Canada, therefore, is only
for imposing as much of her own burdens on
Great Britain, as Great Britain may be disposed
to bear. For everything else, Canada is independent of Great Britain.

The second question is answered by the fact of
the Canadian Legislature refusing to pass the Government Bill for raising the Militia for the defence
of Canada. The majority of the Legislature which
threw out that Government measure, must either
have thought the measure uncalled for, or must
have renounced the duty of self-defence. It proves
either that they do not wish to take up an attitude
of hostility against the United States, either because they think it unnecessary, or because they
think it hopeless, or because they think that
England will do it for them, and save them the
expense.

The Canadians have been well rated by England,
under the leadership of *The Times*, for their conduct
on this occasion. But, as a dependency, they think
they have a right to look for protection to the
country on which they are dependent. And as

an independent nation, for the regulation of their own internal government, they can hardly deserve censure for honestly exercising the privilege with which they have been invested by the Mother Country : otherwise why were they invested with that privilege ?

The real answer to this question is,—because they demanded it ; and if it had been refused, their dependency would have ceased long ago. That was a good reason why the freedom demanded should be granted by the Mother Country ; but it must be an equally good reason why all liability of the Mother Country should then cease, and why Canada, from that time, should hang on her own hook.

The Times admits, that,—" We derive no single advantage from Canada which we do not equally derive, in time of peace, from the United States." And, on this Canadian Militia Bill, *The Times* says :—" Opinion in England is perfectly decided that in the connexion between the Mother Country and the Colony, the advantage is infinitely more on the side of the child than of the parent. We no longer monopolize the trade of the Colonies ; we no longer job their patronage ; we cannot hope from them any assistance for defending our own shores, while we are bound to assist in protecting theirs. We cannot even obtain from this very

Colony of Canada reasonably fair treatment for
our manufactures, which are taxed 25 per cent.
on their value, to increase a revenue which the
Colonies will not apply to our, or even to their
own, defence. There is little reciprocity in such
a relation."

It is not a new discovery, that a state of dependence is unfavorable to the growth of young
communities.

It leads to improvidence and extravagance, and
is as much opposed to real progress in communities as in individuals. It is like the spendthrift
youth who relies not on his own exertions, but
on his wealthy relative.

Our connexion with Canada is opposed to the
highest interests of both nations.

This is not a question of throwing off loyal and
grateful subjects; neither is it a question of their
duty to the Mother Country; nor is it a question
of mere profit and loss. There is no throwing
off in leaving Canada to manage her own affairs;
a right which Canada has claimed and exercised
without any regard to the interests of the Mother
Country. When Canada demanded and acquired
her own Parliament, she took her independence
with all its responsibilities. England has no
ground for remonstrating against a policy hostile to her interests; but Canada has no ground

for claiming British protection. With a population equal to several of the independent Nations of Europe, such as Switzerland, Holland, and Belgium, in the midst of more powerful neighbors, there is no reason why Canada should not be equally successful in maintaining her own independence. But, as *The Times* says:—" It is not in our power to send forth from this little island a military force sufficient to defend the frontiers of Canada against the numerous armies which have learnt arms and discipline in the great school of the present civil war. Our resources are unequal to so large a concentration of force on a single point; our empire is too vast, our population too small, *our antagonist is too powerful.*"

The Canadian Parliament came to the conclusion that Canadian finances could not bear the expense of an armament. England has no right to complain of that conclusion, but that was sufficient reason for withdrawing our armament.

If Canada had not been a British possession, no outrage would have been committed on the English flag, as in the ' Trent ' affair.

The 18,000 men with all the munitions of war sent to Canada, and there supported out of taxes wrung from the hard-earned wages of British laborers, is a gross injustice, opposed to the prin-

R

ciple of utility, and to British policy on every
rational ground. We invite aggression in the full
consciousness of our inability to meet it with successful resistance. We pursue the timid policy
of a neutral power, but without securing the
rights of our neutral position. We spread protection all over the world, for the defence of useless Colonies and Dependencies, and we leave our
own shores exposed to invasion, on any sudden
impulse, by an exasperated and treacherous
enemy. Instead of concentrating our national
strength, and availing ourselves of our insular
position, for our own protection, we make frontiers, and impose on ourselves the duty of defending them all over the world, and we exhaust
our national strength in defending them. We
make costly fortifications and ships without soldiers and sailors to serve them, and we pauperize
our own people by taxes, without securing the
primary object of making our own Country safe
from foreign invasion. By a timid and weak
policy we lower the standard of our Nation, and
by a bold and rash policy we diminish our means
for raising the standard of our Nation and
making it pre-eminent and respected among the
Nations of the world. With natural resources
which, properly employed, might enable us to
defy all the Nations of the world, we expend our

resources in exciting against us the rancorous
jealousy of all the Nations of the world, and we
leave ourselves exposed to all the consequences,
in insults and exactions, nicely calculated to the
limit of our forbearance, which arises only from
timidity, which arises only from the consciousness
of our own danger from hostile combinations
against us, and the consciousness of our own deficient means of resistance.

We submit, without an effort, and even without an offer of friendly mediation, to a blockade,
—imposed by a Nation at war with itself,—which
cripples the staple manufacture of our country,
and casts into sudden destitution a large portion
of our working class dependent thereon, besides
impeding almost every other branch of trade in
our country, and we submit from the fear of
being involved in a war with that Nation, engaged
in a deadly strife with itself for a mere idea ;
or, as the war party in the North themselves express it, ' for the maintenance of their glorious
Union.' We refuse to join our powerful and
politic neighbor, France, in her offer to mediate
for the termination of this wanton waste of
human life, and destruction of property, only
because we are weak and timid, and fear the consequences. We put up with our heavy share of
loss consequent on this malignant and deadly

strife, and we will not raise the strong arm, or
even put out the hand of friendship to interpose and save. We fear more the consequences
unseen, which may follow from our interference
or mediation, than the consequences seen and
felt, which have followed from our neutral and
timid policy.

But, if all our strength now spread over the
world had been concentrated in our own Island,
would this have been the policy of Great Britain?
Would this blockade have been permitted?
Would all the frightful consequences of this wild
civil war, about nothing, have been so quietly
permitted to disturb the peace and welfare of
Europe?

So far as these consequences affect England,
her Colonies and Dependencies are chargeable.

When Canada has nothing to hope from continuing a dependency, will she have anything to
fear from becoming a nation dependent on herself? That her trade would not suffer from her
independence, may be known from the decisive
example of the Independent States of America,
whose trade with this Country has rapidly increased from the day when their independence
was recognized by this Country.

If Canadians dread annexation to the United
States, the danger of annexation will be dimi-

nished when Canada ceases to be a dependency
of Great Britian. That England will some day
get into a war with the United States is only too
probable, and in that case, Canada, as a distant
dependency of Great Britain, would, no doubt, be
in danger. But it is not so clear that the American
people would be so profligate as, without provo-
cation, to invade and annex an independent nation.

The argument, therefore, is, that timely separation, while it is good for both parties, is
especially good for the Colonists. This is the
argument so ably put forth by Mr. Goldwin
Smith, and these are his words: "They have a
fresh start in the world, with a heritage of modern
liberty and civilization, unincumbered by the
feudalism which still presses, and will long continue to press, on the energies of the Mother
Country. Their destiny, as it is the last gift of
Providence, is probably higher than ours, if they
will only go forward as men to meet it, instead
of clinging, like frightened children, to the skirts
of the Old World."

As a plea for keeping up our present Colonial
system on commercial grounds it is said that
"the custom of our Colonists is rather more secure than the custom of foreigners, and that
the trade, for example, of India or Australia, is

not likely to be reduced by fifty per cent. in the course of a few months, as that of the United States has been."

Our Export Trade to our North American Colonies fell from £5,080,000 in 1854, to £2,385,000 in 1855, or rather more than fifty per cent.

In the Parliamentary Blue Book containing the "Annual Statement of the Trade and Navigation of the United Kingdom with Foreign Countries and British Possessions in the year 1861," will be seen the state of our Commerce, Foreign and Colonial, including India, for each year from 1857 to 1861, both inclusive, and the Computed Real Value of the Imports into Great Britain from British North America in the year 1861.

Also the Computed Real Value of the Imports into Great Britain from the United States of America, in the year, 1861 : And the Computed Real Value of the Exports, the Produce of the United Kingdom, from Great Britain to the United States of America, in the same year.

From these Parliamentary Returns, which, however imperfect, must be taken as the best authority, it appears that our Imports from Foreign Countries, in Computed Value, for five years, ending 1861, were nearly one-third more than from British Possessions; and that our Exports to Foreign Countries, in Computed Value, for the same time, were nearly one-third more than to British Possessions.

It also appears that our Imports from the United States of America, in Computed Value, in the year, 1861, were nearly six times more than from British North America; and that our Exports, the Produce of Great Britain, in Computed Value, in the same year, were nearly three times more to the United States than to British North America.

It appears that the computed value of our Imports from British Possessions, in the year, 1861, was, £52,676,010; and from Foreign Countries, in the same year, was, £164,809,014; and that the computed value of our Exports to British Possessions, in the same year, was, £45,139,078; and to Foreign Countries, in the same year, was, £114,493,420.

Nothing can be more conclusive against our Colonial system than these figures. Here are the results of our 'differential duties,' in favor of our Colonial Producers, at the expense of our Home Consumers, to, at least, the amount of the differences, which are, in effect, a tax on our own consumers for articles of inferior quality, so forced into our Home market; and our Export trade to

Foreign Countries is 253·6 per cent. more than to all our Colonies and Dependencies !

In addition to this enormous loss is to be reckoned our actual expenditure, in hard cash, for the benefit of our Colonies. This expenditure is in many millions, sterling, annually; but how many millions, it is impossible to state with anything like accuracy, whilst our Government Accounts of Colonial Expenditure are kept in their present form.

Sufficient, however, is apparent to show that, our total expenditure for our Colonies and Dependencies in the last year, (1862,) including our additional Military expenditure for Canada and New Zealand, cannot have been less than Ten Millions, Sterling, and that it was probably much more.

It is for those who advocate our present system to show that we derive any advantage from this expenditure, either directly or indirectly, commercially or politically.

The fact that we gain no advantage commercially, is here plain enough; and, politically, our Colonies seem to be, in every way, only a disadvantage to us.

For commercial advantage there must be reciprocal benefit; and for political advantage there must be additional strength; but there is neither reciprocal benefit, nor additional strength,· but positive loss of money and strength to the Mother Country, and very doubtful benefit to the Colonies.

In the Parliamentary Return, 1862, No. 475, will be found the names of all the GOVERNORS, LIEUTENANT-GOVERNORS, and Persons administering the Governments of the different Colonies, and their Salaries, in British Money, etc., for the year, 1862.

Also the number of COLONIAL BISHOPS, with the Salaries of each, and the sources whence those Salaries are derived.

In the Parliamentary Return, 1862, No. 396, is given the Name, Rank, Salary and Date of Appointment of each PUBLIC OFFICER employed in the several BRITISH COLONIES appointed and paid by the HOME GOVERNMENT.

In the Parliamentary Return, 1862, No. 387, is given the Expense incurred in maintaining GARRISONS, in each of the CHANNEL ISLANDS, in the years 1810 and 1860 respectively; showing the amount expended for the Pay in each year for Staff and Regimental Officers, Non-Commissioned Officers and Privates, and the numerical strength of each Garrison in each year. Why the salaries paid to the Lieutenant-Governors of Jersey and Guernsey are not included in this statement does not appear. But, after much research and many inquiries, the following has been obtained from the Government officials, as the payments to the Lieutenant-Governors of Jersey and Guernsey:—

THE LIEUTENANT-GOVERNOR OF JERSEY.

	£.	s.	d.
Major-General, as Colonel on the Staff	415	3	9
Allowance as Resident Lieutenant-Governor	173	7	6
Foot Major	82	2	6
	£670	13	9

THE LIEUTENANT-GOVERNOR OF GUERNSEY.

	£.	s.	d.
Major-General, as Colonel of the Staff	415	3	9
Allowance as Resident Lieutenant-Governor	173	7	6
Foot Major	168	7	6
	£757	7	6

Certainly, these payments can.not be said to be extravagantly high, however unprofitable. But it must not be supposed that the sum of £173 7s. 6d. represents the actual benefits of these little Governorships. The Government House, with Coals, Candles, and other perquisites, besides an allowance for hospitable entertainments, (though, doubtless, the hospitality far exceeds the allowance) with many other little undiscovered benefits, all at the cost of the British Tax-payers, are to be added to these nominal Salaries.

To ascertain the Government Expenditure on Alderney, and the other Channel Isles, for Fortifications, Harbors of Refuge, Docks, Piers, and other Public Works, is an impossibility. All that can be said on this part of the subject is, that, for any public good, the whole of the money so expended might as well have been thrown into the sea.

Why any of these expenses should fall on the British Tax-payers is the question which should be answered.

In the case of the Channel Isles it may be said that these works are necessary for the defence of the Mother-Country. If the fact be so, that may be a good answer for the Channel Isles, and it then only remains to be shown that the money has been judiciously expended, an important fact which never has been shown.

But the present question is with our Colonies and Dependencies, and the Channel Isles will be further noticed hereafter.

Why our Colonies and Dependencies should be dependent on the Mother-Country for their resources is the present question.

If the Colonies can maintain their independence only at the cost of the Mother-Country, that is no ground for throwing the cost on British Tax-payers, unless it be shown that they derive some equivalent benefit therefrom.

But it is very doubtful whether the Colonies themselves derive any real benefit from their state of dependence; or, whether that state of dependence be not productive of more injury than benefit to themselves. So far as the Colonies are dependent on Trade and Commerce, the Mother-Country cannot guard them against any changes which affect Trade and Commerce. So far as they are dependent on their own exertions and good conduct, their reliance on the Mother-Country is all against them.

As Mr. Goldwin Smith says: "We have not been able to guarantee Canada against the disaster of civil war; nor have we been able to avert it from the United States; and it can hardly be supposed that, if the old American Colonies had now been under our nominal dominion, we should have been any better able to prevent the conflict between the Free-North, and the Slave-owning South, which causes the sudden fall of our Export Trade to that Country. On the other hand, we artificially expose all these communities to disasters affecting their trade by gratuitously involving them in our wars. If they were independent, their trade with us would still be respected as that of neutrals though their country were at war."

Again, with regard to the true interests of Colonies in Trade and Commerce, Mr. Goldwin Smith remarks with unanswerable force:—" In face of the sudden fall in the export trade to North America in 1855, and in face of the general decline of that trade, notwithstanding the rapid and steady increase of the population of those countries, it is idle to say that the *solidity* of a trade depends on anything but its reciprocal advantages. The Colonist does not trade with us because he is a Colonist, but because at present he can get what he wants better and cheaper from us than from other merchants."*

This truth will hardly be questioned in the present day, and may now be taken as an admitted rule. But it is a disgraceful fact that, for many years, this rule was reversed to us, when by protecting duties we were forced to take Canadian timber of inferior quality at a higher price, and prevented from taking Baltic timber of

* Goldwin Smith, "The Empire."

superior quality at a lower price. This was only
an indirect instead of a direct tax on the Mother-
Country for the benefit of the infant Colony.   It
is for those who advocate this system of fostering
to show the benefit to the Mother-Country.

It is well known that the best system is that
which fosters the Home Trade, and that the next
best trade is that with neighboring Countries,
because in that trade the expense of carriage is
not so great, and the state of supply and demand
are more certainly known.   Of all trade the
worst is that with distant Countries, because the
carriage is expensive and the speculations are
hazardous.

The effects from both these causes have been
fully experienced by our Merchants trading with
Australia and China.

The export trade to Australia has been and is
an increasing trade, but the obvious cause is in the
numerical extension and increase of the markets
in Australia, which the discoveries of gold have
greatly enlarged.   New communities must necessarily for the time import every description of
manufacture; but it is equally certain that they
will in time manufacture for themselves; and
that, in the mean time they will seek the supply
for their wants in the cheapest markets.   In
British North America they are beginning to

manufacture for themselves, and therefore we do not find them so good customers as formerly. But there is no reason to infer that they would not have been as good customers to us if they had been independent of us, and wholly dependent on themselves.

If, by fostering a Colony and helping it out of our own taxes, we help to create a sudden and special trade, which gives our industry an unnatural development in a particular direction, but which, we know, must hereafter fail or decline, and leave our merchants and manufacturers in difficulties, that is a very questionable benefit to the Mother Country.

Any beneficial return from a sense of gratitude for past favors is still more doubtful, as the propensity to Protection is strong in all emancipated Colonists. This evil tendency has shown itself in Canada, and is beginning to show itself in Australia also. Mr. Goldwin Smith gives two reasons for this, and no better reasons can be given. " In the first place, Protection is the natural resort of ignorant cupidity, and ignorant cupidity is the besetting sin of communities intensely commercial and wanting in education. In the second place, these communities are excessively impatient of direct taxation, and therefore if their taxes are high, heavy duties are the inevitable result. Their taxes must be high while their public expenditure is extravagant; and the extravagance of their public expenditure arises in part, from their being inoculated by us with the system of central Government, and the abuses which, under their social circumstances, central Government entails." Such must always be the inevitable result under every government, until the taxes be levied *directly* on the *realised* property of the Country.

Canada can no longer be properly called a Colony, being more properly a Dependency, the limited power of the *Veto* reserved to the Mother Country being more nominal than real. But the fictitious Royalty kept up by British money, and the necessary presence of British Soldiers and Sailors to keep up this fictitious Royalty, for the honor of Great Britain, her Crown and dignity, in return for this nominal power, is a real and substantial tax, of some millions yearly, on all the British People; and that another hundred millions will be added to our National Debt, if we persist in undertaking the defence of Canada, is more than probable.

For these reasons the sooner we get free from these weighty responsibilities the better, and the parties most concerned for their safety, will then be sooner and better prepared to defend themselves.

New Zealand was established as a British Colony, about thirty years ago, on the express understanding that it was to be left to its own resources. But the Colonists contrived to get us into a war with the Maoris, as the Colonists of the Cape succeeded in doing with the Kafirs, and we have now upwards of 6000 British troops in New Zealand, engaged in fighting natives, or in making roads, with a Representative of Royalty, and all the attendant consequences, at the expense of the British tax-payer. Moreover, if the "Confiscation Act" proposed should be passed, whereby the natives will be deprived of every acre of their native soil, there is every reason to expect that they will fight until their race be exterminated; as it is already apparent to them that the loss of their land is the loss of their liberty, and they are not a People to submit quietly to slavery.

If, in the end, we succeed, as, probably, we shall, then we shall have gained the Colony of New Zealand at the price of a costly and exterminating war. But what, then, will our Taxpayers have gained?

If the expenditure of Government be on the principle of producing some benefit in return, directly or indirectly, immediately or prospectively, this is an intelligible principle open to exa-

B

mination and reasonable control; but when, from
the nature of the expenditure, that principle is
not discernible, then there is no guide for directing the examination, or regulating the control.
It is all a matter of chance dependent upon the
judgment and discretion of the Government, or
upon the caprice or fancy of those to whom the
power of judging is entrusted. Whether a few
millions more or less be so expended, must be a
question over which those who pay can have no
control, because of the utility or expediency of
the expenditure they can form no judgment.

It is said that the Colonists may not unjustly
call upon us to pay for their military and naval
establishments, so long as this Country has the
sole control of peace and war.

There is some reason in this, inasmuch as the
power to declare war is, indirectly, the power to
tax. But this is a stronger reason why the Colony
should be free and independent, than why it
should be held in a state of dependence and control, and subject to these consequences.

It would not be reasonable to compel our Colonists to maintain armaments for the purpose of
supporting our policy, and "on a scale dictated
by our views and pretensions, without giving them
a voice in questions of peace and war;" but why
should the Colonists be placed in a position to be

involved in those questions? Why should not the Colonists be free to govern and direct their own affairs, and to defend themselves, without participating in our responsibilities, and imposing on us the duty of their protection?

If our only possible benefit from the connexion with them be through their trade,—and no other can be suggested,—how is that benefit to be increased by increasing our responsibilities and expenditure for their benefit or protection?

It is said that, our Colonies, if given up, would be taken by the enemy. But on what ground could any civilized nation justify the seizure of a free and independent country, against which no cause of war existed? That would be a case of buccaneering, or piracy, which all nations are equally interested in resisting. If our North American Colonies were as completely separated from all connexion with Great Britain as are the United States, how would the attempt at seizure differ from their buccaneering attempt on Cuba? If the United States had been at war with Spain, that attempt would have been justified by the acknowledged rules of war. But being at peace with Spain, that attempt was an act of piracy, which all nations would have been justified in resenting, and ought to have resented.

The sooner that principle is acknowledged by

all the Great Powers of Europe, the better for the peace of the world ; but clearly there can be no chance of peace until that principle is acknow-ledged and enforced ; for, otherwise, the law of the strongest must prevail, and the right must be with the might.

In this view, it must be for the interest of every new community to stand on its own foun-dation, to be responsible for its own acts, and to be dependent only on its own efforts; in short, to be free and independent, and to trade with all nations on equal terms.

Free Trade necessarily implies freedom to carry on trade with all nations, free from all impedi-ments, and on equal terms. The cheapest mar-kets will then determine the choice, and nature has so diversified and distributed her gifts, that the cheapest markets will then be pretty equally spread all over the world ; for, the expense of transport must always be an important ingredient in the question of cheapness.

The progress of the principle of Free Trade is silently revolutionizing the whole world. The old state of things is passing away with the neces-sity for it, if the necessity ever existed. That protection and state of dependency which formerly seemed necessary, is now seen to be less necessary, or not necessary at all. Many now see it to be

injurious to its own object, and the time is, perhaps, near when that will be seen clearly by all.
The only possible ground for maintaining the
present system of Colonies and Dependencies will
then wholly disappear.

Adam Smith foresaw this more than eighty
years ago, but he saw this only through the new
science, the rules of which, it may be said, he
was then reducing into order. If his far-sighted
views could then have been verified by experience, he would, no doubt, have declared them
with more boldness. But his confidence in his
views must have been strong to have enabled him
to declare them as he has. His meaning cannot
be mistaken when he wrote these words :—" Under the present system of management, Great
Britain derives nothing but loss from the dominion
which she assumes over her Colonies. To propose that Great Britain should voluntarily give
up all authority over her Colonies, and leave them
to elect their own magistrates, to enact their own
laws, and to make peace and war, as they might
think proper, would be to propose such a measure
as never was, and never will be adopted by any
nation in the world. No nation ever voluntarily gave up the dominion of any province,
how troublesome soever it might be to govern it,
and how small soever the revenue which it

afforded might be in proportion to the expense
which it occasioned. Such sacrifices, though
they might frequently be agreeable to the interest,
are always mortifying to the pride of every
nation, and, what is perhaps of still greater consequence, they are always contrary to the private
interest of the governing part of it, who would
thereby be deprived of the disposal of many places
of trust and profit, of many opportunities of
acquiring wealth and distinction, which the possession of the most turbulent, and, to the great
body of the people, the most unprofitable province seldom fails to afford. The most visionary
enthusiasts would scarce be capable of proposing
such a measure, with any serious hopes at least
of its ever being adopted. If it was adopted,
however, Great Britain would not only be immediately freed from the whole annual expense
of the peace establishment of the Colonies, but
might settlo with them such a treaty of commerce as would effectually secure to her a free
trade, more advantageous to the great body of
the people, though less to the merchants, than
the monopoly which she at present enjoys.   By
thus parting good friends, the natural affection
of the Colonies to the Mother-Country, which
perhaps, our late dissensions have well nigh extinguished, would quickly revive.   It might dis-

pose them not only to respect, for whole centuries
together, that treaty of commerce which they had
concluded with us at parting, but to favor us in
war as well as in trade, and, instead of turbulent
and factious subjects, to become our most faithful,
affectionate, and generous allies ; and the same
sort of parental affection on the one side, and
filial respect on the other, might revive between
Great Britain and her Colonies, which used to
subsist between those of ancient Greece and the
Mother-City from which they descended."*

The boldness and discernment of this declaration,
considering the time when it was made, are very
remarkable ; and the doubt suggested about the
past and future policy is evidently only a sarcasm
on the wisdom of nations.

Experience has since proved the truth of these
views. "The private interest of the governing
part," is as strong now as it was then. The
reference to ' visionary enthusiasts' can leave no
doubt about the writer's own opinion, and that
the philosopher saw further than the politician
cared more plainly to express. But for the conclusion there was no hesitation, no doubt. The
difficulty, and the only difficulty to that conclusion then was, and is now, ' the pride,' or the

* Adam Smith, ' Wealth of Nations,' vol. 2, bk. iv., p. 443,
0th Edition.

prejudice, 'of every nation,' and ' the private interest of the governing part of it.' For these the
true interests of the nations are sacrificed, and
will continue to be, as long as the private interests
are allowed to prevail over the public good.

The claim of hereditary right by the aristocracy
to Governments, and other high official appointments in the Colonies and Dependencies, has
been too long an undisturbed enjoyment to make
the national prejudice in its favor a matter of
much surprise, and may render it in some degree
excusable, if not pardonable. Nor is this question
confined to the aristocracy, when all the subordinate military, naval, and civil appointments are
taken into the account. But these considerations only make 'the difficulty,' and in no way
affect ' the conclusion' ; and there are now many
who think that this difficulty is to be got over.
Whether or not they are to be set down as
' visionary enthusiasts,' is a question which will
perhaps be settled sooner than many suppose.
In the mean time there can be no harm in carrying on this inquiry into the utility of things. On
the question of the utility of Colonies to the
Mother-Country Adam Smith has no hesitation,
nor does he hesitate to mention as the strongest
reason against the ' visionary enthusiasts,' " that
such sacrifices are always contrary to the private

interests of the governing part of the nation, who
would thereby be deprived of the disposal of
many places of trust and profit, of many opportunities of acquiring wealth and distinction which
the possession of the most turbulent, and to the
great body of the people the most unprofitable,
province seldom fails to afford."

Mr. Goldwin Smith follows up this quotation
from Adam Smith with these true remarks :—
" It is not our soldiers, nor the officers of our
Army, that have an interest in retaining the outlying dependencies of an Empire spreading over
the globe.   On them this Empire entails constant banishment, often in unhealthy climates,
and all the discomforts of a wandering life. They
might guard England without sacrificing all the
comforts of a settled habitation, and all the happiness of home.   More than this, it is in fact to
the extent of the Empire, that they must attribute the wretched inadequacy of their pay.   An
officer of the Navy is very ill-paid compared with
other professions, and considering the hardships
and dangers he has to undergo : an officer of the
army, taking into account the purchase of com-
missions and steps, can often hardly be said to
be paid at all. . . . Nevertheless, though our soldiers and sailors, at least the officers of our Army
and Navy, are ill-paid, our establishments are

the most expensive in the world. And it is the extent of the Empire which makes them expensive. A soldier in a Colony or Dependency costs double as much as a soldier at home, besides all the incidental expenses, such as the cost of Colonial fortifications, and the sudden transmission of troops to distant parts attendant upon outlying and dangerous possessions."

No one can fail to confirm the truth of Mr. Goldwin Smith's remark, "that great changes have come over the world since the time when our Empire was formed and our Imperial policy was adopted; and that, the world being changed, it is at least a fair inquiry whether our policy ought to remain the same. What was wisdom in our fathers, regard being had to the circumstances of their days, may be utter folly in us."

Even those who most rely on the ' wisdom of our ancestors ' must admit that " the most obvious of these changes, and the one which bears most directly on the policy of the Imperial system, is the fall of protection and the progress of free trade." The effect of these changes must be to render further changes absolutely necessary for adapting the old to the new state of things, and for preserving what is worthy of preservation in the old to the new state of things. The more speedily those further and necessary changes are made, the shorter will be the period of transition, which must always be more or less inconvenient, and in many cases injurious, to private interests.

If it be true, with regard to our West Indian Colonies, that the utility which has resulted from them has been very great to our Merchants and others connected with them, it is not so clear and evident that any such has been the result to the British People at large. But this would be a difficult and unsatisfactory inquiry, for, admitting the benefits to the British nation to any extent in former times and circumstances, those times and circumstances are changed, and many of the arguments which might then have been urged with some show of reason for the continuance of the then existing system cannot now apply.

The question is whether, under our existing system, professing to be founded on the principle of free trade, the maintenance of our West Indian Colonies can be continued consistently with that principle, and with the principle of Utility. If our trade with those Islands would be the same, whether held as Colonies or Dependencies by Great Britain, or any other Power, or existing as independent States, it is evident that the cost of our military, naval, and civil establish-

ments in those Islands, and of all our ships on
those stations, for internal government and external defence, is wholly a gratuitous loss to the
British nation ; for, the patronage of the British
Government, for the benefit of private individuals, cannot be admitted as a set-off against
the British tax-payers. Those who wish to know
the annual amount of this cost, in the aggregate,
to the British tax-payers, must find it out for
themselves as well as they can from the details
in the Government Accounts, as given in the
yearly Blue Books : and those who wish to make
out that there is any other source of profit in
these possessions than from trade, must show
that our trade with them would be diminished,
if we ceased to hold them as Colonies or Dependencies ; otherwise the account must be stated
with the whole of this cost to their debit, with
only patronage and *prestige* per contra; and
prestige, as Mr. Goldwin Smith remarks, " is a
French word," which he finds rendered in the
dictionary " illusion," " juggling trick," " imposture."

As Adam Smith said, even in his day, " there
are no Colonies of which the progress has been
more rapid than that of the English in North
America. Plenty of good land, and liberty to
manage their own affairs their own way, seem to

be the two great causes of the prosperity of all new Colonies."

No one now supposes that the progress of prosperity would have been so rapid in the North American States, if they had continued to this day under British dominion.

No one supposes that the prosperity and power of France would have been what they are, if France had been a British Dependency, or occupied by English People. Physical as well as mental character have much to do with this question, and these have been adapted to climate and soil by a power beyond human control. Frenchmen are adapted to France as Africans are to Africa, and many generations must be required for altering this adaptation. Thus Nature points to the place and fixes the population; and though in some cases we see the inferior races disappearing and giving up their places to higher races, yet we see throughout the world broad barriers for preserving the distinctions between the human races, and probably these barriers will never be broken down, but all will be brought to work together in their own various ways, on the principle of utility for the common good of all.

By the principle of Free Trade all over the world this great end will be brought about, and

Liberty will be recognized as a universal principle in establishing the foundation of all human
Governments.

When this principle comes to be clearly seen
and appreciated,—and Englishmen will probably
be the first to see it clearly, and appreciate it
fully,—then Great Britain, by her own voluntary
act, will divest herself of all her Colonies and Dependencies, and thus by concentrating her power
will greatly increase it, and exercise it for good
over the whole world, and in the place of prestige,
or imposture, will substitute solid strength.

Great Britain, when she assumed to herself
the exclusive right of supplying all goods from
Europe to her Colonies, might have forced them,
—as other Countries have done to their Colonies,
—to receive such goods subject to the same duties
which they paid in the Mother Country. But
this was never the policy pursued by Great Britain, at least in modern times. On the contrary,
till 1763, the same drawbacks were allowed upon
the exportation of the greater part of foreign
goods to our Colonies as to any independent
foreign Country. In 1763, by the 4th Geo. III.
c. 15, this indulgence was much abated, and it
was enacted, "That no part of the duty called
the old subsidy should be drawn back for any
goods of the growth, production, or manufacture

of Europe or the East Indies, which should be
exported from this Kingdom to any British Colony or Plantation in America ; wines, white ca-
licoes, and muslins excepted." Before this law,
which passed in disregard of every principle of
justice and sound policy, many different sorts of
foreign goods might have been bought cheaper
in the Colonies and Plantations than in the Mother Country, as the same may still often be at
this day.

In the exclusive privilege to British Merchants
of supplying the Colonies with all the goods
which they wanted from Europe, and of purchasing all such parts of their surplus produce as
could not interfere with any of the trades which
they themselves carried on at home, the interests
of the Colonies were manifestly sacrificed to the
interests of those merchants. In allowing the
same drawbacks upon the re-exportation of the
greater part of European and East India goods to
the Colonies, as upon their re-exportation to any
independent Country, the interests of the Mother
Country were manifestly sacrificed to the interests
of the Colonies, according to the mercantile idea
of those interests. It was for the interest of
the merchants to pay as little as possible for the
foreign goods which they sent to the Colonies,
and, consequently, to get back as much as possi-

ble of the duties which they advanced upon their
importation into Great Britain. They might
thereby be enabled to sell in the Colonies, either
the same quantity of goods with a greater profit,
or a greater quantity with the same profit, and,
consequently, to gain something either in the
one way or the other. It was, likewise, for the
interest of the Colonies to get all such goods as
cheap and in as great abundance as possible.
But this might not always be for the interest of
the Mother Country. She might frequently suffer both in her revenue, by giving back a great
part of the duties which had been paid upon the
importation of such goods; and in her manufactures, by being undersold in the Colonial market,
in consequence of the easy terms upon which
foreign manufactures could be carried there by
means of those drawbacks. The progress of the
Linen Manufacture of Great Britain was notori-
ously retarded by the drawbacks upon the re-exportation of German Linen to the American Colonies.

These were the sound views of Adam Smith;
but, for long after he had made them known, they
were utterly disregarded by the British Legislature, and are now only partially recognized or
acted upon. The history of British Legislation
on the subject of Trade displays the most pro-

found ignorance or disregard of principle, and it is no wonder that a system so long continued and governed by no principle, should be little understood by the people, and be regarded with a favourable prejudice by many who look with satisfaction to results as they are, in total ignorance of the far greater results which, under a more just and wise system, might have been.

"But," as Adam Smith adds, "though the policy of Great Britain with regard to the trade of her Colonies has been dictated by the same mercantile spirit as that of other Nations, it has, however, upon the whole, been less illiberal and oppressive than that of any of them."

If Adam Smith had now been writing on the policy of Great Britain with regard to her Colonies, it is clear, from the tendency of all his remarks, confirmed by the experience of the eighty years since he wrote, that he would have urged the separation of all political connexion between the Colonies and the Mother Country, at the earliest possible opportunity consistently with existing obligations.

With regard to the Colonies of America, he says:—"The policy of Europe has very little to boast of, either in the original establishment, or, so far as concerns their internal government, in the subsequent prosperity of the Colonies of

T

America.   Folly and injustice seem to have been
the principles which presided over and directed
the first project of establishing those Colonies."

In equal folly and injustice they were attempted
to be chained to the Mother Country; but in the
true British spirit they broke the chains, and
worked out their own freedom and independence,
to the everlasting disgrace and humiliation of the
Mother Country, but for the great gain of both
Countries.

As Adam Smith asks:—" In what way, therefore, has the policy of Europe contributed either to
the first establishment, or to the present grandeur
of the Colonies of America?   In one way, and
in one way only, it has contributed a good deal.
Magna virum mater!   It bred and formed the
men who were capable of achieving such great
actions, and of laying the foundation of so great
an Empire; and there is no other quarter of the
world of which the policy is capable of forming,
or has ever actually and in fact formed such men.
The Colonies owe to the policy of Europe the
education and great views of their active and en-
terprising founders; and some of the greatest
and most important of them, so far as concerns
their internal government, owe it to scarce anything else."   The views of that far-sighted Philosopher ought to go far in dispelling British pre-

judice in favour of British policy in regard to Colonies.

It is not proposed that Canada shall cease to be called a Colony of Great Britain, but that Canada shall cease to be dependent on the British tax-payer : " that Canada shall elect her own chief magistrate, coin her own money, decide her own causes finally in her own law-courts, and have the power of making peace and war." If these privileges be dangerous to the Mother Country, why was the privilege of a free parliament conferred on Canada? All experience has shown that two parliaments cannot work together for good under one Crown. There is no reason why, after the separation of the Governments, Canadians, if they desire it, and duly qualify themselves, should not still enjoy all the privileges of British Citizens.

The attempt to maintain two independent Parliaments in England and Ireland was a total failure, and the same experiment in Canada, with the Atlantic between, is not likely to be more successful.

When Canada is really free and independent, and dependent only on herself, there is no reason why she should not enter into a free-trade treaty with Great Britain, and thus form the strongest union of mutual interests, not only

with Great Britain, but also with every other
European Power.

If all our other North American Colonies were
at the same time released from their allegiance to
the Mother Country, they would naturally unite
with Canada for their common protection, and
against any piratical attempt by their more
powerful neighbors they would be protected by
the common interests of combined Europe.

As Mr. Goldwin Smith observes:—" Switzerland, in the midst of armed and aggressive empires, stands secure and inviolable as a nation."

But if all our North American possessions
should, by force or mutual consent, become annexed to the United States,—and *by consent*
seems little likely with the debt now accumulated by the United States, the annual interest
of which already exceeds that of our own,—how
could that affect British interests, or European
interests generally?

Would our trade with Canada be less than it
is? Our trade with Canada has always been
trifling in comparison with our trade with the
United States. Would emigration from our
shores to Canada be less than it is? For one
emigrant from Ireland to Canada, ten Irish emi-
grants seek their homes in the United States.
As Mr. Goldwin Smith asks; what is the " ar-

gument for the present system, except that of '*prestige*'—prestige being, in plain English, a false appearance of strength, known by everybody to be false, which, it seems, has come to be thought the true life of the greatest of nations."

This question has never been answered with anything like a show of reason. 'The Times,' which has set itself up as the great authority on the other side, has the advantage of occasionally putting forth prominent points in leading Articles, to catch the eye of numerous daily readers, and pandering to the popular prejudice. With some the false impressions of these prominent points remain; but in time the false reasoning is forgotten, and leaves the popular Journalist free to take a line of argument quite inconsistent with his former reasoning, but still specious and popular for his purpose. Few take the trouble to turn back to old newspapers, and most readers of newspapers are thankful to be saved the trouble of thinking for themselves on such subjects. *The Times* is powerful for its purposes, but to answer Mr. Goldwin Smith is not one of its purposes, the true answer being not yet the popular. It is, therefore, more convenient, and for the popular Journal more safe, to meet argument by contrary assertion. But the system does not

rest on argument. As Mr. Goldwin Smith sums
up: " It rests on unreflecting pride, ignorant of
the true sources of English greatness.   It rests
on class interests and prejudices, ever triumphant,
by their concentrated energy, over the public
good.   It rests on the routine of offices which
we fondly imagine to be the seats of a superior
intelligence, while in fact they are apt to become,
except for mere administration, the most mechanical of all machines.   It rests upon patronage,
that foundation of adamant, upon which the puny
assaults of reason and justice have so often spent,
and will long spend, themselves in vain."

Such is the system here put to the test of
reason and sound policy in the case of Canada,
and slightly adverted to in our West India possessions and New Zealand.   The system, so
tried, will not stand the test, and is proved to be
bad, because opposed to the principle of Utility.

Many of the foregoing observations apply with
equal force to our Australian Colonies, which
have free representative institutions, and the representative of the Crown present with them.
They have all the internal machinery of English
self-government, and why should they not have
an external government with entire nationality ?
If they cannot take part in the councils of the
British Parliament, how can they be expected to

concur in all the acts which flow from those councils? If they have no voice in the question of a declaration of war by Great Britain, why should they be subject to the imminent danger of a desolating invasion? Their Parliament and ours deliberate under different conditions, and, therefore, are morally sure to come to different determinations. If the English Parliament interfere in questions of military expenditure in Australia, or otherwise in imposing fiscal burdens on the Australians, that is wholly incompatible with their own free institutions; and for them to have a voice in the British Parliament is practically impossible. A large standing army and a well equipped Navy at the cost of the Australians, are as repugnant to the state of society in Australia, as in Canada, and would be as injurious to the interests of the one Colony as to the other. If the cost of such armament is to be borne by the British tax-payers, that would be as repugnant to their state and condition, as injurious to the interests of the country. Separate and independent, with all the rights of a neutral nation, in the case of Great Britain at war, the Australians would be far better able to defend themselves than if under the protection of Great Britain, and much less likely to require defence, or to stand in need of protection.

We draw from our Colonies neither military force nor revenue; but, on the contrary, we dissipate our own military force and waste our own revenue in retaining them, and we aggravate this evil by exciting the jealousy of other nations by an extended Empire. To keep up these costly and unremunerative establishments, and to incur the risk of still more costly wars, we add to the heavy burden of our own over-taxed and suffering people, and we do this to maintain a false appearance of strength, which diminishes our natural strength, and deceives no other nation than our own, but increases the patronage of the Government for bribing the Aristocracy to barter away or withhold the just and natural rights and liberties of the People.

It is said that our Australian Colonies are already free, and have " the same institutions generally " as the Mother Country. But their institutions are directly opposed to the Mother Country in religion, in politics, and in trade. They reject an Established Church, a high electoral qualification, and an aristocratic Parliament, and have manhood suffrage, election by ballot, and democratic assemblies; they reject Free Trade, and pass measures of Protection. " The unity of the Empire " has no existence but in the imagination of our Secretary of State for the

Colonies. He admits that the power of the Crown over our Colonies is gone, but, as the subjects of Her Majesty, he hopes that they will never renounce their allegiance, and separate from the Mother Country. That hope will probably be gratified as long as they are left to enjoy the liberty of self-government, and the privilege of throwing upon the Mother Country the cost of defending them from all enemies, but no longer. Any portion of this liberty curtailed, or this privilege withdrawn, the adult Colony will exercise its power, and take leave of the Mother Country for ever.

The tax, which nominally severed the connexion between the Mother Country and her North American Colonies, was a duty of three pence per pound on tea, imposed for the profit of no special class, but for the general good. Nor was it imposed for remote objects, but to defray in part the expenses of a war entirely American, which had resulted to the benefit of the Colonies, in the conquest of Canada, and thus become a debt not justly chargeable to the British tax-payer alone.

Though the nominal cause was in this small duty on tea, the real cause was in the principle —"Taxation without representation."

There will never be any difficulty in finding a

grievance ready for the occasion, whenever separation is desired, and that will surely be when
the gratuitous supplies from the Mother Country
fall short of the expectation and demand.

And so in the United States, when the South
desired separation from the North: when the
North passed the Morrill Tariff, there was Taxation, if not without representation, at least, in the
absence of representation; for then nearly all the
representatives of the South had ceased to attend
Congress.   But that was not the cause of seces-
sion.   The real cause was in the incompatibility
of interests between the Free States of the North
with the Slave States of the South.

The slave-owning power is essentially and necessarily domineering and aggressive, and the
issue of the civil war, whatever that may be, can
scarcely end in restoring the ascendency of the
slave-owner in his propensities over the politics
of the North.   The people of the North are
brave, powerful, and formidable, if provoked, but
they are an industrious people, among whom
labor is held in honor; and, though a vain and
boastful people, they are too frugal in their habits to indulge their ambition at the expenses of
war.   Such people go to war as they enter into
trade speculation, with a view to profit, and of all
speculations war is the most riskful, and the least

profitable, as they have learnt, and they are not likely soon to forget the lesson.

All the buccaneering propensities of the South in their piratical attacks on Cuba, Nicaragua, and on other occasions, were only trade speculations, with no idea of military glory, and no other object than profit, and if Canada be ever invaded by the North, it will be with that object alone; but the military ambition of the North or the South will never disturb the world.

That the Canadians should be a separate people from the Americans seems manifestly to be desired for the sake of both; but that Canada can ever be made as part of Europe, is as absurd as to suppose that Australia can ever be made as part of Europe; and where society is composed of equals, or all pretend to consider themselves equals, the institutions will be more democratic than aristocratic.

Manhood suffrage is inevitable in a country where all men are equal, or consider themselves so, and there mock monarchy must lack all the dignity of the original, and will never be tolerated; and, without monarchy, there can never be any other aristocracy than that of wealth, which must always be the minority.

Our Australian Colonies are laying the foundation for a great nation in the Southern extremity of the globe; but these, like other nations, will have to go through great trials of their own making, and the sooner they are left to stand alone the sooner they will attain to strength and greatness.

The British Sovereign would no more detract from the honor of the British Crown by renouncing all dominion over the rising communities in America and Australia, than when Calais and Dunkirk were restored to France. But for preserving the natural tie between a kindred people, there could be no time so favorable for withdrawing all interference, as when interference was no longer required or desired.

Mr. Goldwin Smith well remarks that, "Calais was occupied as a landing-place for our invasions of France. When those invasions become hopeless, and had been virtually abandoned, the landing-place became worthless. Yet ambition clung to the possession with an obstinacy, and resented its loss with a fury at which it is easy to smile now. The loss of Calais tarnished the reputation of this Country because it was taken from us by force, instead of being given up when it had become useless."

These last remarks, it will be seen, point to the rock of Gibraltar.

"Gibraltar is, and always will be, a famous

monument of English valour. So are Calais and
Dunkirk. But who wishes that Calais and Dunkirk were ours now? The loss of Calais tarnished
the reputation of the Country because it was
taken from us by force, instead of being given up
when it had become useless. As the value of
Calais ceased with the French wars, so the value
of military posts occupied to force a way for our
trade is ceasing with the reign of monopoly."[*]

We won Gibraltar fairly in war, and we have
good right to hold it if we think it our interest
to do so; but we took it not to extend our territories, but to break the dominant power of
Spain. But great changes have since taken
place in the condition of Spain and all the other
nations of Europe. The reasons, if good, for
taking Gibraltar, have long ceased to be any
reasons for holding it. As a military station it
is very costly, and for any protection to our export trade to the Mediterranean it is useless.

"But money will not measure the cost of Gibraltar. Its price is the implacable and undying
enmity of Spain."[†]

"Not to Spain only but to other nations Gibraltar in our hands is a cause of offence. It is
the symbol of that insulting domination under

* Goldwin Smith, 'The Empire,' p. 206.
† Goldwin Smith, p. 213.

which all nations have smarted in their turn. It
is the throne, in their eyes, of the old tyrant of
the seas." *

How must France view the British Flag floating in its pride over this smuggling station?
And what is Gibraltar now but a smuggling station?

If originally the possession of Gibraltar were
desired by Great Britain to secure the freedom
of the Mediterranean, that object no longer exists,
for the navigation of that sea is free to all nations; and all the States of Europe which bor-
der on the Mediterranean, as well as all other
nations of Europe, are interested in keeping it
free.

On no rational ground can it be shown to be
the interest of any nation of Europe, or of any
combination of European nations, to interfere
with the free navigation of that sea.

If it be said that the possession of Gibraltar is
necessary to us as a protection to the "overland
route to India," it must be shown that that route
would be open to us at all in time of war with
the Mediterranean Powers.

If it be said that the possession of Gibraltar is
necessary to us as commanding the Strait, and
as the key of the Mediterranean, " the answer is

* Goldwin Smith, p. 215.

that there are six good miles of sea-way beyond the effective reach of its guns."*

Captain Sayer, who has recently published a history of Gibraltar, where he has held a military appointment says:—"Restore the fortress to Spain to-morrow—how long would she retain it? Just so long as France might choose to leave her in possession of it."†

But, as Mr. Goldwin Smith answers :—" Why, here is an 'impregnable' fortress which cannot be held by the united force of a nation with sixteen millions of inhabitants, a revenue of £21,000,000, a respectable fleet, excellent naval arsenals, and an army of 160,000 men !"

Captain Sayer, when he wrote, could not have foreseen this answer, and must now see that this admits of no reply.

He says :—" The history of the past century and a half shows that not only was Spain at no time strong enough to retake Gibraltar, but that she was unable to hold it against attack." But, as Mr. Goldwin Smith remarks :—"It was taken from her by surprise at the period of her greatest decrepitude, when the fortifications were almost in ruins, and there was hardly any garrison. It has never been in her hands since. And this is

---

* Goldwin Smith, p. 219.
† 'History of Gibraltar,' p. 440.

the historical proof that she is unable to hold it against attack !"

If France had the power to take what we gave up, she would step " into our seat of odium," and turn Spain against her, as Spain is now turned against England.

We are going a better way than this to make the Mediterranean a French Lake !

As Mr. Goldwin Smith asks :—" If we cannot trust Spain with Gibraltar, how can we trust Denmark with Elsinore, or Turkey with the Dardanelles ? "

Have we any reason to regret our non-interference when France took possession of Algeria ?

Do we look with any alarm at the establishment of French power in Cochin-China, in Tahiti, or in Mexico ? and are these likely to prove an addition to French power, or to impose on other European nations ?

But, if Spain be really too weak to hold her great fortress, why should not the fortress be dismantled, and Spain be bound never to arm it again ?

Why should not a treaty of commerce be signed, as the condition of the cession, giving free entrance for all our manufactures into Spain ; and why should it not be another condition, for the benefit of all nations, that the fortress of Gibraltar should be dismantled, never again to be restored?

And if, in this amicable settlement of an old account long subsisting between England and Spain, a balance should be due to England, why should it not be part of the terms that this debt should be paid by Spain; and that all rights of private property, and all just obligations of England, at Gibraltar, should be respected and fully compensated by Spain?

Or, if a money bargain be preferred, why should not Spain pay over to England the estimated cost of the present works of defence?

In the year 1780 the British Government, with a view to break the alliance then existing between France and Spain, carried on a negociation with the Spanish Government for the surrender of Gibraltar to Spain, on the terms that Spain should yield and guarantee to Great Britain the island of Porto Rico, and the fortress of Omoa and its territory, together with a harbor and territory sufficient for erecting a fortress in the Bay, near Oran. One of the conditions of that treaty was as follows :—

" 4thly. Spain shall not only purchase at the full price all the stores and artillery left at Gibraltar, but shall also pay, before she is put in possession of it a sum not less than £2,000,000 sterling for what has been laid out on the fortifications since Great Britain first possessed it.

A similar offer had been made by Mr. Pitt, in 1756, to surrender Gibraltar to Spain.

On both occasions the negociations went off from no unwillingness on the part of Spain.

If, in 1780, a sum not less than £2,000,000 sterling were a reasonable payment to be made by Spain for what had then been laid out on the fortifications, a sum not less than three times that amount would not be an unreasonable payment for what has since been laid out by Great Britain on the fortifications.

Captain Sayer, though a strong advocate for retaining possession of Gibraltar, fairly admits that, " as a commercial station Gibraltar is rapidly sinking into insignificance."

He also admits that outrages on the British flag by the Spanish Government are frequent ; and, he adds, with a *naïveté* which seems unconscious of the cause,—" It is to be remarked also that British vessels alone are molested, the French flag being invariably respected."*

Captain Sayer has produced a valuable History of Gibraltar, and he has given sufficient evidence to prove that it has been a very costly possession to us ; but he has entirely failed to show that it

* 'History of Gibraltar,' p. 501.

has been of the smallest benefit to us. On the contrary, be has shown that, this possession has involved us in wars which have cost a frightful loss of human life and treasure, and has made Great Britain an object of jealousy and distrust to all the nations of Europe, without one single compensating benefit. He has given his opinion that, " to cede Gibraltar would be to renounce our freedom of navigation in the Mediterranean ; our commerce in those seas would be paralyzed ; we should forfeit the safety of the overland route, depreciate our power in the East, and lose all influence in Morocco ;"* but he has given that opinion without any reason or argument in support of it, and regardless of all the facts which contradict it.

No better answer can be given in this day, than was given by Mr. Bankes in the House of Commons, as thus fairly referred to by Captain Sayer :

On the 5th of December, 1782, Parliament met, and in the speech from the throne allusion was made to the gallant defence of Gibraltar. On the same day in the Commons, Mr. Yorke moved the address to the King, and in the course of his speech referred to the glorious termination of the siege. He announced that a treaty had been

* ' History of Gibraltar,' p. 441.

c 2

opened with the belligerent powers, and that so considerable a progress had been made, that a general pacification might be expected. Mr. Bankes rose to second the motion; and after some preliminary remarks respecting the defence of Gibraltar, thus proceeded amid the silence of the House:—"A peace is the only thing that can save us; and in making this great sacrifices must be made, for national honor is national faith and credit, and our debts are, at all events, to be discharged. Our ambition is not to stand in the way of a peace. We are not to hesitate about giving up this place or that place merely because it has a name, or has distinguished itself in a peculiar manner. If, in making a peace, sacrifices are necessary, sacrifices must be made. If there is any post which is kept as a post of honor more than a post of utility, if there is any place which we have kept as a mark of superiority more than a possession of advantage, a place which costs us more in keeping than it is worth; if there is a place which in particular hurts the pride of the enemy, which is the object of their ambition and desire; that which would instigate them to go to war, and provoke them to continue in it,—surely, that of all others is the place which, in such circumstances as the present, ought to be ceded."[*]

* 'History of Gibraltar,' p. 414.

That the historian of Gibraltar is not insensible to the unfavorable effect to England from that possession, his history gives abundant evidence of.

Referring to the distracted state of England with her North American Colonies, he says :—
" While Spain was thus diligently preparing for the opportunity when she might descend upon an enfeebled enemy, England, apart from colonial disaffection, was a prey to faction, imbecility, and civil commotion. Her prestige, once the terror of Europe, had fallen to the lowest ebb, her representatives abroad were openly insulted in the streets without redress, and even the minor powers assumed towards her an attitude of defiance and contempt. Hated and despised by every European State, virtually without an ally, distracted by agitation at home, and engaged in an attempt to quell an irresistible revolution in a distant colony, the situation of England was critical indeed."*

It is for those who object to this first step towards the permanent peace of Europe, on the sound basis of mutual interests, to show any possible ground of danger to British interests from the cession to Spain, on these terms, of the Rock of Gibraltar in the Spanish Dominions.

* 'History of Gibraltar,' p. 264.

This is a question to be answered by reason, not by prejudice;—on a view of England's policy in the world's affairs as they are, not as they were a century and a half ago;—on a view of Spain, rising in strength and importance as one of the great powers of Europe, and, from her position, the natural and legitimate check upon the increasing power of France; not on a view of Spain sunk into weakness and wholly degenerate, as when the British Flag was planted on the Rock in Spanish dominions.

Spain was once one of the mightiest nations of Europe, and the terror of the world. She may be a mighty nation again, and, to help her to be so, is the true interest of England. England has much more to fear from the weakness than from the strength of Spain. Spain, holding her own and a powerful nation, will be our best guarantee against the Mediterranean ever being a French Lake. That question will be set at rest for ever, when Spain resumes her right position, and Italy is a free and united Nation. And that will be when despotism has passed away, and the power of the priesthood, in temporal affairs, has been broken down.

These are the views to which the principle of utility points, for the peace and prosperity of nations, and the temporal welfare of mankind.

The case of military dependencies such as Gibraltar, Malta, the Ionian Islands, and the Cape of Good Hope, is distinct from that of Colonies, though, to a great extent, it comes under the same question. Whatever may have been the necessity and wisdom in former times of carrying our trade over the world by force of arms, the same necessity no longer existing, the wisdom is less apparent. Trade, being found to be its own best protector, requires no military dependencies for its protection.

The Ionian Islands cannot be called a permanent property, being only a temporary trust ; and a very troublesome and expensive trust it has been to England, without even the smallest return in grateful acknowledgment or profit. But this ungracious and profitless trust being now surrendered to the Greek Kingdom, the less said the better about the wasteful expenditure of British money on those extensive and useless fortifications which will be left to the natural course of decay, and serve only as long enduring monuments of British extravagance and folly.

Malta, possessing great and peculiar natural advantages as a harbor for ships, and having been improved and made available for British Commerce, to an almost unlimited extent, by a vast expenditure of British money, may well be con·

sidered a British Station by right of purchase and
possession, and, as such, may as well be continued
to be held for the benefit of all commercial nations. But, as a fortress, it must ever be untenable and worthless, but at a cost which it could
never repay. As a station connected with the
present overland route to India, it will be convenient as long as that route is kept open, but for
any other purpose it can never be worth the cost
to Great Britain, and, therefore, the whole cost
is properly chargeable against India.

The same of the Cape of Good Hope, as a
Station on our Ocean way to India. But as a
Colony or dependency, whichever it may be,
there is no reason why the Cape of Good Hope
should not be left to govern itself, and to provide
for its own expenses. All that Great Britain now
gains from this costly possession might be better
secured by treaty, without any cost at all to Great
Britain, and to the great advantage of the Colony
itself in every way. In the meantime the cost of
this British possession is also chargeable against
India.

No one proposes that any of the British possessions should be hastily thrown up, but only that
they should be put upon a footing more con-
genial with the spirit of the present time, and
more suitable to the wants or necessities of the

British Empire, than when the Empire was so
unwisely extended over the globe. Not that the
real wants or necessities were greater then than
they are now, but that these are so much greater
and more real now than they were then, that we
are less able to bear the costs and other evil consequences of our former mistakes, and that continuing in those mistakes in the present altered
state of the world, endangers not only the welfare, but the very existence of the British Empire.

The present object is not so much to advocate
the immediate surrender of our dearly bought
foreign possessions, as to draw the public mind
to the consideration of the real value of these
costly appendages, with a view to retaining whatever is worth retaining for the dignity of the
British Crown, or for the profit of the Empire,
by treaties of Commerce, on the principle of Free
Trade, instead of impoverishing the great mass
of the British Working People by ruinous and
unjust taxes, and thereby keeping up the patronage of the government, for the benefit of the Aristocracy of Land and Wealth.

If this question were temperately and fairly
examined, divested of all old prejudices and party
feeling, it would be seen that, in many and most
of these cases we could derive all the benefits
which we now enjoy and much more, without any

of the present cost and responsibility; and that
by concentrating our power for the protection of
our own shores, we should render unnecessary
a vast amount of expenditure for that purpose,
and much more effectually accomplish that most
important object, not only by making that protection certain, which must otherwise be always
more or less uncertain, but also by reducing the
grounds or pretences for invasion.

In this way, it seems that, not only the angry
jealousy of foreign nations would be withdrawn
or mitigated, but that the honor and dignity of
the British Crown would be uplifted, and the
trade and commerce of the country would be
greatly increased over the whole world.

The great reductions which might then be
safely made in our Army and Navy Establishments would alone enable us to dispense with our
Income Tax and Malt Tax, and if a tax of 10 per
cent. on all *realised* property were substituted,
we might then safely abolish all Customs and Excise duties, and every other existing tax. So
great would be the rush of prosperity, with all
the resources of this great country suddenly
opened and let go free, that, most probably, at
the end of the first 5 or 7 years, the property tax,
on the then vastly increased amount of *realised*
property, might be safely reduced from 10 to 5
per cent.

That this would be, in effect, a great revolution, is admitted. But it would be a peaceable one, and for the benefit of all classes, the rich as well as the poor ; and if the effect would be, as it would be, to double, at the least, the purchasing power of the wages of labor, it would, as certainly, double the value of the Land Estates and Rentals generally throughout the kingdom.

It is strange to object to a change because it is great and sudden, if it be a change for the equal benefit of all.

The argument for the change rests upon this ground. If it can be shown that it would not be for the equal benefit of all, then the ground fails, and all that is built upon it falls. But, surely, this is a question deserving the temperate and impartial inquiry of a great and enlightened nation.

But, to carry on the present inquiry into the true policy of Great Britain in regard to her foreign possessions, the case of India shall now be considered.

India,—a dependency—may now be regarded as part of the British Empire, and stands on a peculiar footing, in many respects essentially different from all other British possessions. It must be considered as a conquered country, and has been so treated, as conquered countries were

in ancient times—made to pay the costs of conquering and holding it. Suddenly to renounce
and surrender up a country which has been so
won, would be to renounce and abandon all the
duties and obligations which that conquest necessarily involved.

The first duty is to the conquered and enslaved
people; for, that they have been enslaved, and
much oppressed by unjust exactions, no one
acquainted with the History of British India can
deny. That they are unequal to self-government is
universally admitted. This is not wonderful, considering the state of bondage in which they have
been so long held by their conquerors. Whether
they would have been fitted for self-government
if they had been left alone to themselves, is another question.

Reasoning from all experience, it may be fairly
inferred that, a more free intercourse with civilized
nations, than they have enjoyed under British
rule, would have made them better qualified than
they are for self-government. They are by climate,
religion, and habits of life, a feeble, false, and
treacherous race, and the effect of British rule has
been to keep them what they are, under the mistaken notion of keeping them more easily under
British subjection.

This, at last, has been discovered to be a mis-

take, and it has been dearly paid for. A more
liberal and enlightened policy is now being pursued towards them. But it will be long before
the native Hindoo will be able to appreciate
true honor for its own sake, and until that
time has arrived it would be a bold and rash attempt to trust such an Empire as India to
native government. We have gone too far to re-
cede with honor, even if we could with safety.
We have assumed responsibilities which we are
bound, if we can, to discharge. Whether our
dominion in that country adds anything to our
real strength or wealth is a doubtful question;
but there is no question that, we could not now
abandon it without dishonor.

Mr. Goldwin Smith states, as "our actual advantages, a perennial supply of old Indians spending Indian pensions at Bath and Cheltenham."
He states these as "the main item on the side
of profit; while on the side of loss, we must place
a heavy annual expenditure of our best blood,
wasted in Indian warfare, or by Indian disease;
the paralyzing sense of our weak point, and the
loss of dignity and force thence resulting to our
diplomacy in Europe; and not only the Sikh and
Afghan, but in a great measure the Russian
war."

It is not easy to prove this statement wrong.

But the question remaining to be answered is, as stated by Mr. Goldwin Smith ; " whether the English can convert India from a dependency into a Colony, by settling in it; taking the place of the Mahometans, its last conquerors, and permanently forming the governing and civilizing class. If the climate or any other cause forbid this, the days of our dominion are numbered."

Neither is it easy to prove this statement wrong.

That India should continue permanently to pay at the present rate for civilization, without participating in the benefits of civilization, would be an anomaly which the world has not yet witnessed. And to be always suppressing revolts would be a prospect fearful to encounter, even for Great Britain, at such a distance from the scene of action.

If a fair balance could be struck between the expenditure and the results, it is very doubtful whether the results would compensate for the expenditure, leaving out of the account the enormous sacrifice of human life.

But however the balance may stand, to withdraw British power from India now, would be to leave India to anarchy.

Nor is there any good to be derived from a review of the past exercise of British power in India, unless as a guide to future proceedings.

The retributive justice which seems to be ever in operation in human affairs, has been felt and acknowledged in regard to British rule in India.

The altered policy of the British Government in India opens a better prospect for the future; but, on the carrying out of that policy faithfully, will certainly depend the continuance of British power in India. The ports of India are now open to all the world, and if, through the genius and energy of the British people, we still monopolize the trade, that would not be affected by the abandonment of our Empire in India. But we derive from it no other commercial advantage whatever. All the robbery and corruption under the old Company was never productive of any advantage to the Company or to the Empire. For the investment of capital, our dominion in India gives us no special advantage. We draw no military force from our possessions in India, but, on the contrary, employ a great military force there to maintain them. It is true that India pays for the military force kept there, but that expense is only part of the whole expenditure connected with the military defence of British India.

"The Cape was occupied, and is held by us, merely as a port on the road to India; and the expenses of that station, which have been enormous, must, therefore, be set down to the

account of our Indian Empire. Other English
ships may touch at the Cape, but these ships
might safely be left to the course of nature, and
the interest of the Cape Colonists. It is our
anxiety for the safety of the route to India which
compels us to keep the place in our own hands. The
same may be said of Mauritius. But, moreover,
our great force in the Mediterranean and our military stations there, are maintained partly on account of the necessity, or the alleged necessity,
of overawing the powers which command the
overland route. And, besides all this, our general
policy is influenced, and we are frequently en-
tangled in quarrels, and sometimes in wars, by
causes in which our alarm for the safety of the
Indian Empire has its share. . . . As to the general envy and hatred of the world, which attend
vast territorial aggrandizement, they are by most
people, in reasoning about these matters, set
down as a source of strength, though to others
they may appear to be rather a source of weakness." •

The truth of these remarks is undeniable, and
some others which follow are so true and so full
of subjects for reflection, that these also must be
given in the Writer's own words.

"'There is, however, a revenue of a peculiar

• Goldwin Smith, p. 270.

kind which we derive from India, and which is probably regarded by most people as the chief remaining advantage of the Empire; the salaries which Englishmen receive for governing India, and the pensions which they enjoy when they return from it. The experience of a few years will show whether these salaries and pensions, on the strict and economical footing to which they have been reduced since the government of this country has taken India into its hands and the heavy debt contracted in putting down the mutiny has compelled retrenchment, will really repay Englishmen for undergoing banishment to India and all the sacrifices which it entails. A man is to quit his country just as life is opening upon him; to be separated perhaps for ever from his family; to forget, or at least to be forgotten by, his friends; to spend his days among aliens in a country to which he has no attachment, with little European society, and that little not of his own choosing; and this in a climate where the rate of European mortality is double what it is in England; where life is but half life, and luxury is but a palliation of discomfort. He is to part with his children when they are a few years old, and send them to be reared in a distant country. Very likely he may have also to part with his wife. He is to return only when the best part of life is

X

over, and the power of enjoyment is almost gone, to a land where his place knows him not. Will Indian salaries and Indian pensions on the reduced scale, and under a system of strict purity, which cuts off all indirect means of gain, long seem to Englishmen a sufficient reward for such sacrifices and privations as these?" *

As Mr. Goldwin Smith observes,—" if these were all, these would be a very poor return to this nation for the sacrifice of much of its best blood, and of its best practical intellect, and for the liabilities and dangers which it incurs. It would be a very poor return even if money spent in improductive objects, as most of this money must always be, promoted the general well-being of the people; the reverse of which is the fact."

In an economical point of view it seems doubtful, then, whether our dominion in India has done good to either nation. In a political, or in a religious point of view, that it has done harm can hardly be doubtful.

It seems as if English children were forbidden by nature to be reared in India, and from this we may infer that India is destined to be governed by its own native races. In the absence of any express command, here we may see the index of Providence pointing to His will. How can it be

* Goldwin Smith, p 272.

more plainly pointed out to Englishmen than in the death of their little children?

The British Government has undoubtedly extirpated some barbarous and cruel customs, but it has not introduced Christianity into India, nor taught there the Christian doctrine.

We have taken India out of the hands of the Company, and we talk of the British Empire in India; but we have not really made it part of the British Empire, and, probably, never shall make it part; but, certainly, we never shall until we give to its inhabitants the character of the British people, and for this we must give a free country, governed on free principles.

The only other British possessions requiring particular notice are the Channel Islands. These enjoy the peculiar privilege of self-government under their own ancient Norman Laws and Constitution, free from British taxation, but subject to the appointment of a Lieutenant-Governor in Jersey, and a Lieutenant-Governor in Guernsey, by the British Government under the British Crown, whose salaries are paid by the British tax-payers.

What the British Government gains beyond this patronage, and a few yearly Quit Rents due to the Crown, but scarcely worth the cost of collection, it is impossible to discover.

x 2

What the British tax-payers gain is clearly
nothing more than the profit they may derive
from having their own happy Island made the
place of transportation for the hardened criminals who have become insufferable in their own
native Isles.

As already observed, it is impossible to discover
what these Lieutenant-Governors have to do ; unless in giving hospitable receptions to the few occasional visitors who, enticed by the beauty of the
Isles,—so admirably represented by the native
Artist of Guernsey, Mr. Naftel, in his inimitable
water-color paintings,—venture the risks of those
rocky shores.

No doubt, these gallant Officers are responsible for the military affairs of these little Isles
and Islets, which may be properly regarded as
integral parts of the British Islands ; and to
which, as such, the Duke of Wellington very
wisely attached inappreciable value.

But the fact is, these gallant Officers have no
military affairs to manage, these Isles being without any military defences, beyond those formidable defences which Nature has given in the
rocky coast around.

The only one of the Channel Isles, with any
pretension to military defences, is the little Isle
of Alderney, which is a precipitous rock in the

sea. The sums of public money expended there on fortifications, and a Harbor of Refuge, are of unknown amount, but known to be of enormous amount, and there is only one opinion, that the money so expended might as well have been thrown into the sea. Over this expenditure neither the Military Governor, nor the Chief Civil Magistrate of the Isles had the slightest control. The whole, in conception and execution, was a mismanaged job of the Imperial Government.

The civil affairs of these Isles are managed, and very ably managed too, by the Chief Civil Magistrate, or "Bailiff," as he is called, and the "Jurats," or picked men of the Isles. .

The present Chief Civil Magistrate, or Bailiff, of Guernsey,—appointed by the Imperial Government,—is a Gentleman bred up at the English Bar and highly esteemed. In acknowledgment of his loyalty and public services, he has very recently received the honor of Knighthood. He presides over the High Court, or "La Cour Royale," composed of the "*Jurats*," who administer the Law, and are appointed for life. "*Les Douzaines*" are the representatives of the People, and, with the Jurats, form the Legislative body of the Island.

The whole of their judicial and legislative proceedings are conducted in the French Language.

The Bailiff is assisted by a Deputy Bailiff, who is chosen from the Jurats. This office is now filled by a Gentleman, of high reputation and universally respected, lineally descended from an ancient Norman family. He is the Author of a work entitled, " La Constitution de l'Ile de Guernesey, et de sa Réforme; ou Recherches sur la Nature de ses principes et sur leur application pratique," written in the French language and showing a profound knowledge of the subject. With such a Chief Civil Magistrate and Deputy, it is a singular and rather absurd anomaly, to see the Military Governor, in his military trappings, seated by the side of the Bailiff, and taking part in the legislative and judicial proceedings of ' La Cour Royale,' carried on in the French language, with which the Governor may be, and generally is, wholly ignorant, or but very imperfectly acquainted,—though in the present case he could pass for a Frenchman, if only he looked less thoroughly an Englishman—and taking part in the administration of laws of which he must be wholly ignorant.

Why the Bailiff should not be appointed by the People over whom he presides, and why the Chief Civil Magistrate should not be invested with all the powers now vested in the Military Governor, seeing that his duties are merely no-

minal, are questions which seem to admit of only
one answer.

These small concessions, if made by the Imperial Government, would be gratefully received
by all the Inhabitants of these little Isles, and
though there is no danger of separation, nothing
could more effectually attach them to the Mother Country, to which the positive gain would
be, the saving of the whole of the present annual
expenditure of the Imperial Government under
the head of The Channel Islands. What that
expenditure is nobody seems to know, and it is
no easy matter to discover.

But the result of this and other anomalies,
more clearly discernible in the Channel Islands
than in more distant possessions, is, that the Mother Country is made to fill up, at her own cost,
many gaps in the internal administration of their
affairs, which pass unnoticed and uncontrolled.
Of this the illustration in Guernsey is striking.
Its internal affairs are, for the most part, conducted with admirable judgment and rare consideration for the welfare and comfort of the inhabitants. In the number and admirable state
of its Public Roads, the little Island of Guernsey
is a perfect model, and the Port and Harbor,
with its magnificent Piers and capacious Floating Docks, now far advanced, and all of finely

dressed blocks of Guernsey granite, will be, when completed, well entitled to rank among the finest works of the kind in the kingdom. In loyal British feeling, probably, no British subjects in any part of the world excel the Guernsey People. But the galling sore is in British interference with their ancient Norman Constitution, Laws, and Customs, by the appointment of a Military Governor, a stranger, to over-ride and dictate to them in trifling matters of internal government, in which he can have no knowledge, and ought to have no control.

The collection of Crown dues and Quit Rents, in petty sums, altogether of insignificant amount, taken from, instead of expended in, the Island, is another obnoxious incident, and is productive of consequences really disastrous.

The crying disgrace of this Island,—and it is believed to be quite as bad in Jersey,—is the state of the public Prison, and, consequently, of prison discipline. From the want of space, anything like classification of the prisoners is an impossibility. The most heinous and the most trivial offences can be distinguished only by the longer or shorter duration of imprisonment, in cells unfit for any human creature, and longer or shorter labor at the crank for grinding the air, or helpless idleness, if without labor.

This is not the place for a description of these unwholesome cells, or of the shameful treatment of the prisoners, of both sexes, where even common decency is disregarded, and reformation is never thought of. In none of these cells is there any ventilation and scarcely any light, and in the cells for the refractory, of both sexes, there is less light, and barely sufficient air to support life, and that air is so pestilential that the Gaoler—as he, only a short time ago, admitted to the Writer when he was a chance visitor in the Island,—was always obliged to leave the door open for some time, when he came his first round in the morning, before he could enter to remove the tub deposited therein for the necessities of nature. But the writer witnessed other things which will not here bear the telling.

The inhabitants are very far from indifferent to this state of things, and the excellent and intelligent Chaplain of the Prison has devoted himself for many years to the removal of this disgrace to the Island, but, apparently, with very little success.

The answer to all remonstrances on this subject is, that the British Government ought to provide the necessary Prison accommodation out of the annual revenue which they derive from the Island. The local government has already purchased ample space, adjoining the present prison, for any required extension, and also for a Reformatory for the unfortunate children, but that vacant ground has ever since been lying idle.

The People refuse to be taxed for the building, and the British Government refuses to help towards the erection. Of course, the whole revenue of the Crown from all the Channel Islands is not a farthing in the pound on the sum total of British Expenditure on these Islands, and for the paltry consideration· of these miserable Crown Dues, these disastrous consequences, shocking to humanity, are left unheeded.

This notice,—here quite out of place,—is made on the slender hope of attracting the attention of the British Government, or of some honorable and humane Member of the British House of Commons, for the redress of this disreputable wrong.

As Sir George Cornewall Lewis said ; " A large part of the habits of obedience to a Government rests upon associations with ancient institutions, and ancient names." If this be true of the habit of obedience, it is still more true of the habit of affection. It can never be the part of wisdom to use the one habit for the weakening of the other.

There is another remark of Sir G. C. Lewis, in his Essay on the Government of Dependencies, which may be a fitting conclusion to the present observations: "A nation derives no true glory from any possession which produces no assignable advantage to itself or to other communities. If a country possesses a dependency rom which it derives no public revenue, no military or naval strength, and no commercial advantages or facilities for emigration, which it would not equally enjoy though the dependency were independent, and if, moreover, the dependency suffers the evils which are almost inevitable consequences of its political condition, such a possession cannot justly be called glorious."

This means, simply, that such a dependency, tried by the principle of utility, is found to be a possession not worth holding.

But the Channel Isles are worth holding, and are so important to Great Britain as to be well worth a little more attention and a little less interference by the Imperial Government.

Before concluding the subject under this head, a remark, in a work just published by one of the most distinguished of our living writers of fiction, cannot be allowed to pass unnoticed ; not because he is so distinguished as a writer of fiction, but because he lately filled the high and responsible office of Secretary of State for the Colonies, and was a member of the British Cabinet, and may,

therefore, be supposed to be an authority on this
subject.

In a series of Essays on "Life, Literature,
and Manners," and in the concluding Essay of
the series, entitled, "The Spirit of Conservatism,"
this eminent writer says :—" One of the obvious
advantages of military colonies is the facility
they afford for maintaining therein such military
strength as may be necessary for the protection
of the Empire, without quartering large bodies of
troops in England, to the danger of freedom ; and,
therefore, it is a very shallow view of Imperial
policy to ascribe solely to our colonial wants the
military forces kept in colonies, and exclaim, ' See
what these Colonies cost us !' If we had no troops
in Colonies, we must either be without adequate
military force, or we must obtain such adequate
military force at the risk of freedom, by collecting
and converging it into garrisons at home."

According to this authority, then, we are keeping up the military forces in our Colonies, not for
the protection of our Colonies, but for the protection of our kingdom !

But this assumes that the same military forces
would be required for the safety of our kingdom.
If it be assumed that it would not be safe to
keep so large a military force at home, why should
it be assumed that so large a military force

would be required? This has not been shown.
But the case of necessity supposed would probably be the sudden invasion of our shores. In
that case, how would " the military forces kept in
our Colonies " help us?

The high authority should have explained this ;
but he has not. When he wrote these quoted
words he seems to have forgotten what he had just
written in only a few preceding lines, wherein he
says :—" A conservative policy in England would
vigilantly guard our maritime power, and spare
no cost necessary to maintain a navy superior to
that of any other single European Power ; but it
would regard with great jealousy any attempt to
maintain, in England itself, more than the well
disciplined nucleus and framework of a standing
army."

In that he is right, but, then, where are " the
obvious advantages of military colonies," and
where is the consistency or force of his argument?

CHAPTER XII.

UTILITY.—FOREIGN POLICY.

If the foreign policy of Nations had been conducted with more regard to the principle of Utility, how very different from the present would have been the state of all the civilized Nations of the world !

In former times the struggles of Nations were more for extended empire than for extended liberty. At the present time, with one or two exceptions, the object is reversed.

The mere lust of conquest in one Nation, to invade and despoil another, is no longer the rule. The desire now is more the love of liberty, than the love of aggrandizement. For the love of liberty, the Italians desire to be free from the Austrian and French yokes ; the Poles to be free from the Russians ; the Greeks and all the neighboring provinces and petty States to get rid of the Turks. Who can say that these are not laudable objects, which all the Nations of Europe are interested to promote ? If aggressive tendencies still linger in some of the military Governments, the People whom those Governments oppress no longer participate in such tendencies.

The strongest exception to the unaggressive tendency of civilized Nations at the present time is France. In Russia, the aggressive tendency still exists in the government, but is not shared by the people, though, as a people, politically, they can yet hardly be said to exist.

In the French people there seems too much reason to fear that the passion for military glory and aggrandizement, excited by the conquests of the first Emperor, is not yet extinct.

But, though it suited the second Emperor to declare his principle to be peace, he has ill-disguised his object to make the Rhine a boundary of France.

The designs of Russia on Turkey are too well known to be misunderstood. But the encroaching and paralyzing power of Austria has done more to retard the progress of civilization in Europe, than all the wild ambition and thirst for military glory in France, or even the barbarous despotism of Russia; and more than all has been the desolating dominion of Popery, and the prostrating power of the Romish priesthood. From these crushing effects, by the something like miraculous power of one earnest and honest man,

Italy, at last, has been lifted up from the lowest depth of degradation and misery, to the rank and calling of an independent Nation, and when in possession of her own rightful Capital,—as must be, sooner or later,—she will take her proper place among the great Powers of Europe.

Russia, forced to surrender her ill-gotten share in the dismemberment of Poland, and to restore to Sweden her rightful possession in Finland, will still remain the chief northern Power by her vast and legitimate Empire.

Austria, confined to her own lawful dominions, by the restoration of Galicia to Poland, of Venetia to Italy, and Hungary to the Hungarians, may then resume her proper position and influence as one of the great Powers of Europe, and then Italy and Hungary, as independent Nations, may be her best protectors.

Prussia, made into a petty kingdom by her large share in the spoil of dismembered Poland, must surrender her purloined territory of Posen, and Poland must be restored as an independent kingdom.

The Prussian territory westward of the Rhine, adjoining Belgium and Holland, should then be annexed to Belgium and Holland to form their more convenient boundaries, and a give-and-take line might be drawn between Belgium and

Holland to the mutual convenience and consoli-
dation of both these kingdoms.

By this arrangement the views of the French
Emperor might be met by annexing to France
the remainder of the Rhenish Provinces westward of the Rhine, as far as and including
Coblentz, Mayence, and the intervening country,
together with the Duchy of Luxemburg, and
part of Belgian Luxemburg, and also part of the
adjoining provinces of Namur and Hainault, so
as to form a more convenient boundary line than
the present between France and Belgium in this
direction; thus making the Rhine the boundary
between that part of France and Germany, and
at the same time enlarging and consolidating, or,
at least, not diminishing in extent of territory or
power, the kingdoms of Belgium and Holland.
But, for the security of these arrangements, the
fortress of Ehrenbreitstein, on the other side of
the Rhine, opposite to Coblentz, should be destroyed.

Thus far the western side of the Rhine might
be judiciously restored to France, without encouraging any rash views for restoring that state of
things when the Rhine, from its source in the
glacier of the Alps, to its outlet in the German
Ocean, formed the uninterrupted boundary line
of Ancient Gaul,—if any such views should happen to be now indulged.   Y

England and France, with Spain, and Italy, in possession of Rome, could, no doubt, carry out the reconstruction of the kingdoms of the Continent for the general disarmament and permanent peace of Europe. The only Power that could make even a show of resistance would be Russia, and that would soon be proved to be only a show. Hemmed in on one side by avenging Poland; blockaded in the Baltic by British Iron Ships, and threatened on all her Southern frontiers by the armies of England and France, Russia must submit to surrender these ill-acquired portions of her dominions, or to the dismemberment of her over-grown and unmanageable Empire.

Prussia would then take her proper place among the constellations of Germany, unless, in the meantime, by her own erratic movements, unluckily for herself, she suddenly disappears altogether, and merges into some larger and brighter body.

Poland and Hungary restored would help to preserve the balance of power in the North; and Italy in the South, with the barrier of the Alps, would be a pretty good security against any long flight by Austria, with her clipped wings.

The disarmament and peace of Europe, so purchased, would be no bad bargain, on the principle of general utility, for any party concerned.

Why should Prussia, that sneaking little satellite of barbarous and despotic Russia, be allowed to hold territories and fortresses on the western side of the Rhine, so far away from the centre of her own natural dominions, and so near to the heart of the French Empire?

Until the peace-creating and controlling power of Commerce shall have obtained the mastery over nations, it must always aggravate the evils of military despotism to meet the despot with his own weapons, unless to protect one's own nation from invasion, or to prevent aggressions against the interest of all nations.

The general disarmament and peace of Europe on a permanent basis obtained by such a re-construction of the Chief Continental States, the results to all nations would be incalculably great, and Great Britain, as the greatest of all commercial nations, is the most deeply interested in such an arrangement.

Then would be the timely opportunity to Great Britain for letting go free her own Colonies and Dependencies, able to stand alone in their own independence ; and for re-constructing her own policy, consistently with such changes, by great reductions in her military and naval establishments, and by concentrating her reserved powers for the protection of her own native shores. Then also would be the timely opportunity for abolishing all existing taxes, and substituting the proposed tax of 10 per cent. on all realised property. And then would be the time for the Powers of Europe in this alliance to declare all their Ports free to all the world.

Who can say that such benefits as these would not be cheaply purchased for all nations, and especially for Great Britain, at the price of concurrence and assistance, in meeting so far the views of France, and thereby strengthening and confirming in their integrity the little kingdoms of Belgium and Holland as now established?

Who can look at the Map of France, as at present constituted, and say that the whole of Belgium is not in danger of merging into the French Empire at the first opportunity of a general Continental war? And in that event, where would the Kingdom of Holland be?

Whether or not the restoration of independent Poland can be accomplished without recourse to war, is a question, the answer to which may very much depend on the part taken by Austria. But if Austria will consent, (and, it is said, she did once consent) to make restitution of Galicia, that question is answered. The advantages to Austria of setting up the Kingdom of Poland, as a barrier against Russia, are so great that Austria might

well purchase them at the cheap price of relin-
quishing a territory so unjustly acquired.

There is no country more interested than Great
Britain is in maintaining Austria as one of the
great Powers in Europe. But she can be a great
Power only by progressing in liberal institutions
and a free Government. Here is the golden opportunity of winning not only the respect and
good-will of Great Britain, but of France also.
But once let Russia complete her Railway System, and then the restoration of the kingdom of
Poland will be a much more formidable undertaking, at which all the great Powers of Europe
may well pause. In the present is the oppor-
nity, and, under the alliance of the three great
Powers, Prussia might be dealt with, for a permanent settlement of the peace of Europe, as circumstances might require. Russia then confined
within her lawful boundaries would cease to be
a disturber of the balance of power on the Continent. But if Austria should refuse, and England should draw back, and France remain quiet
much longer? That is a calculation of far more
danger to the peace of Europe than the re-construction under the alliance contemplated; and
to leave this question to the settlement of France
alone would be far more hazardous to the interests of Great Britain, than the bolder policy of

a vigorous co-operation with France for repairing
the mischiefs of the false and timid policy of the
Congress of Vienna.

The right of Prussia to complain of such an
arrangement for placing the peace of Europe on a
permanent basis, would be very much weakened
by the crooked and treacherous policy which
Prussia has so long pursued. But the kingdom
which has been extended by the fraudulent dismemberment of another independent kingdom for
no other cause than self-aggrandizement, would
have little ground for complaint if her boundaries
be adjusted on the principle of general utility,
and her complaint would meet with little sympathy. So far as this arrangement would concern the Prussian territory westward of the Rhine,
it is well known that the change proposed would
be accepted with almost universal acclamation by
the people most concerned ; and as it concerns
France and Belgium, a glance at the map is sufficient to show the great importance of this change
for their mutual interests and security.

By some such means as these only will the
battle of Waterloo ever be forgotten or forgiven
by France, and by these means that famous battle field may be made a triumph for France, and
the foundation of a lasting peace to Europe.

It will consolidate the power of France and

confirm the Emperor on his throne more than
any victories now remaining for him to achieve.
It will present him to the French people as the
founder of the second French Empire, on a firm
basis, by the results of his policy, and will give,
at least, some show of truth to his memorable declaration—" L'Empire—c'est la paix." It will
keep him for ever in the grateful recollection of
the Italian people, as the chief power which lifted
them up from their state of suffering and degradation, under the most atrocious tyranny, to liberty,
and restored the Kingdom of United Italy.   It
will establish him and his dynasty in the heart of
every loyal Pole, as the chief power which restored
the Kingdom of Poland ; and his name will stand
in History, as the ' Great Emperor :' for, tried by
the principle of utility, his reign, in its results,
will have exceeded in greatness, the results of the
reign of the first Emperor, and at a much less
cost.

Thus, out of much evil will be brought about
the greater good, and whatever may have been
the motives of men, the designs of Providence
will be seen to have prevailed for universal good.

The difficult question of the Turkish Protecto-
rate is one which it is not easy to see the way out
of, and, perhaps, the time has not arrived for
getting out of it, without raising other and greater

difficulties. Our only motive for supporting the
declining Empire of the Turks in Europe is, the
fear that the power of Russia, which always ad-
vances and never recedes, will increase with the
advance of its territory in the Eastern and Southern parts of Europe, and the greater distrust
of that overgrown, barbarous, and treacherous
power, than of the feeble, capricious, and corrupt
dominion of the Turks.

In every region, from the Danube to the Eu-
phrates, the Turkish administration is, and always has been, feeble, capricious, and corrupt.
Bosnia and Bulgaria, as well as Syria and the
Lebanon, are exposed to all that grasping Governors and intriguing underlings can effect. No
reflecting person can require further evidence to
convince him that Turkish authority is a cruel
wrong to the populations over which it rules, and
to the fine and fertile regions which they inhabit.
No one can doubt that for four centuries the European provinces have been subjected to a rule
which has degraded the Christian population, destroyed every industry but the commonest agriculture, and checked even this by imposts and
exactions, by the insecurity of property, and the
impossibility of obtaining justice at the tribunals.

It is not to be expected that the instincts and
habits of twelve centuries will be eradicated by

the lectures of European Statesmen, or by the *liberal* manifestoes of the Sublime Porte. It is
only by wasting away and their loosing their hold
on the Christians, that any material improvement
is to be looked for in the dominion of the Turks
in Europe. It is to the continuance of this process that we must look for real progress, and not
to any nominal reform of laws which are to be
administered by Turkish judges and officials under the government of a Turkish Pasha. As long
as two populations, Mussulman and Christian, are
intermingled, with the one essentially dominant
over the other, the idea of equal justice or social
equality is but a dream. Equality between the
whites and the blacks of America is not more impossible than between the conquering religion
and these who are tributaries to it.

On what ground the British Prime Minister
'confidently relies' for the 'stability and prosperity' of the Turkish Empire upon 'a solid
foundation,' does not appear. But the British
public, relying on the British Prime Minister's
confidence, hasten to put down their money on
the promise of payment by the Turkish Government, without British guarantee. It, therefore,
remains to be seen whether Her Majesty's Government have taken such effectual measures for
placing Turkish affairs 'on a fair footing,' as will

justify this confidence. But, at all events, after
the great sacrifice of life and treasure to prevent
the Turkish Empire from falling into the hands
of the Northern Despot, he would be a more bold
than a wise statesman who advised the withdrawal of British power without some sufficient
guarantee against that long threatened danger.
The great resources of the Turkish Empire are
certainly no guarantee for its security, but are
strong evidence against the character and government of the Turks. If the country possessed
less natural resources there might be more hope.
But seeing that its great resources have only made
it a greater object for seizure,.without adding to
its power for self-protection, any argument from
great resources seems to afford small ground for
'great expectations,' and small comfort for the
contributors to the Turkish Loan.

To form a rational ground for expecting
Turkish regeneration, we must take strong and
active measures, not only for the protection of
the Christian population, but also for their admission into the highest offices of the State, with
a view ultimately to the substitution of the
Christian Gospel for the Koran in Turkey in
Europe. For this a long time must be required,
and, in the meantime, England must maintain, as
well as she can, the independence of Turkey, if

necessary, against the world. With the honest help of France this will not be difficult, but for this it will be wise in England to consult the wishes of France, where these do not conflict with the real interests of England.

When the Victory of Free Trade is universal, as it soon may be, with the willing cooperation of England and France, the freedom of commercial intercourse among Nations will increase the feelings of sociability and good-will, and extend all the other innumerable blessings of civilization over the world, more than any of the victories which have ever been achieved by warfare since wars first began.

This is the practical application of the Principle of Utility which Nations have yet to learn, and to lead the public mind to this view of the subject is the object of these few remarks.

Much more might be said, and many important topics have been intentionally omitted to avoid the risk of weariness. The intelligent reader who has followed thus far, will be well able to apply this principle for himself; and if the view here presented be favorably received, the further application of this principle may be given at a future time.

It is hardly necessary here to consider the probable results of a European Congress of Crowned

Heads, the probability of such a Congress being
so very remote.   Still less probable is such a result, as here proposed, if such a Congress were
assembled.

The practical question is, whether or not such
an arrangement for the peace and prosperity of
all the Nations of Europe could be brought about
by the combined power of England and France,
with the aid of such other Nations as may choose
to lend their help.

That France, Spain, Italy, Belgium, Holland,
Hungary, Poland, Sweden, and Denmark, might
be brought into this Alliance with England is not
improbable, if the objects, here proposed in their
behalf were guaranteed to them.

To France, would be given the great object of
her ambition, in the Rhenish Provinces, and
Luxemburg.

To Spain, the great object of her desire in
Gibraltar.

To Italy, the addition of Rome and Venetia
would make United Italy complete.

To Belgium, the new territory taken from the
Rhenish Provinces and some few adjoining parts
from Holland would be ample compensation for
the territory yielded to France.

To Holland, her share in the Rhenish Provinces,
with the give-and-take line, would be ample com-

pensation for her concessions to Belgium, and would make a more convenient and natural boundary than the present.

To Hungary and Poland, the restoration of territory and independence would be like the restoration to new life of a great People crushed by the weight of despotism, and the addition to Europe of a vast extent of new and fertile country long desolate under the oppressive rule of tyrants ; and these two new Kingdoms would help to readjust the balance of political power in Europe.

To Sweden, the re-possession of Finland would be only the restoration of her own,—the recovery of the most ancient and most highly-prized jewel stolen by Russia from the Swedish Crown.

To Denmark, the secured possession of Schleswig and Holstein would be only her just reward.

The main question would be between England and France.   But if the designs of France be not mistaken, this partial restoration of the boundary of the former Empire would carry due weight in the Councils of the present Empire.

To Great Britain, so far as her true political interests are concerned, these new divisions in the map of Europe are really of small importance.

But to her the disarmament and peace of Europe on a sound basis are of the greatest importance.

If to these important objects, secured by special
treaty with all the Powers so united in self-inter-
ested alliance, were added the guarantee of all
these Powers that, henceforth and for ever, all
the Sea-ports of their respective Kingdoms should
be open and free to all the world, Great Britain
might well be satisfied with such an arrangement
which, under wise government, would secure to
her pre-eminence in prosperity and power over all
the nations of the world.

The free concession of Gibraltar to the Spani-
ards, and of Canada, with all our North American
possessions, to the Canadians, would go far to
buy their concurrence with these terms ; and the
concession at the same time of independence to
all our other Colonies, ready to accept it, would
hold them to the Mother-Country by a stronger
bond than dependence will ever make, and then
one of the greatest causes of the jealousy of the
Nations of Europe towards England would be
withdrawn.

Although the concurrence of Russia to such
arrangements is out of the question, and the consent of Austria and Prussia is not to be looked
for, yet it by no means follows that they would
resort to war against so powerful a combination.
Diplomacy would still be open to them. It would
still be open to treat with Austria and Prussia for

their mutual aggrandizement out of the mean little kingdoms and wretched little Principalities which constitute the strange anomaly of the German Confederacy, and are for ever creating such confusion in the affairs of Germany.

For what purpose of good can the existence of such feeble little kingdoms as Bavaria, Würtemberg, and Hanover, or such contemptible little Principalities as Nassau, Homburg, and Baden, be prolonged?

How is the welfare of Europe concerned in the preservation of these monarchies without majesty, or of these Grand-duchies which condescend to replenish their petty treasuries by sharing in the infamous profits of their Gaming Tables?

Why should not these petty potentates, who really have no property of their own, be placed upon the retired list, on half-pay?

If Austria and Prussia are to be bought,—and who can doubt it,—why not let each bid for her division of this spoil?

They could not object on the ground of spoliation, for they shared in the spoil of Poland, and were the despoilers.

That would inflict much less wrong than war, and would right, as far as now possible, a great wrong.

Russia, perhaps, cannot be bought in this

question. But what could Russia do, with all Europe against her, but yield and make the best of it?

Much more might be said on this part of the question, and not without some show of authority from the highest quarter.

But this is a delicate part of the question, and the veil, if ever to be wholly lifted, must be lifted gradually.

For the purpose of restoring Confidence among the nations of Europe, and effecting a general disarmament, it must be admitted that no Congress is necessary, the power of accomplishing these objects being in the Emperor of the French. He can, of his own pleasure, withdraw his troops from Rome, and, by diminishing his own army, he can effect a corresponding diminution in all the armaments of Europe. He knows that nobody thinks of attacking him, and that every one fears he will attack them. He knows that he is the sole cause of the enormous armaments of Europe, and that he only and not a Congress can remove them. He must submit to have his sincerity questioned, as long as his acts are at variance with his words.

But as all Europe knows this as well as the French Emperor, and as all Europe does question his sincerity, the useful question now is, whether

it be not better to buy his concurrence and co-
operation on his own terms, and thus to secure
all the objects, rather than to wait for the chance
of accomplishing them in indefinite time and the
course of events, with all the risks, and the certainty, in the meantime, of all the evils of the
present state of things, with the probability of
many more and greater evils. That the peace
and disarmament of Europe could be long secured
by the deliberations and conclusions of any Congress that could now be assembled, nobody supposes. Is it not better, therefore, to meet the
difficulty at once by consenting to pay the price
for a firm alliance, strong enough to secure these
and all other objects of European policy for the
peace of Europe on a sound basis?

This may suffice for the present purpose, merely
as a hint to show the fitness in the utility of
things, as well in regard to Foreign as Domestic
Policy.

CHAPTER XIII.

CONCLUSION.

THE conclusion of all Moral Philosophy is, that
God wills man's happiness through the exercise
of his faculties, and that his only means of fulfilling the Divine will is by exercising his faculties
in accordance therewith. This is man's duty,
and is proved to be so by the evil consequences
which follow from his own neglect.

The fulfilment of this duty, therefore, pre-
supposes freedom of action. He must be free to
do everything which is directly or indirectly
necessary for enabling him to fulfil the Divine
will. Especially he must be free to come and to
go, and to work, to get food, raiment, and shelter,
and to do everything requisite for the due satisfaction of every mental and bodily want. Without
this he cannot perform his duty, or fulfil the Divine
will. He has Divine authority for claiming this
freedom of action, and, therefore, this is his natural *right*.

This being the equal natural right of all men,

the freedom of each man must necessarily he bounded by the like freedom of all men, and the restraint necessary for this equal freedom must necessarily be equal, to be consistent with the Divine will. Hence it follows that, every man has a right to enjoy the fullest liberty for the exercise of his faculties compatible with the like liberty to every other man ; and that every moral being has an indefeasible right to the " pursuit of happiness." In other words, he has a right to have his moral interests considered and respected, and not to be treated as a being having no moral interests of his own,—a mere "living tool," as the slave is called by Aristotle, or a "chattel personal" as he is called by the American law. Every moral being has a right to be treated by the community as a person, and not as a thing.

If this be a sound principle of moral right,— and it can hardly be otherwise if consistent with the Divine will,—it must be a Divine right in the sovereign government to enforce this principle.

The term *right*, in this application, means *justice*. An act which conforms to the Divine law, is emphatically called, *just* : an act which does not, is emphatically called, *unjust*. An act which conforms to the Divine law, as known through the principle of utility, is found to be useful : an act which does not conform to the Divine law, as

z 2

known through the same index, is found to be pernicious. Consequently, " an act which is just or unjust," and "an act which is useful or pernicious," are nearly equivalent expressions. An act which a sovereign government has a right to do, it has a Divine right to do: if it have not a Divine right, it has no right at all. An act which is useful the Divine law, as known through the principle of utility, has conferred on the sovereign government a right to do: an act which is pernicious the Divine law, as known through the same exponent, has not conferred on the sovereign government a right to do. Consequently, an act which a government has a right to do, is an act which is generally useful ; and an act which a government has not a right to do, is an act which is generally pernicious. And so, a sovereign government has not a Divine right to tax its subjects, unless the scheme of taxation accords with general utility: for every Divine right springs from the Divine law expressed, or the Divine will implied ; and, in the absence of any express command, general utility is the index to the Divine will. Consequently, when the advocates of Divine right object to try it, on any particular application, by the principle of utility, they object to the only test by which it is possible to determine the reality of the right itself.

Whether a sovereign government consist of one person, or many persons, we cannot infer that the government lies under moral or legal duties, or has moral or legal rights against the interests of its own subjects.

The proper purpose or end of a sovereign political government, or the purpose or end for which it ought to exist, is the greatest possible advancement of human happiness, or welfare; and, if it would accomplish its proper purpose or end, it must advance, as far as is possible, the weal of its own community.

" The good of the universal society formed by mankind, is the aggregate good of the particular societies into which mankind is divided : just as the happiness of any of those societies is the aggregate happiness of its single or individual members. Though, then, the weal of mankind is the proper object of a government, or though the test of its conduct is the principle of general utility, it commonly ought to consult directly and particularly the weal of the particular community which the Deity has committed to its rule. If it truly adjust its conduct to the principle of general utility, it commonly will aim immediately at the particular and more precise, rather than the general and less determinate end."[*]

[*] Austin, ' On Jurisprudence,' p. 264.

The general and particular ends never, or rarely, conflict; but are perfectly consistent, or rather are inseparably connected. An enlightened regard to the principle of utility, implies an enlightened regard for the common happiness or welfare of nations; whilst the stupid patriotism which looks exclusively to country, and seeks its interests at the cost of other countries, grossly misapprehends the principle and fails in its object.

If a sovereign political government were formed and regulated on the principle of utility, and the community were adequately instructed or enlightened, the habitual obedience to the government which would be rendered by the community would proceed from their conviction that this principle was carried out for their benefit. And, even if they thought the government faulty in some particulars, yet if the conviction continued that this principle were honestly intended to be carried out for their benefit, a fear that the evil of resistance might exceed the evil of obedience, would be their inducement to submit. But if they distrusted the government, or deemed its principle imperfect, they would not persist in their obedience, if they thought that a better government might probably be got by resistance, and that the probable good of the change outweighed its probable mischief.

As every society is inadequately instructed or enlightened, the habitual obedience to its government which is rendered by the bulk of its community, is partly the consequence of custom, and partly the consequence of prejudices, which have no foundation whatever in the principle of general utility.

But if the *permanence* of every government be owing to the people's consent, and if that consent be given by the bulk of the people from the conviction that the government is conducted on the principle of general utility, the *permanence* of the government is better secured than when it depends on the obedience rendered by custom or prejudices, which, being governed by no principle, are apt to change.

It is, therefore, of the first importance for the permanence of every government, that it should be formed and conducted on the principle of general utility, in order to obtain the consent of the inadequately instructed or enlightened from their own experience of the benefits, as well as from custom or prejudices; and then the consent of all proceeding from the same principle, will not only make the government more permanent, but, bringing it into closer conformity with the Divine will, of which that principle is the index, will also make the government the instrument or channel for conveying God's blessings to the People, instead of making it the instrument of injustice and oppression, in opposition to His will, His will being the Happiness of all Mankind.

The duties of the subjects towards the sovereign government, are partly religious, partly legal, and partly moral; and if the principle of utility were carried out for the general good, the habitual obedience of the subjects to the sovereign government would probably follow.

The duties of the sovereign government towards the subjects are known through the principle of utility. The government is bound by the Divine law, as known through the principle of utility, to advance, as far as possible, the common weal or good. Its moral duties towards the subjects are, to observe and to enforce the observance of the laws which its own community imposes upon it, consistently with the same principle.

It follows, therefore, that the duties of the subjects towards the sovereign government, and the duties of the sovereign government towards the subjects, originate respectively in the Divine law, as indicated by the principle of utility, in positive law, and in positive morality. We account sufficiently for those obligations, and sufficiently impress the necessity of their observance, when we refer them to those sources. No higher source or ampler solution of the origin of those mutual obligations can be required, than that they are imposed by the express command or implied will of God. . Those writers who resort to ampler solution must draw their conclusions, directly or indirectly, from these same sources.

This was the view taken by Sir William Blackstone, when he wrote, "that the laws of God (whether they are revealed, or are indicated by general utility) are superior in obligation to any other laws : that no human laws are of any validity if contrary to them : that all human laws which are valid, derive all their force, and all their authority, mediately or immediately, from those divine originals."

From this is to be inferred that, no human law which conflicts with the law of God, is obligatory or binding. But this we know to be contrary to the fact; for, many of our laws on which Sir William Blackstone wrote his Commentaries were as contrary to the laws of God,—whether revealed or indicated,—as human laws could well be ; and although many of these have since been repealed, in consequence of the almost universal indignation expressed against them for the outrages which they committed against the feelings or instincts of human nature, yet many of these laws still re-

main, to the disgrace of civilized society, being
wholly irreconcileable with Divine law, as far as
that is known to us. But, however that may be,
no one supposes that human laws are, *therefore*,
less binding or obligatory, so far as human life or
welfare are concerned.

It is remarkable, as Mr. Austin observes, how
few writers have distinguished between laws properly so called and laws which are such only
in a metaphorical sense—the laws of nature, as
the expression is understood by physical inqui-
rers, meaning the uniformities of co-existence or
succession in the phenomena of the universe.
Among other eminent writers in our own country
who have fallen into this confusion, Blackstone is
conspicuous, and among eminent French writers,
Montesquieu. As Mr. Austin remarks: ' We are
frequently warned by a certain class of writers
against disobeying or violating the physical laws
of organic life, as if it were not the very meaning of a physical law that it may be unknown
or disregarded, but cannot possibly be violated.'

The force of this distinction and the importance
of observing it in all inquiries of this nature must
be evident to every one when attention is thus
called to it. The confusion and contradiction into
which Sir William Blackstone has so frequently
fallen for want of attention to this distinction are

apparent in his admirable Commentaries on our Laws. If he had said that, a human law which conflicts with the law of God *ought* not to be imposed, and is *morally* not *binding* and not *valid*, he would have said what everybody now feels to be true. But to say that a human law which conflicts with the law of God, is therefore not *binding*, or not *valid*, is sheer nonsense, when the unfortunate victims are hanged, transported, or shut up in prison.

Was that law not *binding*, or not *valid*, under which the husband of Mary Jones was carried off by the Press-gang, leaving destitute his young wife, under 19 years of age, with two small children?

Was that law not *binding*, or not *valid*, under which that poor distracted young wife was carried to execution, with her baby in her arms, and hanged at Tyburn?

The case, as reported, stands thus: "She was very young (*under nineteen*), and remarkably handsome. She went to a linen-draper's shop in Ludgate Street, took some coarse linen off the counter, and slipped it under her cloak. The shop-man saw her, and she laid it down. *For this she was hanged.* Her defence was, 'that she had lived in credit, and wanted for nothing, till the press-gang came, and stole her husband

from her; but since then she had no bed to lie
on—*nothing to give her children to eat, and they
were almost naked*; and, perhaps, she might have
done something wrong; for she scarcely knew
what she did."

"*The Parish officers testified to the truth of
this story.*"

"When brought to receive sentence, she be-
haved in such a frantic manner as proved her
mind to be in a desponding and distracted state,
and the child was sucking at her breast when
she set out for Tyburn" [gallows].

Well and truly did Sir William Meredith exclaim, when he brought this case before the House
of Commons : "I do not believe a fouler murder
was ever committed against law, than the murder
of this woman by law."*

This case occurred in the year 1777, in the
reign of our King George the Third, of blessed
memory. In the following year he showed symptoms of insanity.

That murderous law was binding and valid
enough to destroy many hundreds of precious
human lives.

"It was not many years ago—it was in the
year 1814—that one Edward Pollo was executed
at the new gaol, Chelmsford, for cutting down a

* "The People's Blue Book," p. 519, 2nd Edition.

young cherry-tree, in an orchard, or rather plantation, at Kelvedon, in Essex, the property of a
Mr. Brewer. The Judge hanged this offender by
the law of inference, remarking,—" That a man
who would wilfully cut down a young cherry-tree
would take away a man's life." That Judge was
—Mr. Justice Heath. The man who confirmed
that sentence, and ordered it to be carried out
in execution, was our Prince Regent, afterwards
King George the Fourth. His Prime Minister
then was Robert Earl of Liverpool; and the
Keeper of the Royal Conscience was John Earl
of Eldon. St. Paul said of Alexander the Cop-
persmith :—" The Lord reward him according
to his works !"*

In the same year, (1814,) " a Recorder of London declared it to be the determination of the
same Regent, to make an example for the offence
of stealing from a shop or from the person, and
he took the opportunity of making the example
in the case of a child of ten years of age, actually
at the moment lying under sentence of death, in
Newgate, for stealing from the person.

" The Recorder—let it not be forgotten—was
Silvester. Let it not be forgotten that Arch-
bishops and Bishops voted against the repeal of
that law. Let it not be forgotten that, on that

* " The People's Blue Book," p. 288, 3rd Edition.

occasion, the same Lord Chancellor, Eldon, exclaimed : "There was no knowing where this was to stop, and that the public ought to know, once for all, in what the criminal code consisted, that their Lordships might not, from time to time and from year to year, have *their feelings distressed* (!) by discussions like the present."

"This fierce struggle actually continued, from poor Mary Jones' case in 1777, down to the year 1818. But it is gone at last, and their Lordships' *feelings* since then have been '*severely distressed* from time to time' by the indecorous perseverance of men who know no better, rude and unpolished men, who would not understand why laws, not to be acted on, were still to be retained, and uncouthly thought that the caprices of mankind, even of ministerial mankind, were not to be trusted ; credulous and timid men who weakly suspected that what had been, might be, that another Regent might be ill-advised by another Keeper of his Royal Conscience, or by another Recorder of London, and that a future Ludgate might obtain 'the comfort' of another immolation."*

Who, now looking back to any one of those appalling cases, would not rather have been the victim than one of the jury who found that verdict,

* "The People's Blue Book," p. 521, 2nd Edition.

or the judge who passed that sentence, or the
King, or the Regent, who confirmed it?

One is almost led to believe that cases so appalling to every human feeling could have been
permitted by the Divine being, only for the purpose of touching the heart and opening the eyes
of the hard-hearted and the blind, that they
might be able to see their God!

These execrable laws are some of the many
instances of laws formed on men's notions of the
principle of utility.

The men who made these laws were not more
wicked, perhaps not more cruel, than other men,
and were reputed the most learned of their time.
They all had their peculiar evil habits, and some
of them were peculiarly low habits, now confined
to the lowest and most ignorant,. but, perhaps,
they were not more immoral than many of
their own class. Judges do not now habitually
swear in public, nor mutter oaths and curses
from the judicial bench. They have never been
addicted to stealing after they had attained to
the bench, though some few instances are on
record of their having been convicted of stealing
before they had attained to that elevation ;—
afterwards there could have been no occasion.
But the instances of taking bribes (happily now
unknown) were formerly of very frequent oc-

currence, and the inference that a Judge who
would take a bribe would steal, is not more
forced than Judge Heath's inference, on which
he hanged his man.

But what are all the Judges, but weak erring
men, no better and no worse than the common
run of men, and less guilty of many crimes,
only because lifted out of the temptations to
commit them, having less opportunity and lei-
sure time for committing them, if so disposed;
formed and fashioned in their narrow views of
justice and mercy by the laws which they administer, made by men as weak and erring as
themselves, much more after their own false
notions of the principle of utility, than under
the safe guidance of the Christian doctrine which
they disregard. That any one who has studied
and reflected on the sad history of the past administration of human affairs should place so much
confidence in human authority is truly astonishing !

It is not to disparage those men, who were no
better and no worse than other men, that these
remarks are made ; but to show the weakness
and absurdity of looking up to them, or to any
other erring men, with their narrow notions and
false principles, as our infallible guides for human
government.   What are the opinions of the best

men worth, if not formed in accordance with the
revealed will of the Divine Ruler, or in conformity
with the principle of Utility, as an index to the
Divine will, in the absence of more express command ?

Who now believes that it was in accordance
with the revealed will of the Divine Ruler, or in
conformity with the principle of utility, as an
index to that will, to hang a child of ten years
old for stealing a pocket-handkerchief from the
person ; or to shoot dead, or maim for life, man,
woman, or child, for robbing an orchard ?

But who then doubted the wisdom of those
great and learned men who made and maintained
the laws which so long continued to perpetrate
such atrocities ?

Who can now look back without astonishment
and horror at the marvellous stupidity of the men
who talked and acted as they did ?

And yet those men were counted the wisest
and the best, and ruled over this happy country
for——God only knows how long ; for, such
men have always ruled over this happy country !
Who knows when they began ? Who can say
when this happy country was ruled by other than
merciless and bloody laws ? And, yet, all good
people have always been thankful for the blessings
they enjoy under the glorious British Constitution!

2 A

Nor were they altogether wrong, on a comparison of their condition with that of the people of other nations. But comparisons are unsatisfactory, without a standard, and that is nowhere to be found in any human authority.

Binding in blood, but not in conscience, are all merciless and cruel laws; and valid they are for the increase of crime and human misery; but valid for nothing else.

Adverse to general utility are all such laws, and yet they have been and are enforced in every age and nation, and were known by Blackstone, through the very exponent which he himself adopted, to conflict with the law of God.

The plea to the indictment, ' that the law is adverse to utility,' and ' that, by necessary consequence, it conflicts with the law of God, and therefore is not *binding* or *valid*,' would not avail to stop the executioner in his duty.

This plea was often tried in the case of our Corn-law, and though that law brought starvation to the people it was not the less binding or valid.

The law which makes it criminal in a trader to buy certain goods in France, and bring them here for sale, though adverse to the moral law and to utility, is still binding or valid.

The law which takes from the hard-earned wages of labor to save the pockets of the Landlords and Capitalists, though adverse to moral law and to general utility, is still binding or valid.

The legislature claims and exercises the right to take, to any extent and for any purposes it thinks fit, the people's property, though many of the purposes are against the people's interests, and the bulk of the people have no voice in the question.

Sir William Blackstone admits that to be a violation of the British Constitution, but the law which confirms the practice is still binding or valid, and, in spite of the numberless oppressions and miseries which ensue, the practice is still persisted in.

Sir William Blackstone wrote: "No human laws are of any validity if contrary to the law of nature; and such of them as are valid derive all their force and all their authority mediately or immediately from this original." This is good for teaching that a legislature does not necessarily exercise a divine right, but only a temporal power for a temporary purpose; but it is bad for teaching that, however exercised, it is invalid. It is good for teaching that it may be righteously resisted when it exceeds its lawful limits, and defeats its designed purpose; but it is bad for teaching that it may be resisted with impunity.

The same authority says:—"No subject of

England can be constrained to pay any aids or
taxes even for the defence of the realm or the
support of the government, but such as are imposed by his own consent, or that of his representative in Parliament." But the great bulk
of the subjects of England are constrained to
pay taxes which are imposed without their own
consent, or that of their representatives in parliament. Their consent is not asked, and as they
have no Representatives of their own choosing,
they have no voice in the question. It is said
that they are too ignorant to be safely trusted
with a voice in such a question; but, then, they
ought not to be made to pay. No voice, no choice
—would, perhaps, be accepted by many,—perhaps, by the bulk of the workers,—if their wages
of labor were exempt from taxation. But no voice
and no choice, but to pay or go to prison, when
the great burden of taxation is thrown upon the
workers by those who are not workers, is as manifest a violation of the British Constitution as it
is of the moral law, and of the principle of utility.
To affirm that a man may not be taxed unless he
has directly or indirectly given his consent, is to
affirm that he may refuse to be so taxed. But
that is a mockery, if his refusal be followed by
his punishment. If he have no vote, he can express neither assent nor dissent. If it be thought

uusafe to give him a vote because he is incompe-
tent to determine for himself whether to consent
or refuse, it must be inconsistent and unjust to
assume his consent when it is manifestly for his
interest to refuse it, and the more so when those
who assume his consent know it to be for his interest to refuse. The only fair presumption is, that
his right to vote is withheld from him because
it would be exercised for his own interests, and
against the interests of those who withhold from
him this right; that it is unsafe for their interests,
according to their view of their own interests,
not that it is unsafe for his interests, or for the
interests of the greatest number. But to test
the truth of their view, or their own belief in it,
and to preserve their own consistency and claim
to fair dealing, if he be excluded from a voice in
the question, he should be exempted from the
tax. On no other ground can the withholding the
right to vote, except as a punishment, be justified.

But if it can be shown,—as it has been shown,
—that it is as much for the interest of those who
are consumers only, that the producers should not
be taxed, as producers, as it is for the producers
themselves that, as such, they should not be
taxed, then, still more manifest is the trickery of
the pretence that, it is unsafe to allow the free

exercise of the constitutional right of voting
equally to all who are under no legal disability.
If it be essential for the safety of the community
that property should be duly represented, as nobody disputes, it must be no less essential that
labor, which is the only property of the bulk of
the people, should also be duly represented. The
necessity in both cases must be the same; but, at
least, the necessity in the one case cannot make
it unnecessary in the -other. The necessity for
representing the rights of property, cannot be a
justification for leaving unrepresented the rights
of labor, from which all property originates, and
on which, therefore, all property depends. The
influence of property, rightly exercised, must
always be paramount, if property be made to
confer the right to vote; but that admission con-
fers no ground for denying the right of manhood
suffrage, which is a natural right to every community, consistent with moral right and the principle of utility.

That men are selfish and will employ the
power placed in their hands for what they believe to be their own advantage, with little regard
for others, requires no proof. Assuming, then,
that men are selfish,—and they are often proud
and pitiless,—it may be assumed that those who
possess the power will, if they can, use it for their

own selfish purposes. In all countries, in all times, this has been sufficiently exemplified, and not the least so in those countries which are considered to be the most civilized. In France, before the first revolution, the *tiers état*, or working classes, were little better treated than slaves, the greatest portion of the burdens of the State being imposed upon them, many of the most onerous upon them exclusively, and their lives and property being at the will of their masters.

In Scotland, the Chiefs formerly claimed and exercised the power of life and death over their clans, and it was no unusual occurrence for lairds to kidnap the common people and export them as slaves.

In Ireland, it was the common practice of landowners to hunt and shoot down papists as wild game.

In England, the legislature has furnished plenty of examples.

The Act 9th George I.—significantly named the "Black Act," declares that any one disguised and in possession of an offensive weapon "appearing in any warren or place where hares or conies have been, or shall be usually kept, and being thereof duly convicted, shall be adjudged guilty of felony, and shall suffer death, as in cases of felony, without benefit of clergy."

Who, but the Landowners, made that law?

Who, but the Landowners, made the Game Laws, the Corn Laws, and many other laws; and for what, but their own advantage, as they ignorantly supposed?

Who, but the Landowners, made the Inclosure Laws, and divided the Commons among themselves and their neighbors, regardless of the claims of the poor Cottagers?

Who, but the Landowners, made the law which estimated a man's life at the value of a sheep's life?

Even in 1833, the legal estimate of a man's life was only 40s. Lord Suffield, in the House of Lords, on the 2nd of August, 1833, said:—"I hold in my hand a list of 555 perjured verdicts, delivered at the Old Bailey, in fifteen years, for the single offence of stealing from dwelling-houses; the value stolen being, in these cases, sworn above 40s., but the verdicts returned being to the value of 39s. only. If required, I will produce the name of every one of these 555 convicts, and show the value proved to have been stolen."

This became too horrible to be tolerated any longer. But what was the remedy? A repeal of the law? No such thing. If that were the result, "the people of England," as Lord Wynford said on a similar proposal, "could not sleep in safety in their

beds." No, but the legislature revised its arithmetic. Man, made in the image of his Maker, rose in
the money market. Human life was extravagantly
averaged at five pounds. A rise in the article of
no less than sixty shillings a head! But still, the
obstinate juries demurred to the valuation. Perhaps, as for mere blood, they thought the price
too low; or, it may be, they remembered that
an immortal soul was included in the estimate.
Again, therefore, to the scandal and disparage-
ment of public justice, they applied the only remedy in their power. Disregarding the actual
amount stolen, they substituted for the old 39s.
" Guilty of stealing to the value of £4. 19s."
. . . . The jury remembered that, in the previous
May, (1831) a man had been executed under this
very statute, and they shrank from the work of
extermination.

Such was the spirit of our cruel laws, and such
their equally calamitous administration, when one
of those men appeared whom Providence occasionally sends on earth to mitigate the misery of
his fellow-creatures. This was Sir Samuel Romilly,
a profound lawyer, a learned jurist, a wise and
humane legislator, the friend of Bentham, the co-
operator with Brougham, the associate of every
man, and the advocate of every measure, likely
to ameliorate the social condition of his country.

302 UTILITARIANISM.

Nauseated by the scenes he had witnessed on his
circuit, he determined that, so far as in him lay,
our monster code should lap human blood no
longer. . . . He set about his Christian work with
caution. . . . He commenced with that murderous
statute of the Good Queen Bess—the 8th Eliz.
c. 4,—which made the privately stealing from a
person a capital offence! Under this most monstrous enactment, a hungry boy who stole a pocket-
handkerchief was liable to be executed.

The repeal was carried almost in silence; one
solitary Irish member muttering 'innovation.'
Thus encouraged, in the Session of 1810, he attempted to repeal the statute of William, which
made a private theft in a shop, to the amount of
five shillings, punishable with death. This bill
escaped through the Commons not without opposition, but was defeated in the Lords, by a majority of thirty-one to eleven. Posterity will
scarcely give credence to the fact, that in this
majority are to be found an Archbishop and six
Bishops! But the Church stood not alone. The
sages of the wool-sack and the Bench, added the
law to the Gospel. It is almost incredible how
wise men, and learned men, and good men, unex-
ceptionable in all life's relations, could have clung
to prejudices so injurious! Lord Chief Justice
Ellenborough exclaimed against the bill as an inno-

vation, declaring that he knew not where such speculations were to stop, and strange to say, with rare
sagacity naming the very bill (12 Anne, c. 7) the
repeal of which was next to pass the Commons !

It may not be without advantage to those
who pin their faith upon human authority, just
to advert to the astounding fact, that the then
judicial bench of England were, without exception,
against the repeal of this sanguinary statute. "I
trust (exclaimed the Lord Chief Justice Ellenborough) your Lordships will pause before you
assent to a measure pregnant with danger to the
security of property. The learned judges are
unanimously agreed that the expediency of justice
and the public security require there should not
be a remission of capital punishment in this part
of the criminal law. My Lords, if we suffer this
bill to pass, we shall not know where to stand—
*we shall not know whether we are on our heads, or
on our feet ! !* My Lords, I think this, above all
others, is a law on which so much of the security
of mankind depends in its execution, that I should
deem myself neglectful of my duty to the public
if I failed to let the law take its course." Thus,
with the assent of all the judges of England and
by the Votes of seven dignitaries of our Christian Church, it was again decided that human
life was justly forfeitable for a private theft to the
amount of five shillings in a shop !

Again, next year, in 1811, the bill, carried through the Commons, was rejected by the Lords, led by three of the most eminent Judges. Again, in 1813, undaunted and indefatigable, he introduced this bill, carried it through the Commons, and lost it in the Lords; an Irish Archbishop, on this occasion, displacing the English one, and five of the Episcopal bench supporting him. Again, in 1816, the Commons passed, and the Lords, little being said, again refused it. In 1818, for the last time he triumphed in the Commons, but death, alas, arrested him in his struggle, and he left to others the consummation of his labors, and the glory of his example.

Since the repeal of these bloody laws, the people have slept, at least, quite as safely in their beds,—notwithstanding Lord Wynford's fears. But that same Lord Wynford, when Chief Justice of the Common Pleas, held that it was lawful and right to shoot men, women, and children, dead with spring guns, or to cut off their legs with steel traps for robbing an orchard. Fortunately, the Legislature, at last, thought otherwise, and made those cruel proceedings no longer lawful.

As long as such laws as these are made and administered, it is no wonder that the people are brutal and depraved in their excessive misery.

Who can forget the outcry raised on the mere hint of a mitigation of the law relating to forgery? All England was panic-stricken. The Banks must stop, public credit would be a thing of history, commercial confidence would vanish into air! Such were the predictions of bankers, merchants, and traders,—of every counting-house—of the whole Exchange; and they prevailed, not unnaturally, for the commercial world were entitled to all deference on the subject; but they prevailed not long. These cruel laws were repealed—repealed after torrents of blood had been shed—after the jury-box had been desecrated a thousand times. They were repealed —and, wonderful to relate, on the petition of the Bankers of every City and Exchange in England, *except London.*

The petition of the Bankers virtually abolished punishment of death for forgery, in 1830. It was high time, and only just in time. This important petition was entrusted to Mr. Brougham, no hasty innovator, but a true reformer, cautious of change, of which, when approved, he was indefatigable in the accomplishment. In this petition neither the Bank of England, nor the Bankers of London joined—an unenviable reminiscence. The petition was signed by Bankers, and the Bankers only, of 214 cities and towns of

the United Kingdom; 233 Banking-houses, 36
Joint-Stock Banking Companies, and 502 individual Bankers affixed their signatures to this
petition, which Mr. Brougham advocated with
talent and energy worthy of himself and the occasion; his speech, say the journals of the day,
was 'splendid, impressive, and unanswerable.'

In the Session of 1832, capital punishment
for forgery was abolished, except in cases of Wills
and Powers of Attorney relating to the Public
Funds.   We have already alluded to the motive,
the selfish motive in which this movement of the
Bankers originated.   We give now the very
words of the petitioners,—invaluable words,
speaking trumpet-tongued, how insane the folly
is which can seek, by unjust and cruel means,
the protection of property or the repression of
crime.

" Your Petitioners find by experience that the
infliction of death, or even the possibility of the
infliction of death, prevents the prosecution, conviction, and punishment of the criminal, and thus
endangers the property which it is intended to
protect.   We, therefore, earnestly pray that your
honorable House will not withhold from them
that protection to *their* property, which they
would derive from more a *lenient* law."

The foregoing examples are taken from "The

People's Blue Book" (2nd Ed.) where they were chiefly quoted from a small work on 'Capital Punishments' by that eminent Criminal Lawyer, and no less distinguished Orator, the late Mr. Charles Phillips.

In proportion as mankind became wise, in exact proportion to that wisdom should be the extinction of the unequal system under which they now subsist. Government is, in fact, the mere badge of their depravity. They are so little aware of the inestimable benefits of mutual love as to indulge, without thought, and almost without motive, in the worst excesses of selfishness and malice. Hence, without graduating human society into a scale of empire and subjection, its very existence has become impossible.

It is necessary that universal benevolence should supersede the regulations of precedent and prescription, before these regulations can safely be abolished. Meanwhile their very subsistence depends on the system of injustice and violence which they have been devised to palliate. They suppose men endowed with the power of deliberating and determining for their equals; whilst these men, as frail and as ignorant as the multitude whom they rule, possess, as a practical consequence of this power, the right which they of necessity exercise to prevent (together with their own) the physical, and moral, and intellectual nature of all mankind.

It is the object of wisdom, on the principle of utility, to equalize the distinctions on which this power depends, by exhibiting in their proper worthlessness the objects, a contention concerning which renders the existence a necessary evil. The evil, in fact, is virtually abolished wherever *justice* is practised; and it is abolished in precise proportion to the prevalence of true virtue.

The whole frame of human things is infected by an insidious poison. Hence it is that man is blind in his understanding, corrupt in his moral sense, and diseased in his physical functions. The wisest and most sublime of the ancient Poets saw this truth, and embodied their conception of its value in retrospect to the earliest ages of mankind.

The experience of ages which have intervened between the present period and that in which the Founder of Christianity taught, tends to prove His doctrine, and to illustrate theirs.

There is more equality because there is more justice; and there is more justice because there is more universal and true knowledge.

To the accomplishment of such mighty ends were the views of the Great Teacher extended; such did He know to be the tendency of His doctrine—the abolition of artificial distinctions among mankind; so far as the love which it becomes all human beings to bear towards each other, and the knowledge of truth, from which that love will never fail to be produced, avail to their destruction.

After His disappearance, the system of equality was attempted to be carried into effect by His followers. " They that believed had all things in common." (Acts ii.)

The practical application of the doctrine of strict justice to a state of society established in its contempt, was such as might have been expected. After the transitory glow of enthusiasm had faded from the minds of men, precedent and habit resumed their empire.

Men to whom birth had allotted ample possessions, looked with complacency on sumptuous apartments and luxurious food, and those ceremonials of delusive majesty which surround the throne of power, and the court of wealth. Men from whom these things were withheld by their condition, began to gaze with stupid envy on pernicious splendor, and by desiring the false greatness of another's state, to sacrifice the intrinsic dignity of their own. The demagogues of the infant republic of the Christian Sect attaining, through eloquence or artifice, to influence

2 B

among its members, first violated (under pretence of watching over their integrity,) the institutions established for the common and equal benefit of all.

These demagogues artfully silenced the voice of the moral sense among them, by engaging them to attend, not so much to the cultivation of a virtuous and happy life in this moral scene, as to the attainment of a fortunate condition after death ; not so much to the consideration of those means by which the state of man is adorned and improved, as an inquiry into the secrets of the connection between God and the world—things which they well knew were not to be explained, or even to be conceived. The system of equality which they established necessarily fell to the ground, because it is a system that must result from, rather than precede, the moral improvement of human kind.

It was a circumstance of no moment that the first adherents of the new doctrines of Christianity cast their property into a common stock. The same degree of real community of property could have subsisted without this formality, which served only to extend a temptation of dishonesty to the treasurers of so considerable a patrimony. Every man, in proportion to his virtue, considers himself, with respect to the great community of mankind, as the steward and guardian of their interests in the property which he chances to possess. Every man in proportion to his wisdom, sees the manner in which it is his duty to employ the resources which the consent of mankind has entrusted to his direction.

Such is the annihilation of the unjust inequality of powers and conditions existing in the world; and so gradually and inevitably is the progress of equality accommodated to the progress of wisdom and of virtue among mankind.

Meanwhile, some benefit has not failed to flow from the imperfect attempts which have been made to erect a system of equal rights to property and power upon the basis of arbitrary institutions. They have, undoubtedly, in every case, from the instability of their formation, failed. Still, they constitute a record of those epochs at which a true sense of justice suggested itself to the understandings of men, so that they consented to forego all the cherished delights of luxury, all the habitual gratifications arising out of the possession or the expectation of power; all the superstitions with which the accumulated authority of ages had made them dear and venerable. These are so many trophies erected in the enemies' land, to mark the limits of the victorious progress of truth and justice.

2 D 2

But, until truth and justice be more plainly recognized and established by laws and regulations made in conformity therewith, it is a manifest mockery to talk of putting into practice the doctrines of Christianity for the government of our Home or Foreign Affairs; and to attempt it would be absolute absurdity.

It is not difficult to see that those doctrines carried out, would make all governments very simple and easy; but, to produce the good fruit we must graft from the true stock.

To teach the People the practice of truth and justice, the laws and regulations by which they are governed must be founded on truth and justice. In what human government has that experiment ever been tried?

To off-ward the evil is one thing; to right the wrong is another.

The law which inflicts the penalty of death for murder, or theft, or any other crime, even if it do off-ward the evil, which is more than doubtful, certainly does not right the wrong. Such a law proceeds on the principle of retaliation, of injury for injury, and that is vengeance, for which we have, not only no divine authority, but a positive divine prohibition, and this principle is as much opposed to the principle of utility, as to the Christian doctrine.

Whilst the law sets the example of vengeance, can it be a wonder that the people follow it? Our criminal law does not pretend to right the wrong, and often aggravates it.

In the laws regulating Civil affairs, or government, it is difficult to discern the principle of utility, or the principle either of truth or justice. The manifest rights of the People are imperfectly acknowledged, and, therefore, are imperfectly respected. A natural consequence is, that the People but imperfectly acknowledge or respect the rights of each other. The natural right of every individual to enjoy the produce of his own labor is quite disregarded. Property is heavily burdened with Taxes, but Labor is far more heavily burdened. These taxes, unjustly raised, have been most shamefully misapplied in ruinous wars and profligate expenditure; and, moreover, after deducting the direct costs of collecting, and the indirect losses from the mode of raising these taxes, less than one-third ever reaches the Exchequer. How much of that is properly applied can only be guessed.

" Assuming the tax-payers to be six millions, out of a population of thirty millions, (a large allowance), this is equal to a tax of £33. 2*s*. 4½*d*. a head. Of this sum, £10. 17*s*. 8*d*. and no more, finds its way into the Exchequer. This is in the proportion of 1s. to 3s. 0½d., and, to be exact, a small fraction more than half a farthing more. Therefore, for every shilling paid into the Exchequer for Taxes, three shillings and a halfpenny are taken out of the pockets of the People, and the difference is not only their loss without any benefit to the nation, but is to the great injury of the Trade, Manufactures, and Agriculture, and, consequently, of the whole property of the Kingdom, and of the People of all Nations of the world! And, be it remembered, this calculation is made on the *net* revenue."

"On the ethical part of the question, or the loss and injury to the nation from the demoralizing tendency and inevitable effect of our Revenue Laws, every one must form his own estimate, for we can never fully appreciate our loss under this head, until we can compare the results of a happier state of things with our experience of the past."[*]

Not only is the tendency of our Revenue Laws demoralizing, but such is the actual and inevitable effect, in frauds and perjuries innumerable, and even in crimes of the most atrocious character. It is astonishing that, in the most highly civilized Country in the world, crimes and even trivial offences have been punished with a severity

[*] "The People's Blue Book," p. 90, 3rd. Ed.

unknown in the most barbarous country, and yet
laws have been made, and are still retained with
persistent obstinacy, tempting to the commission
of those very crimes and offences, and actually
exciting public sympathy in favor of the criminals
and offenders !

As Adam Smith said in his time, regarding
smuggling :—" The law, contrary to all the principles of justice, first creates the temptation, and
then punishes those who yield to it, and it commonly enhances the punishment too, in proportion to the very circumstances which ought certainly to alleviate it—the temptation to commit
the crime."

Nearly a century ago, Adam Smith laid it
down as an admitted axiom that, " Every tax
ought to be so contrived as both to take out and
keep out of the pockets of the people, as little as
possible over and above what it brings into the
Treasury of the State."

Now, the effect of our system is, to reduce the
purchasing power of the Wages of Labor throughout the kingdom, about two-thirds, for all the
necessaries and conveniences of life. Thus, the
skilled workman, at five shillings a day, receives
in money value, measured by its purchasing
power at present prices, in comparison with what
would be the purchasing power of the same wages

under the system of *direct* taxation proposed, in
the proportion of about 1*s*. 8*d*. to 5*s*. for the
skilled laborer, and about 10*d*. to 2*s*. 6*d*. for the
common laborer.

These proportions show a difference something
like that between the itzebou and the kobang.
The principal silver coin of Japan is the itzebou,
representing about 1*s*. 8*d*. of British money; and
the gold. kobang, which was intrinsically worth
£1. 2*s*., could be obtained for four itzebous, or
6*s*. 8*d*. of our money. The merchants, of course,
at once detected this difference in the specific
value of the silver and gold coins, and discovered
in it a mine of wealth, compared with which the
returns of commerce would, they thought, be altogether unworthy of their attention. The merchants accordingly immediately converted their
silver dollars into itzebous, and their itzebous into
gold kobangs, realizing at once a profit of about
200 per cent. Four silver itzebous (a dollar and
a third in weight) would, it was found, purchase
a kobang of gold, exchangeable in China for
18*s*. 4½*d*. The merchants then found themselves
unexpectedly able to triple their capital by two
very simple operations, which they could re-
peat several times a year. The Government was
distracted and at its wits' end how to evade or
to meet these unexpected requirements, which

they felt were opposed to justice and fair dealing.*

Our Landowners are converting their silver dollars into itzebous, and their itzebous into gold kobangs, at the expense of the Government. Our Government are at their wits' end, but, not feeling this to be opposed to justice and fair dealing, they think to throw the loss upon that ignorant portion of the people which has no voice in the affairs of the State. The Landowners do not see that the whole loss must ultimately fall on themselves, and that, in the mean time, the ignorant people are wronged and ruined.

Nor is the existing state of society in Japan, any more than with us, calculated to confer 'the greatest happiness on the greatest number.' The general aspect of the population is described to be one of poverty in harsh contrast to the amazing richness and fertility of the country :—"Few signs," wrote the British Minister in 1861, "of absolute destitution meet the eye, but masses of population with nothing evidently beyond the barest necessaries of animal life, a roof covering the area of a few mats, on which groups of eight, ten, or more men, women, and children crowded in the doorway as we passed, must be all huddled

* Quarterly Review, for October, 1863 ; Article "Japan," page 470.

together more like cattle than human beings, at night, and with just as little provision for comfort or decency. Some few of the larger towns had a better aspect, and a superior style of house in the principal thoroughfares, but only where there were signs of trade. The inhabitants of the purely agricultural districts and towns were all poverty stricken. From such general features I draw the conclusion that although the fertility of the soil is great, and turned to the best account by a plentiful supply of labor of the cheapest kind, yet little superfluity is produced, or, if there be any, it is absorbed almost entirely by the Daimios and their retainers, who are the non-productive classes, and proprietors, I believe, of nine-tenths of the soil. Of peasants or other landed proprietors, out of the Daimios class, there seem to be few, if any, except under altogether exceptional circumstances. Judging from the manifest poverty of the frugal laborer, the whole produce of the soil, save the barest pittance necessary to support life, must go to the Daimio."

There is in this description of the condition of the productive and non-productive classes in Japan a painfully striking similarity with the same classes in England, Scotland, and Ireland. Certainly, our Daimios and their retainers, who are the non-productive classes, are proprietors of nine-tenths of the soil.

It is not intended to suggest any interference
with their possessions, but only to direct attention to this great inequality, which seems to be
also a striking characteristic of the half-civilized,
half-barbarian, and wholly pagan state of Japan.

Let those who wish to carry on this comparison commence their course of reading with the
Preface to the collected Reports of Mr. Simon,
(late Officer of Health of the City of London,
and now Medical Officer of the Board of Health,)
on the Sanitary Condition of the City of London.
He says : " I would beg any educated person to
consider what are the conditions in which alone
animal life can thrive ; and to form for himself a
conscientious judgment as to the need for great,
if even almost revolutionary, reforms.   Let any
such person devote an hour to visiting some very
poor neighbourhood in the metropolis, or in almost any of our large towns. Let him breathe its
air, taste its water, eat its bread.   Let him think
of human life struggling there for years. Let him
fancy what it would be to himself to live there,
in that beastly degradation of stink, fed with
such bread, drinking such water.   Let him enter
some house there at hazard, and—heeding where
he treads, follow the guidance of his outraged
nose to the yard,—if there be one,—or the cellar.
Let him talk to the inmates : let him hear what

is thought of the bone-boiler next door, or the slaughter-house behind; what of the sewer-grating before the door; what of the Irish basket-makers upstairs—twelve in a room, who came in after the hopping, and got fever; what of the artisan's dead body, stretched on his widow's one bed, beside her living children. Let him, if he have a heart for the duties of manhood and patriotism, gravely reflect whether such sickening evils, as an hour's inquiry will have shown him, ought to be the habit of our laboring population: whether the Legislature which his voice [*his* voice! whose voice?] helps to constitute, is doing all that might be done to palliate these wrongs; whether it be not a jarring discord in the civilization we boast—a worse than pagan savageness in the Christianity we profess, that such things continue, in the midst of us, scandalously neglected; and that the interests of human life, except against wilful violence, are almost uncared for by the law."

This is strong language from a Government Official, but this is the best sort of answer to be given to the hired writers and calumniators of Mr. Cobden and Mr. Bright. Nobody really supposes that they ever suggested any interference with the Land in this country, or that the suffering People, for whom they spoke, and for

whom they have devoted their whole political
life, ever thought of disturbing the Proprietors
in their quiet possession. Nobody really supposes that, if these suffering classes could tell of
their wrongs and sufferings before the great
Council of the Nation, by Representatives of
their own choosing, these grievances would long
be unredressed. Nobody really doubts that there
is a remedy. All know that there is a remedy,
but many fear it. They fear it for themselves,
though they profess to fear it only for their country. Many, perhaps, are sincere in this profes-
sion, and deplore the present evils, but they are
blind to the real danger, and see not the greater
evils which their ignorance and cowardice have
brought upon the country, and are threatening
to overwhelm it in one great common disaster.
That may not be very near, but it is no less certain of coming if our present system of injustice
and inhuman cruelty be continued.

This is not the place for details of the deprivations and sufferings of the poor working classes.
Such details must be sought for in the volu-
minous Reports of Official Authorities,—in the
Records of our Poor Laws,—in the well-authen-
ticated statements of our numerous Charitable
Institutions, and Benevolent Associations,—must
be sought out and seen in all their horrid re-

ality. But few can so enter into this inquiry
nor ought they to attempt it. To those who
cannot do so for themselves, as well as to those
who trouble themselves but little about what appears little to concern them, the experiences of
such a man as Dr. George Johnson, Fellow of
the Royal College of Physicians, may not be
without a painful interest.

In a Lecture on "Over-Work, Distress, and
Anxiety, as causes of Mental and Bodily disease
among the Poor ; and on the means of counter-
acting these injurious influences"; he says :—

"I have already described in some detail the
effect which over-work, anxiety, and sorrow have
in depriving the patient of natural, refreshing
sleep. . . .

"But when we, as medical men, have done
all that we have it in our power to do for these
over-worked, anxious, sorrowful, and nervous pa-
tients, we often feel that there are certain facts
and features in their history with which we have
the means of dealing but very unsatisfactorily.
It is quite impossible for us to give a medicine
which will be an efficient substitute for food.
Yet we clearly see that wholesome nutritious food
is the only remedy for many of the diseases which
we are called upon to cure by drugs.

"But I am convinced by long and careful ob-

servation, that the mental anguish of many of
these poor men and women is out of all proportion greater and more intolerable than any physical sufferings they may have to endure. True
it is, that their bodies are often worn down by
hard labor, poisoned by impure air, and ex-
hausted by want of proper food; but, worse than
all this, is the black despair which settles upon
them when they find themselves beneath a thick
cloud of sorrow, or surrounded by a hopeless en-
tanglement of debt and difficulties, from which
they see no way of escape, with, perhaps, no one
to lend them a helping hand, or to speak a word
of encouragement or sympathy. What wonder
is it that in circumstances so cheerless and so
desperate, men, and, alas! women too—many
of whom have grown up in utter ignorance of
the very rudiments of Christianity—should fly
to the gin-shop to escape from their wretched
homes, to drown in the oblivion of drunkenness
the cares and troubles which daily become more
intolerable, or to seek temporary relief from the
physical exhaustion occasioned by excessive labor
in the impure and over-heated atmosphere of their
workshops!

" It appears to me, that in this state of things
we have a sufficient explanation of the necessity
for a continual increase of prisons and lunatic

asylums—institutions which it would be well
that we should all learn to look upon as monuments of neglected duty. We may be well as-
sured that if we were more diligent in our efforts
to educate the young, and to visit and relieve the
sick and the distressed, we should less frequently
be called upon to erect costly buildings for the
reception and maintenance of criminals and lu-
natics. Crime and sickness are very expensive ;
and the principles of economy, no less than the precepts of Christianity, instruct us that we should
act wisely if we did more to prevent these evils."

Monuments of neglected duty, indeed, are our
prisons and lunatic asylums ; but educating the
young, or visiting and relieving the sick and the
distressed, will not prevent these evils. These
evils have their roots too deeply down to be torn
up by any such efforts of individuals, however
diligent.

For the removal of these evils our first efforts
must be for enforcing the amendment of our unjust and cruel laws, against which all palliatives
are but temporizing and very questionable measures.

This eminent authority, in the same Lecture,
attributes the fearful increase of insanity in our
crowded manufacturing Cities and Towns, and in
our destitute Agricultural districts to the " para-

lysing influence of fear and anxiety" on diminished bodily strength, by hard work and insufficient food.

"It happens to us almost daily to meet with
instances of these nervous symptoms in needle-
women, who frequently work the whole day and
half the night in hot and ill-ventilated rooms,
who rarely have an opportunity for taking exercise in the open air, and whose earnings are often
so small as barely to suffice for the maintenance
of themselves and others who may be dependent
on them."

How these nervous symptoms are increased by
intemperate indulgence in stimulating drinks, it
is needless to dwell upon. But according to this
authority, confirmed by all experience, these
nervous symptoms originate chiefly in mental
anxiety occasioned by the distressing circumstances of poverty, and consequent despondency.
Delirium tremens and insanity are results. Any
one would think that, in seeking the remedy, the
first thing to be done is to seek the cause. But
this never has been done for these evils. And
what is the use of further inquiry into the cause,
when no one doubts it? How far palliatives to
such evils are desirable may be doubtful, the tendency of all palliatives being to relax the efforts
necessary to removal. It is not to be assumed,

even on the authority of the Rev. C. Kingsley
that, "it is a cruel Utilitarianism to refuse to
palliate the symptoms because you cannot cure
the disease itself," unless the meaning be—because it is incurable. It is not by palliatives;
nor by drawling expressions of pity for them as
the lower and more indigent classes, doomed to
toil and slavery; nor by stirring them up to
throw off the yoke and turn the tables upon
mankind; nor by holding out of sickly hopes
that times will soon be better; nor by casting of
the blame upon their own wasting and improvi- .
dence, that these evils will ever be removed or
materially relieved. It is even to be feared that
the tendency of such palliatives as these is to
multiply and perpetuate rather than to remove
or to reduce these evils.

The first sentence of Him who came to preach
glad tidings to the poor was: "Blessed are ye
poor, for yours is the kingdom of heaven." But
it was not to the poor indiscriminately that the
kingdom of heaven was promised. Against this
mis-interpretation our Evangelist has guarded
well, by saying that "He lifted up his eyes upon
His disciples," and said, "Blessed are ye poor,
for yours is the kingdom of heaven." To all
those who were disciples was that promise made;
not to the hungry, the wretched, and the forlorn,

without distinction of persons, and as it were by
caste; but to the rich as well as the poor,—
and to the poor especially for their comfort, con-
solation, and encouragement,—by character and
respect of righteousness; not by respect of the
lowness and wretchedness of their station.

"Let no man be deceived : it is not the physical
attributes of poverty, but the moral attributes of
poverty, which draw on the fulfilment of the promises. It is not the slender pittance, the lowly
roof, the toilsome day, nor the coarse fare which
make men meet for heaven; nor yet voluntary
fasting and a coat of sackcloth, stripes of pe-
nance and a bed of stones, as the Church of
Rome long did and still doth beguile men to believe. Heaven is not an Arcadia in which none
but poor shepherds are, nor a Utopian common-
wealth where none but men of low and level conditions are. That is all folly and delusion, by which
the poor are cunningly taken and craftily wound
into the snares of the tempter. But it is the slender
pittance enriched with the faith of Christ and
the hope of heaven, it is the coarse fare seasoned
with contentment and partaken with a blessing,
the toilsome day spent with a light heart and a
pleasant countenance as the good appointment of
God, and all the scantiness of poverty made up,
made sufficient and more than sufficient, through

the exceeding plenty of the grace of the gospel of Christ. This it is which hath departed (alas! that it should have ever departed) from the generality of the poor of our cities; this it is, and this alone is the estate of poverty to which any hope of heaven can be permitted; for how can heaven be expected there, where no reverence is paid to the tidings of it, no preparation made for the coming of it?"

Such were the words of Edward Irving, a man who, when among us, was much heard of and little known, but whose memory, to the few who did know him, must be held fast by the remembrance of all those great and endearing qualities which command the love and admiration of mankind.

But what is to be said for those who preach the plenty of the grace of the gospel and reduce the scanty pittance of the poor to enrich themselves; who tell the worn laborer to bear the toilsome day with a light heart and a pleasant countenance, and to be content with his coarse fare, which, at the best, is all that his wages ever can provide, that their own Rent-rolls may be kept up? What they may expect is with equal clearness promised.

They who make the Laws which deprive the laboring classes of the means of subsistence, and those enjoyments of life intended for them as the rewards of their honest labor, will as surely be held responsible, if not here, as certainly hereafter, as the promised blessing will hereafter be fulfilled to those who live and die within it. The duty of obedience to the Laws is nowhere more strongly enforced than is the duty of equal justice to all, in the making of Laws. The love of your neighbor as yourself, is expressly given as the definition and test of Charity,—not almsgiving,—and this love is not only declared to be the highest of all the Divine commands, but also to be the only true test of love to God.

Where is this love to be found as a characteristic in any of our Laws affecting the Poor? In our Poor Laws? These are but a make-shift to patch up the rents made in our social state by other and less well-meaning laws, without which patching up our social state, even such as it is, could not have held together. The whole of our social system is little better, as regards the working poor, than a miserable compound of ingenious contrivances to hide the injustice of inequality. The rich make the Laws in their own favor, and they settle the compensations, according to their own notions, for the poor. As if anything could compensate a People for unequal and unjust laws! They allow them no voice, and give them no choice.

This reminds us of the old story of the white man and the red man :—' You take the buzzard, and I'll take the turkey ; or, I'll take the turkey and you take the buzzard.'

What innumerable tracts are published and circulated to prove the blessings of poverty—as if poverty were something to be desired!

How endless are the allegorical interpretations of scriptural subjects to inculcate this deception, which nobody believes in,—which nobody ought to believe in,—and which so many excellent men, both Churchmen and Laymen, have so contemned and ridiculed!

Conspicuous among the Churchmen, and no less conspicuous for piety and learning than for wit and wisdom, was the Rev. Sydney Smith. Unsparing was he in shooting forth his shafts of pungent ridicule against all this sort of religious cant and hypocrisy. Another learned and excellent Churchman, in America, Theodore Parker, has left us an example of this kind of warfare worth preserving. He says: " How ridiculous the allegorical interpretation is of such books as Solomon's Song, Daniel, the Apocalypse, etc. Here is an example from a common nursery tale : 'This is the house that Jack built.' This bears a double meaning. 'The house that Jack built' is the Christian Church ; Jack, the builder, is the

head; Jack is the vulgar for John, which is the English for *Johannes* : the etymology indicates God's
gift. The 'Malt' is the Doctrines of the Christian
Church, as containing the spirit of Christianity.
The 'Rat who ate the malt' is the Catholic clergy,
symbolized by the Pope. The 'Cat who caught
the rat' is Master Luther, symbol of the Reformation. The 'Dog that worried the cat' is the
opponents of the Reformation, especially the
priests, of whom Loyola is the symbol. The
'Cow with the crumpled horn, that tossed the
dog,' is the French Government, which drove
out the priests, and the crumpled horn denotes
the Gallic cock, and thereby seems more clearly
to denote the French Government than any
other, for the crumpled horn is much like the
crest of a cock. The 'Maiden all forlorn' is
Liberty. The 'Man all tattered and torn' is the
French people, enamoured of liberty, and court-
ing it (in a most *feline* fashion) in the Revolution. The 'Priest all shaven and shorn' is
Lafayette; *shaven* because divested of his dignity
and wealth by the revolution itself; *shorn* as de-
spoiled of *his liberties* and shut up in an Austrian
dungeon, etc."*

This is no ridicule of sacred subjects, but hold-

* Life and Correspondence of Theodore Parker, vol. ii.
p. 26.

ing up to ridicule those who weakly and ignorantly, or designedly and presumptuously, use sacred subjects for their own foolish or sinister
purposes.

Our system is literally starving and demoralizing the great mass of the working people, and
as long as the system is continued great numbers
must prevent any palliatives from ever producing
more than inappreciable temporary relief. Tried
by the principle of Utility, for the 'Greatest Happiness of the Greatest Number,' it is impossible
to reconcile this system with any of the ordinary
rules of common sense. Instead of being a system of equal justice for union and social order, it
is a system of inequality and injustice, ever working disunion and disorder. It is a system at
variance with every Divine Command expressed
and implied, and, therefore, cannot stand.

The important truth intended to be conveyed
in these remarks is strikingly exemplified in the
present condition of Ireland, a country depend-
ing almost exclusively upon agriculture.

The difficulty is very great of obtaining statis-
tical facts which fairly represent the actual condition of such a country as Ireland. But these
seem to have been collected with unusual care
and industry by Dr. Neilson Hancock, formerly
Professor of Political Economy in Dublin Uni-

versity, who was directed by the Lord Lieutenant
to examine into the statements made as to the decline of Ireland, "with a view to ascertain the
real truth as to the state of the country." This
has been done by Dr. Hancock, and he has given
the result in what appears to be a carefully prepared "Report on the Supposed Progressive Decline of Irish Prosperity," which has lately been
printed by the Government printer in Dublin.

Examined by all the tests which can be brought
to bear on the subject, and taking the year 1849
as the close of the famine period, it appears that
the economical condition of Ireland was one of
steady improvement up to 1859, and that, notwithstanding the enormous emigration in those
ten years, the total number of acres under crops
of all kinds had increased by 320,000.

With this evidence of increasing prosperity
many secondary indications are afforded in the
official returns, and during the same period about
1000 miles of railway have been opened for trafic.
This gradual economic progress is confirmed by
various other returns examined by Dr. Hancock.

The conclusion to be drawn from all this evidence is, that a large increase of wealth had
flowed into Ireland during the period of improvement that set in after the famine crisis, or between the years 1649 and 1859.

But, what share of this increased wealth came to the laboring population of Ireland? Let Dr. Hancock answer this.

Before the famine, the wages of the adult laborer were from five-pence to ten-pence a day, the average being scarcely above seven-pence, and even at that rate thousands were seeking work in vain. The present rate, in the rural districts, runs, or was at the date of this Report, from a shilling to fifteen-pence a day. Agricultural wages in Ireland, therefore, do not yet suffice to keep a man and those dependent on him in substantial food. But notwithstanding this improvement in the condition of the agricultural laborer in Ireland, more than 80,000 persons emigrated from Ireland in 1859, and nearly twice that number in 1863. During this period of improvement in the condition of the laboring classes, the returns show a falling-off in the number of crimes, including all but trivial cases, amounting to 76 per cent. The cases reported by the police were, in 1849, — 14,908, and this number steadily decreased until, in 1858, it was reduced to 3,492.

But, in 1859 the tables turn and give painful evidence of a change for the worse. Crime has increased to nearly its former level. All the former signs of prosperity have nearly vanished, leaving evident signs of depression everywhere.

This is accounted for, according to Dr. Hancock, by a considerable diminution in the extent of land under crops, and the falling-off on potatoes and wheat, attributed to unfavorable seasons. Dr. Hancock estimates the losses of the agricultural class in 1661, by comparison with the average of preceding years, at more than ten millions, sterling, and the hopes of a favorable change of seasons in 1862 were disappointed.

All the official returns show a falling-off in prosperity and a corresponding increase in crime, since 1859, and it is painful to add that the past year, which has been a season of unusual plenty in most parts of Europe, and in England especially, has brought no visible relief to the distressed people of Ireland. The decline in Irish prosperity since 1859 is an admitted fact, but this is said to be traceable to causes over which Laws and Governments have no control, and that Emigration is the only means by which the depressed condition of the laboring class in Ireland must ultimately be raised. In other words, more laborers must be sent away, that those which remain may get better wages.

There is something in this suggestion for the benefit of those who remain, though how this can improve the bad seasons is not so apparent. But is the blame properly laid on the bad seasons, or

on the over-number of laborers? Is the one or the
other, or are both these together, or is something
else, the cause of the falling-off?

In many parts of Ireland the complaint is of
diminished tillage from diminished number of
hands. Further Emigration will not help this
complaint.

The difference of seasons between England and
Ireland can hardly be so great as to account for
the great difference of the actual results in the
two countries. Perhaps there is a greater difference between the people than between the seasons.
And yet, most of the hard work in England is
done by the poor Irish. The Irish laborer is not
more delicate than the English; nor less industrious, at least, out of Ireland; and if less
industrious in Ireland, why is he so? Is it that
the reward for industry in Ireland is less than in
England or elsewhere? Is it that the wages of
the agricultural laborer in Ireland are insufficient
for the subsistence of himself and family? Is it
that the Irish laborer is discouraged, depressed,
disheartened, desperate? If so—why? Can any
one believe that the seasons in Ireland are to
bear the blame of all this? Can any one believe
that the people themselves are to bear all the
blame? Why are the Irish so prosperous in America and starving in Ireland? Why are they so

eager to escape from their native land, to which
their attachment is so strong as to be proverbial ?
There must be some other reason for this—some
primary cause. The seasons, if any cause, can be
but secondary. Scotland can hardly be said to be
better off for seasons, whatever may be said for
England and Wales. There must be some other
cause than bad seasons to account for the state of
Ireland ; some primary cause, and that not in the
nature of things, but in the abuse of the nature
of things, in a disregard of the natural utility of
things, in a mis-use of nature's gifts, and a disregard of the condition. The primary cause,
therefore, whatever that may be, may be altered
and removed by human means; the secondary, if
the seasons, never can be. It is a strange way
of setting about the alteration to reduce the
strength of the country. Here is a country, famous
for its natural fertility, not half cultivated and
not half-peopled, and to make it more prosperous
the number of its people must be reduced !
Many complain that there are not enough of
people for the cultivation of the land, and for
gathering the abundant harvests when ripe. They
are answered—" reduce the number of the people
—Emigrate !" Others complain—" there is too
much land under tillage "—and, to meet the
seasons, the answer is,—" turn it into grazing

land !" But, turn any way, the agricultural population in this agricultural country are starving, and
all agree in crying out—'Emigrate!' Well—
Emigration has been going on at a great rate for
a great many years, and is now going on at a still
greater rate, and Ireland has been going down
and is still going down in prosperity at a corresponding rate, with occasional variations, but
these so rare and slight as to be regarded only
as remarkable exceptions to the general rule.
No doubt, emigration may be carried on to such
an extent as to raise the rate of wages, but to
raise wages by such means must diminish profits,
and if it be now unprofitable to bring into cultivation uncultivated lands, it must then be still more
unprofitable, and then the attempt will not be
made, and much land now cultivated at a profit
will then go out of cultivation, being unprofitable.

It will be better to try the new system of raising the wages of labor by abolishing all taxes on
labor and profits until the profit be realised. In
no other way than this will prosperity ever be
brought to Agricultural Ireland, and the mischief
of ages can be but slowly repaired by any legislation. When that mischief is repaired the sooner
Poor Law Relief is abolished in Ireland the better.

How the agricultural laborer in Ireland, or

in England or Scotland, in the best of times, sup-
ports himself, his wife, and children, on the wages
of his labor, is a question not to be answered by
any one who has never tried; but it is easy to
imagine the evil results from this state of things.

It is easy to see that, after providing for house-
rent and clothing, leaving out warming and
lighting, the means for living must be of the scan-
tiest, and it is not much to be wondered at if, on
such living, the race should degenerate both phy-
sically and morally—if manly strength and
womanly good feeling and influence should grow
feeble—if they should occasionally poach and
pilfer,—or smuggle and steal, and sometimes even
commit acts of violence,—if not for themselves, at
least, for their half-starved little children ; for to
suppose that a man or woman so situated, or children so brought up, will display the physical
vigor of the well-fed Anglo-Saxon race, or will
not appropriate to their own use the property of
others, if they think they can do so with impunity, is only to betray a singular ignorance of
human nature.

Who would not do the same under the same
circumstances?

Why, there is not a man in the House of Lords,
the Bench of Bishops included—there is not a
man in the House of Commons, the present Prime

Minister and Chancellor of the Exchequer included,—there never was a Lord Chancellor on
the woolsack, nor a Judge on the Bench—not
even the Judge who hanged poor Mary Jones for
intending to steal a bit of linen from a shop to wrap
around the infant in her arms—not even that other
Judge who hanged the man who wilfully cut down
a young cherry-tree, *because* " a man who would
wilfully cut down a young cherry-tree would take
away a man's life,"—nor that Lord Chief Justice
of England, who did " not know whether he was
standing on his head or his feet "—nor that Lord
Chancellor, who would have hanged a child of ten
years old for stealing a pocket-handkerchief—nor,
last and least, that well-remembered Chief Justice of the Common Pleas, who would have shot
or mutilated man, woman, or child, for stealing
an apple from an orchard—of all these there is
not one who, under the same circumstances would
have hesitated to poach and pilfer,—to smuggle
and steal, and, if necessary for the object, to commit violence ! Who would hesitate when their own
little children were starving around them ? Society must go on trying to prevent it, but they
had better try some other means than penal Laws,
which never have been and never will be found
effectual.   They had better try something new,
for the old system has utterly failed.

In England the great mass of the People are ignorant, over-worked, and under-fed. In Scotland they are no better off, and in Ireland they are worse off.

In this state of things, is it a matter of wonder that ignorance and wretchedness go together?

If the strength and prosperity of a Nation are to be estimated by the number and condition of its people, how will Great Britain and Ireland come out in this estimate?

Who will say that enormous Capitals accumulated in the hands of a comparatively few individuals constitute the real wealth of a Nation? If there be any ignorant enough to say so, let them look for the answer in the state and condition of France previously to the great French Revolution. They will not find in England anything to equal the accumulated wealth then in the hands of some of the old French nobility. But they will find greater destitution then in the mass of the French people than now in the mass of people of Great Britain or even Ireland, and, perhaps, more ignorance. Even the poor Irish have not yet been reduced to eat grass, and in Ireland, Education is, perhaps, more extended among the poor than in England. That great inequality between the rich and the poor was, in France, the consequence of unequal and unjust laws; and the consequence of that evil was the great French Revolution, which, now, looking back, appears to have been a necessary consequence.

With such an example before us, can it be wise to wait for such a result? Is it not wiser for the wealthy to take into consideration the condition of the poor working classes, before they take it into consideration for themselves, especially, if they be very ignorant as well as very poor?

Mr. Cobden, in his speech at a recent meeting at Rochdale, said: "I don't know a Protestant country in the world where the masses of the people are so illiterate as in England. This is no bad test of the condition of a people. It is no use your talking of your army and navy, your exports and imports; it is no use telling me you have a small portion of your people exceedingly well off. I want to bring the test to a comparison of the majority of the people with a majority of the people in other countries. Now, I say with regard to some things in foreign countries we don't compare favorably. The condition of the English peasantry has no parallel on the face of the earth."

Mr. Bright, following at the same meeting, said:—"I ask, shall we believe that it is an unchangeable decree of the Most High that more than one-half of the population of this country

shall live in houses of not more than £5 yearly
value, and that their children shall grow up in
comparison with those of the wealthy classes to a
large extent uncared for and untaught ; that life
with them shall be but one long struggle to live,
and that the sunshine which falls across and
athwart our path shall only to them be the gild-
ing of the land which they see afar off, but which
they can never hope to attain ?"

Many think that the state of things here described is not " the decree of the Most High," but
the natural consequence of our own system.

Many think that this is a remnant of the old
feudalism, and believe with Mr. Bright that, " if we
were fairly represented, feudalism with regard to
the people of England would perish, and the
agricultural laborer throughout the United Kingdom would be redeemed from that poverty and
serfdom which up to this time have been his lot."

Many think, with Mr. Bright, that " such laws
as we have, are intended to bring vast tracts of
land into the possession of one man, that one man
may exercise great political power."

Many think, with Mr. Bright, that "such a
system is a curse to the country, and dooms the
agricultural laborer to perpetual poverty and degradation."

The Editor of the *Times* says,—this may be

2 D 2

regarded as " Mr. Bright's proposition for a division among the poor of the lands of the rich."

Mr. Cobden, answering for Mr. Bright, says,
—this is " a gross literary outrage," " a groundless and gratuitous falsehood," " a foul libel,"
" a calumny," " pre-eminent unscrupulousness,"
" slander," and such like.

These are strong epithets, and such never help
a case. As a matter of taste, many will disapprove
of them. But, as a matter of fact, many will
agree with them. Not the writers for the public
press generally, because there is something of
personality in these epithets applicable to editors
of newspapers in general. By a sort of *esprit
de corps*, they all, or nearly all, rush to the
rescue of their chief. But that is a very immaterial part of the question. This is something
more than a question of good taste or good tact
on the part of Mr. Cobden, or of good feeling
or good sense on the part of the Editor of the
Times, now known as Mr. Delane, though, to
those who are indifferent to the sport, it was quite
immaterial whether the fox were un-earthed or
not. But to all in this country it is a matter
of much interest to know whether Mr. Cobden
or Mr. Bright really are in favor of a division
among the poor of the land of the rich ; or,
whether they, or either of them, have used words

fairly open to this construction. It is quite immaterial to the country what the writers in the
Times, the *Saturday Review*, or any other newspaper writers, may think, but if they think fit
to give utterance to their thoughts, through
channels at their command, in terms calculated
to deceive the public, and to injure, in public
estimation, the two best, and best proved, friends
of the People and the Country, by assertions
which are both untrue and calumnious, then this
becomes a question of very great public interest.

In the words here quoted from Mr. Bright's
speech lies the whole gravamen. He prefaces
these words with the startling assertion that,
"more than one-half of the population of this
country live in houses of not more than £5
yearly value, and that their children grow up, in
comparison with those of the wealthy classes, to
a large extent uncared for and untaught, and that
life with them is but one long struggle to live."

This may be true, or not, but as issue is not
joined on the assertion of fact, it may be taken
as true.

Mr. Bright, confining his remarks to the system,
which, he thinks, works out these undisputed results, then proceeds to show *how* this system
works.

Here issue is joined.

Mr. Bright thinks that this system tends "to bring vast tracts of land into the possession of one man;" and that one man holding such vast tracts of land "may exercise great political power." Moreover, he thinks that such is "*intended*" by the system.

This is matter of opinion, but, probably, more than half the people of the United Kingdom are of the same opinion with Mr. Bright on this question. But to this question only the *probable* answer can be given, until all the people, competent to answer it, shall have been polled.

Mr. Bright thinks, and probably the majority of the people think with him, that if we were fairly represented, this state of things "would be redeemed." He does not say,—' would be redeemed by a division among the poor of the lands of the rich.' He does not use a word which, by any forced construction, can be held to imply such a meaning. He simply says that, "the agricultural laborer throughout the United Kingdom would be redeemed from that poverty and serfdom which up to this time have been his lot." If his meaning is to be inferred from his words it is simply this;—that if the laborer were left in possession of the wages of his labor, without any deduction therefrom by taxes, he would be able, out of his savings, and by co-

operation with others like himself, to come into
competition occasionally with the rich landowner
for the purchase of small bits of freehold land,
an advantage which the agricultural laborer
can never hope to acquire under the present
system.

For saying this, and, we can only infer, meaning
this and nothing more, Mr. Bright, and his friend
and leader, and, therefore, defender, Mr. Cobden,
have ever since been hooted and hunted by nearly
the whole pack of the public press, hounded on
by a cry as unmeaning as if they had literally
shouted,—Tally ho !

Has anything been heard so stupid as this since
Milton wrote ?—

> "I did but prompt the Age to quit their clogs
> By the known rules of ancient liberty,
> When straight a barbarous noise environs me
> Of owls, and cuckoos, asses, apes, and dogs:
>
> .   .   .   .
> .   .   .   .
> .   .   .   .
>
> But this is got by casting pearls to hogs ;
> That bawl for freedom in their senseless mood,
> And still revolt when truth would set them free."
>
> .   .   .   .

That one of the clever writers in the *Saturday
Review*, should have joined in this senseless cry,
and written the following, in their No. 424,
under the heading " Accusation and Denial," is

surprising:—" It was wholly unnecessary for
either of the two agitators to commit themselves
to the statement that a division of the land would
be the first result of a Parliament reformed according to their ideas." *The* statement! What
statement? This statement? Where is anything
like it to be found in Mr. Cobden's speech, or in
Mr. Bright's speech?

The writer then goes on to reason, according
to his ideas, on his own fictitious statement. He
quotes Mr. Bright's words, already given, referring
to that system which is the curse of the country,
and dooms the agricultural laborer to perpetual
poverty and degradation, and then adds:—" Mr.
Bright promises that, with a Reformed Parliament,
the agricultural laborer shall *be redeemed from
that poverty*." Consequently, Mr. Bright promises
that a Reformed Parliament will put an end to
this system of land being held by a small number of persons. Consequently, Mr. Bright did
propose " to divide among the poor the lands of
the rich."

Such is the reasoning of the writer of this Article
in the *Saturday Review*. This is *consequently*," to
divide among the poor the land of the rich!"
Can any comment be required on such a '*consequence*' as this? The writer himself describes this
as " a demonstration in the little-go fashion," and

truly it is so ; but it is not by such demonstrations that the *Saturday Review* has been brought into fashion, nor are such demonstrations well calculated to retain a distinguished position, even among the fashionable readers of the day.

It would, however, have been more polite if Mr. Cobden had imputed the " groundless and gratuitous calumny " to a confusion of intellect, and to have retorted the charge of false logic, rather than the charge of " groundless and gratuitous falsehood."

On other parts of Mr. Cobden's and Mr. Bright's speeches the Editor of the *Times* is not more fortunate. He admits that they have " succeeded in mitigating our Tariff, and that of the neighboring countries "—that they have " certainly cheapened grain of all kinds and enlarged the circle of demand for British Manufactures. But here begins and ends the work."

And a very good work too.

Ought not that work to have been enough to have protected Mr. Cobden and Mr. Bright from such a commentary on their speeches in the *Times*, as this ?—

" The language so often repeated, and so calculated to excite discontent among the poor and half-informed, *has really only one intelligible meaning.* ' Reduce the electoral franchise ; for when

you have done so you will obtain an Assembly
which will *seize* on the estates of the proprietors
of land, and *divide them gratuitously among the
Poor.'* . . . It may be right to reduce the franchise, *but certainly not as a step to spoliation."*

If there be any meaning in language, these
words admit of only one construction.   But the
writer, who must know what he did mean, now
disavows having imputed to Mr. Cobden or Mr.
Bright the design of promoting by violent, illegal,
or immoral means a redistribution of the land of
this country.   Mr. Delane only thinks that the
speeches on which he so commented are open to
this construction.   But ought he not, as the
Editor of the popular journal of the day—ought
he not, as a sensible man, as a Gentleman—and
he is both—to have taken into consideration
these admitted services to his country, and have
tried to hide, rather than have exposed to public
view, such a construction, even if open to it?

Mr. Delane has not ventured to assert more
than that there are some passages in these speeches
open to his construction.   He has not ventured
to declare that he believed *his* construction to be
their meaning.   He has not ventured to say that
he believed that Mr. Cobden or Mr. Bright meant
to incite the People to agrarian outrage.   And
who would have believed Mr. Delane if he had

said so? He has, therefore, insinuated what he dared not to assert, and he has insinuated what nobody supposes he himself believes.

This conclusion admits of no argument, and is open to no explanation. Of what, then, does Mr. Delane stand self-convicted? If he have not learnt elsewhere, he might have learnt from Cicero—" In primis hominis est propria veri inquisitio atque investigatio."

What more could Mr. Cobden or Mr. Bright have done than they have done, or do than they are doing? They tell the people that, without extending the Elective Franchise, no Government in this country can do much more for them. They tell the People that, without Reform in Parliament, the confederacy of Landowners and Capitalists in this country is too strong for any Government, however well disposed, to stand against them. They do not tell the People, that the Landowners have too much land, or the Capitalists too much capital, but that the present system prevents the humble working-classes from getting any of either. They tell the people that a Reform in Parliament would lead, by constitutional means, to a peaceable change in this system. They tell the People this, not to lead them into agrarian outrage,—i.e., murder and robbery,—but to lead them away from ever thinking of such a thing.

Who, then, puts this thing into their heads?
Not Mr. Cobden or Mr. Bright, but Mr. Delane,
himself. Who raises this cry, and hounds on the
Public Press to make this cry echo throughout
the kingdom—who, but Mr. Delane, himself?

These Editors charge Mr. Cobden and Mr.
Bright with inconsistency, when they say;—"the
masses of the people are illiterate, and they are
entitled to choose their representatives in Parliament"—not *because*, but *notwithstanding*.

Well—they are illiterate; but, then, they are
heavily taxed. Their ignorance does not exempt
them from taxation. Why should their ignorance
exclude them from the franchise? What is the
criterion of ignorance? Who has fixed that criterion? Who are the judges, and are they dis-
interested? Who do the real work of the country? Who are the producers of the wealth? Who,
but the unrepresented masses of the People?
Why should property alone confer the franchise,
and those who confer the property be excluded
from the franchise? Why should property be
represented, and not the labor which produces
the property?

What has education to do with this question?
However great the reproach to the rich, that the
poor are so illiterate,—what has that to do with
the question of the franchise? The poor always

will be illiterate as long as they are kept on the verge of pauperism.

Many, as well as Mr. Cobden and Mr. Bright, believe the first step to the remedy to be by a Reform in Parliament. Mr. Delane does not believe in this. But this is a question to be answered by the People, not by the Editor of the *Times*, or by any other journalist.

Many believe that this question, if it could have been answered under the protection of the Ballot, would have been answered and settled long ago. It may yet be answered sooner than Newspaper Editors expect, and in a manner which they are not prepared for.

In the *Times* Newspaper, of the day before, under the head "Foreign Intelligence, France," is the following :—

" The impulse given to French Commerce and Industry by the abolition of the system of protection is becoming every day more manifest to the Manufacturers of Paris. The Exports from the 1st of January to the 1st of October equal in amount the entire exports for the year 1862. England and Belgium have particularly contributed to this development of French industry. England has taken lace, plain and figured silks, merinos, articles of ladies' dresses, mercery, ribands, linen and cotton cloths, bleached and

unbleached; gilt and plated bronzes, jewelry,
clocks and watches, porcelain, wrought steel,
stained paper, engraved music, a quantity of chemical ingredients, such as potash, chloride of
lime, nitrate of soda, and sulphate of copper;
refined sugar, dressed skins, and a variety of
basket-work.

"It is expected that the exports to England
this year will amount to 100,000,000 fr. more
than last year.

"The Exports to Belgium for the first nine
months of the present year are equal to those of
the entire twelve months of 1862. The exports
consisted chiefly of fine pearls, gilt bronzes,
wrought metal, plated ware, cutlery, tin, caout-
chouc, fine and common porcelain, chemical and
surgical instruments, pianos, potash, nitrate of
soda, sulphate of magnesia, alum, cream of tartar,
acetate of copper, common carmine, isinglass, wax
candles, and carriages. Other nations in Europe
and America have by their purchases assisted in
swelling the French Exports to 2,500,000,000 fr.,
which it is expected they will amount to by the
end of the year.

"Although there is generally a falling off at
this season of the year in the manufacture of
machinery in the great Iron-works about Paris,
orders are being daily received for locomotives

for the Italian and Spanish railways. The construction of iron bridges likewise employs a great number of hands. Orders for handsome carriages are every day increasing. Those engaged in the building trade were never more prosperous, for as fast as one house is finished another is commenced. The construction of the docks of St. Ouen occupies numerous workshops; while stone-cutters are preparing the granite which is to serve for the foundation, the iron rafters for the store-houses are being forged in the neighborhood. A large order has been received from Milan for the apparatus required to light that city with gas. The manufacturers of stained paper cannot find sufficient hands to execute the orders on their books. The decorators and gilders of porcelain are equally well employed, and the men are engaged in the manufacture of pianos frequently with extra hours. Skilled cabinet-makers capable of carving articles of furniture are in a similar position. Woollen spinners are fully employed, and cotton spinners are beginning to find employment. Manufacturers of perfumery find it difficult to supply their customers."

In the *Times* Newspaper, of the day before, is given the account of a man, apparently aged 60, who was found by the Police in a dying state in a street in London. He was taken to the Station-house, and died the same night.

"The *post-mortem* examination showed that there was no fat in the body. The stomach was empty. The cause of the death was an effusion of serum on the brain, coupled with want of food and exposure to the cold." That means *starvation*, and to that effect was the Verdict of the Jury of Inquest.

It is much to be feared that this is not a singular case, but it is a case for serious reflection, when descriptive of the state and condition of a large proportion of the population in our Cities, Towns, and Rural Districts, and at a time of more than usual plenty and prosperity. This, at least, should lead to an inquiry into the actual condition of our Working People, and into the truth of Mr. Cobden's unqualified assertion that, "the condition of the English peasantry has no parallel on the face of the earth."

But a few days before the occurrence of this death from starvation and cold in the streets of London, the Writer of these pages was in Paris, looking into every street and purlieu of that splendid Capital; and although he saw the unmistakeable signs of poverty mingling with costly magnificence, yet he met with none of the squalid misery of London, nor one person begging alms, nor one drunken person.

As a fact, trivial but characteristic, he will mention that, from an opposite window he watched, for thirty-five minutes, watch in hand, a poor paralysed man reclining on the stone pavement under an archway to the entrance into a fashionable 'magasin des modes' in the Rue de la Paix, and grinding a small hand-organ, but in no other way asking alms. During those thirty-five minutes he saw fifty-two persons stop and drop some coin into this poor man's hand. Who ever saw the like of that in London? Nobody ever will see it, whilst Charity is made compulsory by Law. If only a single sou were dropped by each of these fifty-two arrested passers-by,—and, probably, of these many dropped double that amount,—this man received in half an hour more than an English laborer, on the average, receives for a full day's work.

It is not that the French are a more charitable people than the English, but that Law interposes fewer impediments to the natural current of charitable feelings for the poor in France, than in England.

There is, perhaps, no civilized country in Europe where the deserving poor are so neglected and so destitute as in England, Scotland, and Ireland. In no part of the United Kingdom is there any Charitable Institution for the poor afflicted with Incurable Bodily Disease. Nor is there any Cha-

2 E

ritable Institution for the Sick Children of the
poor, with the single exception in that dreary
and confined locality, Great Ormond Street,
where, a few years ago, a private house was converted into a Hospital for Sick Children, by a
few benevolent persons who have since supported
it by their voluntary contributions. In France,
and in almost all other countries of Europe such
Institutions are established and maintained on a
noble scale of national benevolence.

How, in a country larger than our own, and
with a population larger than in our own, with
an amount of taxation and expenditure larger
than our own, though with less capital than in
our own, and with no legal provision for the
poor, who are entirely dependent on the voluntary contributions of the public, there is less of
individual misery from destitution, and more of
the actual enjoyment of life, than in our own, is
a question worth inquiring into.

But how it happens that we have starvation in
the streets of our metropolis, and a large portion
of our working classes but little above the level of
starvation, and this in a time of general prosperity, as it is called, whilst we are expending
millions of money on our National Defences,—
is a question which it is the duty of Englishmen to inquire into.   " It is no use your talking

of your army and navy, your exports and imports; it is no use telling me you have a small portion of your people exceedingly well off," when you have a much larger portion of your people living but little above the level of starvation, and some actually dying of starvation and cold in your public streets and highways, lanes and alleys. If it be true that "the condition of the English peasantry has no parallel on the face of the earth" for wretchedness, why is it so? Can it be wise to go on expending millions of money for our external defence, when such an enemy as starvation is working against us from within? Surely, this is a question to be inquired into by the People!

This is the question which, sooner or later, English Gentlemen will have to face.

After all the attempts for improvement of the social state, it must be admitted that society is governed much more by false than by true principles; by expedients and substitutes rather than by sound rules. When abuse has arisen from the neglect of a principle, it is a very common error to abandon the principle and adopt some expedient with reference to the particular abuse, which is the beginning of endless botching. Of this the instances are very numerous both in the practice of government and in legislation.

2 E 2

Of these instances, Prison discipline is the most striking. This, like many other subjects which occupy public attention, is not worth the time and expense which are bestowed upon it. All the attempts which have been made to reform criminals in prison have been attended with signal want of success. On this question, one of the most able and experienced of the Police Magistrates of the Metropolis many years ago thus recorded his experience: "I believe that after the immense expense that has been lavished upon the attempt, the instances of reform really attributable to the system do not amount to one in five hundred; and if it were calculated how many might have been saved from a prison at all by the application of the same means to the purposes of good government, it must be concluded that prison discipline with a view to reform is a great deal worse than useless." But still, against all experience, the attempt continues in the same wrong direction, regardless of principle, and botching by expedients.

If principle were regarded it would be seen that the sole end of imprisonment ought to be punishment, to deter from crime, and punishment by a separation from the world with all its advantages, that the greater the contrast, the greater may be the punishment. But the reform

system, however strict the discipline, must necessarily be made up with a degree of attention and
indulgence which must mitigate the pain of imprisonment, and diminish the dread which ought
to operate as a lesson to the criminal himself,
and a warning to others. Unfortunately, to the
neglected wretches, who form the bulk of prisoners, the outside world offers so few advantages that the prison offers no terrors, and the reform prison has all the advantages in the contrast,
with the one exception of restraint from vicious
courses. They do not like confinement and re-
gularity, but then they find so many sets off in
the attentions they meet with and the comforts
provided for them, and their physical state becomes so much improved, that when they come
again into the world, their retrospect is far from
one of unmixed repugnance to a prison life; and
if they return, as they generally do, to their vicious courses, the sufferings they bring upon
themselves must make them often wish for a re-
newal of restraint with its attendant comforts,
compared with their frequent privations. Where,
then, is the punishment or the reform within the
walls of a prison ?

Any attempt to unite reform with punishment,
as a system, must always be unsuccessful, being
reconcileable with no principle. Punishment

must be punishment, and then it seldom works reform; nor is that the object, the object of punishment being to deter. To work reform is a very different object, and is to be effected only by very different means. Those means are not within the legitimate jurisdiction of the Law, and never have been and never will be brought within its jurisdiction. To unite the means for both objects can end only in the failure of both, and that has been the result of all such attempts.

If it be asked, then, what is the best mode of prison discipline for diminishing crime, the true answer is, first reform the Laws and the Government. Make imprisonment a real punishment, as short as may be, but certain, and for murder, in all cases, certain for life. Thus will be avoided those sad and solemn inquiries into sanity and insanity, for which there never can be any standard, there being no true test; and thus will be attained the great object of certainty of punishment following conviction, and the present chances against conviction will be diminished. To make the inside of the prison a real punishment, the standard of comfort outside, to the classes most concerned, must be raised. The advantages from which they are separated must be real, not imaginary. This can be done only by leaving the laborer in possession of the full wages of his

labor, and that can be only by the abolition of
all Customs and Excise duties, and all other *indirect* taxes. In this way and in this way only
can the standard of comfort be raised to those
classes which furnish chiefly the inmates of prisons, without destroying that feeling of independence which is essential for the due appreciation
of the true standard. This way has never yet
been tried, though it is pointed out by the principle of general utility, here the only index to the
Divine will.

Long experience has proved that prison discipline is no cure for systematic crime. All systematic crime arises from defective government,
and is beyond the reach of prisons. The reform
must first be in the government, and then the
question of prison discipline will be found to be
in very narrow limits, by making imprisonment
and its deprivations a striking contrast to liberty
and its enjoyments. A necessity for severe punishments is a scandal to a government. When
the inside of the prison is the chief subject of
attention, what most concerns us on the outside
is the subject of neglect. Govern well, to make
a contented and happy people, and crime will
be unfrequent, and simple confinement sufficient
punishment. Individuals above the neglected
mass are not deterred from the commission of

crime by any consideration of degrees of severity of confinement, but by confinement itself; and if there were no neglected mass, there would be no necessity for what is called prison discipline; it would be so little required that it would be little thought of. Great as is the quantity of crime, the wonder is that it is not much greater, considering the quantity of neglect, and thence the inference is strong that the diminution would be great if attention were given in the proper direction. The principal means of accomplishing this is by moral influence, to be derived from an improved system of government. This is the only system for a free and Christian country, and to this we must come.

The severe and cruel system has been tried long enough, and has proved a total failure. For some centuries society was to be improved by terror of torture, burning and hanging. That was found to make men more like wild beasts than human beings in their treatment of each other. For another long and dreary period transportation was tried, and the crowded and pestilential prison, which was to many slow death, and to all contamination physical and moral. The abominations which arose out of this system at last worked other changes. Transportation was abandoned when the place for throwing out the refuse could no longer be found, and jail-fevers were found to spread beyond the prisons. For all these shocking contrivances of human imbecility, others were substituted. Hard labor, mitigated by Tickets-of-leave, or licences to thieve and throttle, then came to be tried, and prisons were converted into penitentiaries, combined with reformatories, the one destroying any good effect from the other, and making both worse than useless. This last improvement brings us down to present time with its results in an illiterate, degraded, pauperised and partially brutalised lower class of our population, and a pampered upper class dazed and bewildered by the fast-flowing floods of guilt and wretchedness around them, and a helpless Government sitting in silent contemplation of the misery which they are powerless to relieve. But, probably, we must come to worse before we come to better; nor shall we ever come to better until we have learnt to see, in the utility of the things of this world, the index to the Divine will which desires to have and will have all things, not in common, but open and free to all for the common benefit of all.

If the inquiry were pursued with careful attention in the direction to which this index points, it would be seen that there is a certain price for

everything, and that any attempt to force it below produces a contrary effect, though it may
cause a division of the payment. Individuals
may contrive to lower wages, and may throw the
difference, with the increased cost of labor, upon
the public—the State may inadequately remune-
rate those it employs, and thereby keep down
the amount of taxation; but the means of paying
the taxation will be inevitably diminished in a
greater proportion. It is in the nature of things
that pauperised laborers should be dearer than
independent ones, and that public servants inadequately paid should be either unequal to their
duties, or negligent or corrupt in the discharge
of them. The best rule for obtaining labor, of
whatsoever kind, at the cheapest rate, seems to
be, first, to render the service as agreeable and
respectable as its duties will permit, and then to
offer in open market the lowest direct remuneration which will induce the best qualified spontaneously to engage themselves, and willingly to continue. If the subject were closely pursued, it
would appear that, by rendering the various offices
of labor as little irksome as may be practicable,
and by approximating by all possible means the
direct wages of labor to the cost of labor, pauperism and crime might be very considerably reduced.
The hope of an immediate and adequate reward,

and the certainty of the secure enjoyment of it,
are indispensably necessary to obtain labor at the
lowest price, and however high that price may
be, still it is the lowest possible. By a law of
nature the slave is the dearest of laborers, and
the man whose heart is in his work the cheapest;
even the horse, when going home, in the hope of
eating its corn in comfort, is able to accomplish
more than by any urging of the whip. Heart,
supported by hope, and kept constant by prudence, constitutes the perfection of the laborer.
Arthur Young said that, he should prefer an
Essex laborer at half-a-crown a day to a Tippe-
rary man at four-pence.

In this view, the inquiry so pursued must lead
to the conclusion that it is of the first importance
not to impose upon labor any burden in addition
to that which is unavoidable in the nature of
things, and also to do all that is possible to make
labor less burdensome, by supporting the physical strength by those means which Nature has
so abundantly supplied for that very purpose, and
moreover by encouraging, as far as possible, that
hopefulness which is so essential for the cheerful
endurance of any burden, by a reasonably fair
share in the just reward, or an adequate remuneration out of the profits. In this view it will be
seen that, to impose any additional burden on

the necessary weight of labor, is to depress labor
to the incalculable loss of the Nation, however much to the apparent gain of the Government, and must be attended with incalculable
misery to the laborer, especially that misery which
leads to crimes and offences innumerable, the consequences of which must not only deprive the
Government of all its apparent gain, but must
leave it also in an actual and incalculable loss.

It is, therefore, no fallacy and no exaggeration
to say that, low and unremunerative wages and
profits, with consequent pauperism, are the sure
signs of bad government, and that these are the
inevitable consequences of our system, which,
being radically defective, admits of no palliatives,
all such being really only false expedients for
prolonging a state of things in opposition to the
Divine will and intention, which must sooner
or later be carried out by all Governments, or
they will certainly be overthrown, to make way
for wiser Governments to justify the ways of
God to man. In the mean time Nations will be
seeking for peace and security, but they will
never find either. They will find no peace at
home, no cessation of trouble from abroad. The
means which they use they will continue to use,
and those means which are only aggravating their
difficulties will continue to aggravate them, until

all are confounded in the confusion which themselves have created, and then exhaustion will produce relief, and relief will be in change. May that change come in time to prevent the overthrow, and may it be such a change as to make the relief permanent!

It is a common saying that, "poverty is no sin;" but nine times out of ten poverty is a sin, or approaches very near to it, if by *poverty* be meant *destitution*, and if *sin* be neglect of a Divine command.

But of all taxes, of all drawbacks upon enjoyment, assuredly those are the worst which diminish the means or discourage the efforts for self-subsistence and self-advancement. To escape the injurious effects of such taxes as these no station in life is too high, none too low. In all classes, each in his degree is the victim. The mischief spreads by reaction, and all must suffer. The poor have no encouragement to accumulate, and though they see ruin in old age, they see it only in the far distance, and then they see the Parish, the contemplation of which prepares and qualifies them for that last resource. How many give up the struggle for subsistence in despair, and plunge into that state which, with better encouragement, it would have been the labor of their lives to avoid!

If the rule be,—and who can doubt it?—that
human beings are born into the world with a
capability of self-dependence, how unwise must
be all those human laws and regulations which
operate as obstacles to diminish that natural capability so wisely and so mercifully provided!

To help those who are helping themselves—to
relieve the few, whom unavoidable calamity has
overwhelmed, or overtaken too late in life to be
retrieved by self-exertion, is a gratifying duty,
which, in this country more than in any other,
would be cheerfully and readily met and performed; but to lay down a general and indiscri-
minate rule that the old are to be maintained, the
fatherless to be provided for, the sick to be taken
care of, the young to be educated, and all out of
a public fund, to be provided by the industrious
and thrifty, the well-to-do and the rich, is to
render null and of no effect God's ordinances in
favor of industry, prudence, and foresight in the
ordinary changes and vicissitudes of life.

There is no excuse for poverty so weak as that
of old age: it is the very reason why a man should
have made provision against it. It is the strongest
inducement to industry, prudence, and foresight.
It is the rule of our nature for our self-protection
—it is one of the most essential for the well-being
of society—but we in our wisdom annul that rule

of nature, and substitute another and wholly artificial rule of our own, which not only encourages improvidence and idleness in those who are so disposed, but also involves others, not so disposed, in the same consequences, and too often in the worse consequences of despair. If the fatherless be held to be legally entitled to relief, the parental feeling of obligation to provide for children will be weakened or destroyed, and imprudent marriages will be encouraged. If the sick are to be taken care of by law, one of the chief uses of health will be perverted or neglected. Particular cases of old age, protracted beyond the usual period, children left destitute by extraordinary circumstances, or sickness of uncommon violence or duration, furnish legitimate objects for the voluntary care of relatives, friends, and neighbors, and that resource, if left to free operation, would always be found at least amply sufficient.

Legal provision by a general law against particular and occasional casualties, such as these, either make the mass of misery it can but very inadequately relieve, or is a wretched expedient for remedying that demoralization and debasement which arise out of defective government, and which under a wise government would have no existence. Give men fair play, by just and equal laws, and they will want no help from

government. Leave them to the full consequences
of their own actions, and they will exhibit human
nature according to a standard much higher than
that which any system of poor-laws, or any other
human contrivances, can establish. But, for the
full effect of the natural laws, no artificial restrictions must be placed upon them. They must
not be tampered with. The rights of labor must
be most specially regarded and preserved. Any
interference with those rights must be prejudi-
cial, nor can any be justified if this principle be
admitted.

This is the principle of Utility, and this is the
index to the Divine will, which must prevail in
the end.

The best security for every country is in a
strong and contented people, and a people who
are but half-fed, half-clothed, and miserably
lodged, cannot be either united, strong, or contented.

Such is the present state of the great bulk of
the agricultural laborers and working classes
generally in this country.

If every working man had a little property,
some provision against misfortune and old age,
and something to leave to his children, he would
have a stake in the country, and thus become a
supporter of order, and this would place our in-

stitutions on a basis so sound that nothing could shake them.

The working classes would then become as provident as they are now improvident. Many of them would render themselves independent of labor, and almost all would be partially so, and then, when the demand for labor should fall below the proper remuneration, they would keep withdrawing in proportion to their means, till the demand returned to its former standard. When it rose above the average, those who had become independent would return to labor or would remain at it, as the additional remuneration tempted them, till the extra demand ceased, or if permanent, till it was met by increased population, and this is the state in which labor would be the cheapest and most satisfactory.

Though a provident population must have more resources than an improvident one, yet it will be much more difficult to form or keep up combinations among a class strong in their own provident resources, than when weak, and without resources through their own improvidence.

In the former case, the interest of each individual is more distinct, and, therefore, not so easily drawn into the mass; each is calculating his own individual benefit, and being, in the meantime, to a certain degree independent,

2 F

is not so easily drawn into the mass, and will not readily make a certain sacrifice for an uncertain benefit; he is in a position of progressive comfort, from which it is difficult to disturb him, and his prudence and constant occupation make him little liable to become the dupe of the discontented and designing.

In the other case, the life of the improvident is an alternation of privation and indulgence, and they are ever ready to undergo the former for the chance of the latter; they listen readily to the plausible and the artful, and are constantly exposed to their evil designs. They have no fixed purpose or ultimate aim to keep them steady, and their individual interest being worth little to them, they are ready on every occasion to throw it into the general lot, and make common cause with those who have as little to lose as themselves. A provident people is the best calculated to resist unjustifiable aggression, and an improvident people to commence it.

The first object, therefore, of every government should be to give the people individually a personal interest in the welfare of the country, and for this there seems to be no way so effectual as to give every individual who has attained to the age of manhood and maintained his own independence by his own labor, or who is capable of doing so, a free voice in the affairs of government, that, by thus sharing in the responsibility, each may have a personal interest in the result, and all may have a common interest in the general welfare, by enjoying a fair share of the prosperity, according to their degree, and also bearing a fair share of the necessary burden according to their means, when by their own labor and skill they have acquired the means, and then by an equal rate, but distinguishing, and always preserving the distinction, between property and the labor and skill which make the property; for, to rate labor and skill as property, is to diminish the means of production, and also the inducement to produce, by taking from the labor and skill before the profit has been realised.

A State is quite justified in taking, for its necessities, from property and profits when realised; but nothing can justify a State in imposing any portion of its burden upon the labor and skill which create the property; and it is manifest that, to impose any part of the burden on the property before the profit is realised, must be injurious to the owner, and, if to the owner, to the State, which is only the aggregate of all owners, and is intended to represent as well as to maintain the common welfare.

On this principle, carried out in practice, the

State really represents and maintains the common welfare, and for the security of a country this is a basis so sound that nothing can shake it, and no external defences can equal it. Then it would be made apparent to all that, "The welfare of the People is the highest law,"—for it is the observance of this law, which makes a united and contented People, and a Country's best security.

How little the present state of England, Scotland, or Ireland, affords to make a united and contented people is a question on which there will be a difference of opinion, and it may be admitted that we stand favourably in a comparison with any other country. But little is gained by this admission, when the natural advantages of our position are taken into the account, for it must be admitted that, our country ought to stand much higher than it does in this comparison.

If the natural advantages of our country exceed those of any other country, certainly our National Debt in amount very far exceeds that of any other country, and though it may be true that, we are better able to bear our burdens than other countries are to bear theirs, yet it is undoubtedly true that there is more actual pauperism, and, perhaps, more individual wretchedness, in our country than in any other civilized country of the world.

But if it be true that a united and contented people constitute the strength of a country, it is not less true that pauperism is the weakness. Pauperism at all times was a pressing danger in ancient Rome, and ultimately effected its downfall; nor was that scourge of ancient Rome ever mitigated in its force by the agrarian law of the Gracchi, and their successors. But of an agrarian law, as it seems now to be generally understood, or, at least, as it seems to have been understood by the parties to the recent controversy arising out of Rochdale, there is no record in ancient or modern history. The Roman agrarian laws never even pretended to interfere with private property, and the agrarian law of the two Gracchi applied only to the distribution among the poor Roman citizens of the property said to have been left by a King of Pergamus expressly for their benefit.

That anybody in these days should be found to advocate an agrarian law, in its vulgar acceptation, or a division of the lands of the rich among the poor, is incredible. Nobody really believed anything so absurd; but experience has long ago proved that nothing is too absurd for the service of one political party against another.

But there is too much good sense in this country
to be so deceived, even among those who make
no pretension to classical knowledge, and, in the
end, even the most ignorant distrust those who
attempt to deceive by representing as true what
they do not themselves believe.

But though we have nothing to fear from the
example of the agrarian law, yet we have much
to fear from the example of the effect of pauperism in the downfall of ancient Rome, and this
appeals much more to the rich than to the poor,
and much more to their good sense and good
feelings, than to their ignorant fears and personal
selfishness.   The downfall of ancient Rome was
no loss, but a great blessing to the whole world.
But the signs of that coming event were long
foreshown, though unheeded.   Some of the same
signs are to be seen in our own time for our own
warning, and there is no reason to doubt that
they will be followed by the same consequences,
if unheeded till too late.   .

"It is a noticeable and very remarkable fact,
if the returns of the Income Tax are to be relied
on as anything near the truth, that, out of a population of thirty millions, less than three hundred thousand persons are in possession of incomes beyond £100 per annum, or *about one per
cent. !* Incredible as this fact may seem, yet so it

appears to be by the Parliamentary Return, No. 119, Session 2, 1859. But if this be anything near the truth, what must be the suffering of this immense proportion of the population, from an additional charge of 300 per cent, and upwards on many of the necessaries and conveniences of life, bearing on an income of £100 a year or less? Take the loyalty and patriotism of the country at as high an estimate as any one pleases, these *percentages* must, at least, have a very depressing effect. Without following the inquiry further, this may be sufficient for the present purpose, which is, to show what are the best National Defences of every country; and the only true answer, that the best National Defences are those laws and regulations which contribute in the highest degree to the WELFARE OF THE PEOPLE."*

The present question for the Nations of Europe is, whether or not war be an absolute necessity for the French Emperor. Certainly, the Empire represents no principle like liberty; no tradition like legitimacy; no faith like theocracy. The Empire represents a fact,—a power created by the will of the people.

Whether this fact be necessarily invading,— whether this power can maintain itself only by

* "Our National Defences : What Are They?" p. 39.

action, by assimilating to itself the life of others, and thereby strengthening itself;—whether glory and territorial aggrandisement be the only things that the Empire can give to France in exchange for liberty,—these are the questions.

Where power consists in a chief and an army, war is the normal condition of its being. To delude oneself into the hope that the Empire will be peace, is against the experience of all history. The alliances of the Empire, as at present constructed, can be only with despotism. Alliances are founded upon identity of principles or interests. The continued existence of the Empire of France, as it now is, demands the triumph of Imperialism in Europe. The natural alliance for the French Emperor is with Russia, and Austria: it would be with Prussia, if the Rhenish Provinces, destined, according to Imperial tradition, to belong to France, were not in the way. Between England, and the French Empire, there is no real bond of union.

In face of the ascending movement of Imperialism; in face of the new Holy Alliance of despotism; in face of the dangers which threaten England, and the liberty of Europe, England's fears will, probably, keep her neutral. But how long can this neutrality be maintained? Can England stand quietly by and witness the partition of the Mahomedan possessions in Europe and Africa, between the three Imperial and despotic Powers?

Morally, neutrality is the abandonment of every function, of every mission, of every duty, which is to be fulfilled on earth; it is a mere passive existence, forgetfulness of all that sanctifies a people, the negation of the common right of nations, egotism raised to a principle—it is political atheism. A people cannot limit its own free action without falling, without denying the progress which it is called to advance. Politically, the neutrality of a State is its nullification. It does not lessen a single danger, but condemns a State to front it in isolation. History points to States that neutrality has drawn to ruin—Venice, for example; not one that neutrality has saved from war or invasion. By inscribing a negation upon its own flag, a nation does not avoid death, but adds dishonor to it.

Imperialism, which means *despotism*, is the most urgent danger of Europe. Europe must combat it—conquer, or die in the attempt.

Imperialism cannot be resisted by caressing it, diplomatising with it, endeavoring to bind or limit its action by hypocritical alliances, or conditional concessions. It must be resolutely met; but it must be met fairly. If France persuade herself that the Empire is a fact with which no one can contend; if the People be convinced that there is no support for them anywhere, Europe is lost.

So says Mr. Goldwin Smith; and all this is true. These are the signs of the times. The only way to destroy this most urgent danger is by isolating it, and snatching from it the arms by which it is preparing to conquer Europe.

But, how is this to be done?—And by whom? By England—not by neutrality, nor by war; but by being prepared for war, and determined to preserve peace; by making the people lay down their arms, and thus isolating Emperors, and despots.

The re-settlement of Europe cannot be much longer deferred, and in that territorial question England cannot remain neutral, without abandoning her position among the Nations.

In the meantime, England had better be prepared to take her proper part. Instead of an Imperial Association of despotism, it may then be a fraternal Association of all the great Powers of Europe. But for this there must be a great principle, and there is but one by which they can hold together.

That one is, the mutual interests of the Nations—the Welfare of the People—the united proclamation of UNIVERSAL FREE TRADE.

This, at once, makes the bond of interest which will unite the whole together. Against this no Association against the liberties of the People can stand; for, Armies will be disarmed, and dispersed, and self-interest, guided by reason and conducted with discretion, will prevail; and behind all this will be the irresistible moral and physical power which England will exert—England, the head and leader in the progress of Civilization, to whom all the Nations are now looking with so much anxiety and earnest expectation,—England cannot be neutral.

If there be much to fear in the present aspect of affairs, there is also much to hope for; and not by shrinking from it is the danger to be avoided.

As Burke, on a similar occasion, once said: "Early and provident fear is the mother of safety; for, in that state of things, the mind is firm and collected, and the judgment unembarrassed; but when fear and the thing feared come together and press upon us at once, even deliberation, which at other times saves, becomes one's ruin, because it delays decision; and when the peril is instant, the decision should be instant too."

But, if there be much to hope for, it is from Christian Education, free institutions, and social reforms. Then no zeal will be called Christianity which is not hallowed by Charity; no faith Chris-

tion which is not sanctified by Reason. For this
end, no effort should be spared to advance general instruction, and civilization, and increased
commercial intercourse between the nations, until the character of merely military conquerors be
reduced to its proper dimensions, and until society be impressed with just notions of moral
obligations and the blessings of peace.

No one can reflect on the relative positions
of England and France, without seeing that the
Anglo-French Alliance is the best safe-guard of
peace and prosperity for the world—the palla-
dium of the liberties of the West. Both nations
have an equal interest in supporting each other.
Both should endeavour to avoid everything calculated to excite jealousy and to renew antagonism, for the benefit of despotism: Divided they
may destroy their own glory, and must destroy
their own prosperity : united, their true glory
will be in the peace and prosperity of the whole
world. France has much to gain by a more in-
timate and extended intercourse with liberal
England ; nor would England be a less gainer by
a cordial and complete understanding and free interchange of productions with France.

It is this industrial intercourse which has maintained international relations between England
and the United States ;—it is this which will

restore tranquillity to the Italian Peninsula;—
and it is this which will ultimately secure the
peace of the world.

In this way, and in this way only, wars will be
brought to an end. The folly and the wickedness of wars, and the shedding of human blood,
will then be seen. To suppose that this effect
can be produced by any other means, or that
this effect can be produced suddenly, is simple
weakness.

Against this folly and wickedness Dr. Johnson
thus expressed his opinion :—

"The wars of civilized Nations make very slow
changes in the system of Empires. The public
perceives scarcely any alteration, but an increase
of debt, and the few individuals who are bene-
fited are not supposed to have the clearest right
to their advantages.

"If he that shared the danger enjoyed the
profit, and, after bleeding in the battle, grew rich
by the victory, he might show his gain without
envy; but, at the conclusion of a ten years' war,
how are we recompensed for the death of multi-
tudes, and the expense of millions, but by con-
templating the sudden glories of paymasters, and
agents, contractors, and commissioners, whose
equipages shine like meteors, and whose palaces
rise like exhalations ?"

So wrote, a long generation ago, one of the wisest and best specimens of a moral Englishman.

To the amount of time and capital wasted in war, and preparations for war, we are all witnesses.

Reckoning our own Costs of War only, from the war with France in 1691, to the Peace of Ryswick in 1697, down to the year 1859,—being a period of 169 years, of which 67 years were war, and 102 peace, our capital expenditure for war was, £910,589,522.

Our payments in hard cash for interest only, during the same period, amount to £2,130,882,179.

Loans . .	910,589,522
Interest .	2,130,882,179
	£3,041,471,701

Thus, making together for our own COSTS OF WAR, paid in loans and interest, exclusive of increased taxation, in 67 years, the incomprehensible sum total of THREE THOUSAND AND FORTY ONE MILLIONS FOUR HUNDRED AND SEVENTY ONE THOUSAND SEVEN HUNDRED AND ONE POUNDS, sterling, and between TWENTY FIVE

AND THIRTY MILLIONS, sterling, to be paid yearly for ever !

These figures are taken from the Tables made by Mr. Henry Lloyd Morgan (the well-known Investigator of the Government Accounts,) from the Public Accounts furnished by Government; and, as Mr. Morgan adds:—

"This is for *simple* interest *only*; yet even this gigantic sum represents only a comparatively small portion of the actual costs of war; moreover, it must be remembered that all this has been abstracted from the working capital of the country, therefore, in reality, 'compound interest' should be charged to represent even the outlay for payment of the simple interest; to which must be added a much larger sum for *extra* taxation levied to carry on war."

If the capital and skill wasted in war and preparation for war, "were in the flat sea sunk," though that would be useless, it would not be so deeply injurious as so to employ them. The subject of war, indeed, cannot be thought upon without calling to our recollection those events which paralysed Europe from the year 1793 to 1815, and without reviving all those bad passions which should be extinct. Additional taxation, both upon France and England, must take place; the effect would be the withdrawal from both

countries of so much capital as is expended,—a
loss which must be followed by very disastrous
consequences.

Nine millions, sterling, are said to be required
by France for costs of war in Mexico, and three
or four millions more for costs of war in Cochin-
China. And these wasteful costs have been
incurred with a floating unfunded Debt of nearly
Forty Millions, sterling; exclusive of State liabilities, in guarantees to Railway Companies, for
some millions more; and all this with a Revenue
of Eighty Millions, sterling, a year. Such is the
cost of Imperialism to the French People!

This, though not alarming, may well be taken
as a warning to mend the ways. But the French
are not a people to be content with such an expenditure of their money, and to have nothing
for it. They mean to have something for it.
They had Nice and Savoy for their costs of
Magenta and Solferino. What they will have
for their costs at Rome is yet to be seen.

War cannot be conducted now, as it was by
the first Napoleon. No Power in Europe can
do it. You cannot make the country conquered
bear the cost of the conquest. The thing is impossible. With States, as with individuals, the
day of reckoning comes round; and when, in
their sober moments, men calculate the relative

advantages of immense armaments, and the illu-
sions of military glory, with the cost of the taxes
to pay for such exploits, they come to take a
calmer and more discreet view of the comparative
advantages, than they could be expected to do
in the moment of excitement.

The interest of Europe is not that any one
country should exercise a peculiar influence; but,
the true interest of Europe is to come to some
common accord, so as to enable every country to
reduce those military establishments which belong to a state of war, rather than of peace.

It is much to be wished that the councils of
every country would willingly propagate such a
doctrine. There is a great revolution in Public
Opinion on public affairs of late. The peace of
forty-eight years, the intercourse of commerce,
new connections, new interests, which have
sprung up therefrom, have effected a great
change in public affairs. If France were in any
danger of an unjust aggression, the security of
France would not be found in the number of her
regiments, but in the mind and public spirit
with which she would rise, as one man, to revoke
and repel the danger.

It is the same with that magnificent country
which has abolished the name and distinctions
of separate States:—Germany, at this moment,

2 G

from Hamburg to the Tyrol, and from Berlin to the southern confines, burns with a spirit which would intimidate and overbear any invader, if the people were only united—but they are not.

But those southern confines are not well defined, nor fairly maintainable against France, and until this cause of discord be removed, by the restoration of the Rhine boundary to France, as it is, the peace of the Continent can never be regarded as established on a firm and secure basis.

These are some of the securities against aggression—some of the securities for peace; and on these the late Sir Robert Peel relied much, in reference to his great movement towards Free Trade, when referring to the will of Providence, which has given to every country a sun, a climate, and a soil, each differing one from the other, in order that they may feel their reciprocal dependence by the exchange of their respective produce, thus causing them to enjoy in common the blessings of Providence.

"It is thus that we find in Commerce the means of advancing civilization, of appeasing jealousy and national prejudice, and of bringing about a universal peace, either from national interest, or from Christian duty."

There is something in these words, "universal peace," which seems not applicable to this world.;

and yet we may sometimes catch such a glimpse
of the whole truth as to believe that, even in this
present world, this is something more than a
mere fancy.

Viewed in the broad results, it will be seen
that, all these questions admit of safe answers
when tried by the principle of general utility.

But this is a test resting on human experience,
and can be applicable only to human affairs.   It
is, at best, but an index to the Divine will, where
no surer revelation has been given, and necessarily imperfect, because resting on human experience, and, therefore, subject to the variations of
human opinion.   No certain rule being given for
ascertaining to what this index really points, it
must always be more or less an imperfect guide
for human government.

If the soul were furnished with *innate practical
principles*—if man were endowed with a *moral
sense*, or gifted with a *peculiar organ* for acquiring a perfect knowledge of his duties—the duties
imposed by the Deity would be subjects of immediate consciousness, and completely exempted
from the jurisdiction of observation and induction, and then we should not be left to construe
the Divine Commands by the principle of general

2 G 2

utility. To a great, and, we must presume, sufficient extent, we have access to that *moral sense* through the Divine will revealed, and we are guided and directed to the true interpretation by a *common sense*, or a *practical reason*; but, without the Divine revelation, we know that these are very imperfect and often very erroneous guides, being necessarily subject to all the infirmities of our nature.

As we are not gifted with that *peculiar organ*, we are left within the jurisdiction of observation and induction for many of the important duties of life, and this throws upon us the necessity of resorting to the principle of utility, how defective soever it may be; and that it must often be very defective, and to a great extent uncertain, is apparent, being in so great a measure dependent on the common sense or practical reason with which our observation and induction are conducted. On these occasions we must gather our sense of our duties, as we can, from the tendencies of human actions; or remain, at our own peril, in ignorance of our duties.

This may be a great help to the knowledge of the Divine will, in the absence of a Divine command, or, as Mr. Austin calls it, 'an index to the tacit command of God,' through the works of Nature, though this is, as Mr. Austin adds, 'but

the help of a glimmering light, in profound darkness;' and, he might have added that, even this
glimmering light is borrowed from the stronger
light of revelation.

This may help to present the Principle of
Utility in its true light, and all that can be said
for it is, that it is a safe guide to follow when it
can be seen to be in conformity with the Divine
will as revealed; and that, although it have no
necessary relation to Happiness, a due observance
of the Utility of things may help to lead human
beings to Happiness.

Beyond this, the Principle of Utility can never
be carried for good, and to attempt to carry it
farther, is the vain attempt to make it a substitute for the Christian doctrine.

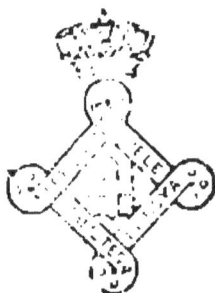

INDEX.

———

W.

Y.

Z.

THE END.

JOHN EDWARD TAYLOR, PRINTER,
LITTLE QUEEN STREET, LINCOLN'S INN FIELDS.